A PRACTICAL APPROACH TO
COMPUTER SIMULATION IN BUSINESS

A PRACTICAL APPROACH TO COMPUTER SIMULATION IN BUSINESS

L. R. CARTER
Senior Lecturer in Management Science, Slough College of Technology

and

E. HUZAN
Principal Lecturer in Computing and Director of the Computer Unit,
Slough College of Technology

A HALSTED PRESS BOOK

JOHN WILEY & SONS
New York

Published in the USA
by Halsted Press, a Division
of John Wiley & Sons, Inc.
New York

© George Allen & Unwin Ltd   1973

Library of Congress Cataloging in Publication Data

Carter, L   R
  A practical approach to computer simulation in business.

  "A Halsted Press book."
  Bibliography: p.
    1.   Management—Simulation methods.   I.   Huzan, E.,
joint author.   II.   Title.
  HD38.C372   658.4'035   73–11017
  ISBN 0–470–13729–0

Printed in Great Britain

Contents

page

Preface   11

1. Introduction to the Principles of Simulation   13
   Simulation   13
   Random Numbers   14
   Simulation Example   14

2. The Place of Simulation in Management Science and Operational Research   20
   Approaches to Management   20
   The Development of O.R.   21
   The Basic Concepts of O.R.   22
   Use of Models in Business   25
   Applications of O.R.   26
   The Relationship of O.R. to Statistics and Work Study   27
   Resume of O.R. Methods and Techniques   27
   Summary   31

3. A Review of Some Statistical Concepts   33
   Probability   33
   Expectation   36
   Frequency Distributions   37
   Significance Testing   49

4. Building Simulation Models   52
   Terms of Reference   52
   Identifying Relevant Factors   54
   Constructing the Inter-Relationships   62
   Validation of the Model   69
   The Ideal Simulation Program   74
   Summary   75

5. The Use of Fortran for Computer Simulation Studies   76
   The Use of Computers for Simulation   76
   Introduction to FORTRAN   77
   The FORTRAN Coding Form   78
   Basic Definitions in FORTRAN   80
   Sample Program (ELEM)   90
   Detection and Correction of Errors in FORTRAN Programs   97

Contents

page

Summary of Program Development   100
Standard Frequency Distributions—FORTRAN Programs   100
Further facilities in FORTRAN   101
Use of Magnetic Tape   102
Implementation of BASIC FORTRAN on the ICL 1900 Series   103
Further Examples   104
Use of On-Line Terminals   105

6. The Use of CSL for Computer Simulation Studies   109
Introduction to General Simulation Languages   109
Historical Notes   109
Introduction to CSL   110
Data Structure   112
Simple Data Operations   114
Simple Transfer Statements   115
Complex Conditional Statements   117
FIND Statements   118
Distribution Sampling Functions   119
Histograms   122
FORTRAN Statements and Segments   123
Compilation and Execution   124
A Complete Program   125
Further CSL Examples   135
CSL Structural Words   135

7. Queueing Systems   136
Introduction   136
Queueing Theory   136
A Dispatch Problem   140
A General Queueing Simulation Program (SIMQ)   149
Simulation Program of Refuelling Aircraft (BOWS)   153
Simulation Program of Two Mobile Patrols (PSIM)   155
Simulation Program of a Repairing and Re-issue Cycle (SOMB)   160

8. Forecasting and Inventory Control   165
Introduction   165
Forecasting   165
Exponential Smoothing   173
A Simple Forecasting Program (FORE)   179
Inventory Control   181
A Program that Simulates Alternative Inventory Policies (STAN)   190

9. Simulation of Other Systems   194
The Simulation of Alternative Maintenance Policies (ELEM)   194
Production Control   198
Profitability Analysis   211

		page
10.	Summary and Conclusion	219
	Developing and Using a Computer Simulation Model	219
	Suggested Exercises	220
	Conclusion	220
	References and Bibliography	221

Appendixes

FORTRAN Programs

1.	CAPF	223
2.	COMF	226
3.	ELEM	228
4.	FORE	232
5.	LOAD	237
6.	SIMQ	241
7.	SUBF	244

BASIC Programs

8.	PRAC	251
9.	PRAS	254

CSL Programs

10.	BOWS	258
11.	PSIM	263
12.	SOMB	267
13.	STAN	270
14.	SUBC	273

15.	A Dispatch Problem: Table of Lorry Loading	280
16.	Random Numbers Tables	284
17.	Chi-Square Tables	285
18.	Normal Tables	286
19.	Poisson Tables	287
20.	Formulae for a 'simple' Queue	290
21.	Runs Test Tables	292
22.	*r* Tables	293

Index	295

Preface

The purpose of this book is to introduce the general principles of simulation as applied to business. Today, simulation techniques are playing an increasingly important part in the solving of industrial and commercial problems, in such areas as production, maintenance, marketing, distribution, finance etc. The ultimate aim being a model of the complete company which can be experimented with and examined by simulation.

To achieve this aim a certain amount of expertise is required, and this book has been written for managers, systems analysts, industrial engineers and operational research workers who need to know where to start. It is intended that readers should be able to use simulation to solve simple problems after working through the examples given in this book. Very little mathematical knowledge is assumed and the treatment is kept simple. Apart from assuming that the computer is a familiar tool, the book is intended to be a self-contained introduction to simulation.

The basic principles of simulation and the relation between simulation and other management science techniques are dealt with in chapters 1 and 2. Some basic statistical theory which needs to be known before simulation can be applied is given in chapter 3. Readers who are familiar with general statistical theory may find this chapter useful mainly as a review of certain statistical principles that are pertinent to simulation. For readers with little knowledge of statistics, this chapter serves as an introduction to the statistical principles involved and indicates the areas for further reading.

The practical aspects of simulating a situation are covered in chapter 4, from establishing the terms of reference to validating the model. The use of computers for solving simulation problems is dealt with in chapters 5 and 6. Three programming languages have been used to write the simulation programs in this book. They have been chosen to illustrate the three different types of languages available, i.e. FORTRAN (a universal scientific language available on most modern computers), BASIC (a commonly used conversational language available on many terminals), and CSL (a special purpose simulation language available on several different machines). Although there are many other suitable languages for simulation, they can be broadly categorised into these types. While a comprehensive treatment has not been given, sufficient details have been included for the reader to follow the programs listed in the

Preface

appendixes, and to attempt to run some simple computer simulations. The problems of simulating particular types of systems such as queueing, forecasting, inventory, production control, maintenance, and profitability analysis, are discussed with examples in chapters 7, 8 and 9.

We wish to thank Professor Samuel Eilon, Head of the Department of Management Science, Imperial College of Science and Technology, for allowing us to base the program CAPF (simulation of alternative plant capacities) on an example described on page 351 of his book *Elements of Production Planning and Control,* published by Macmillan, New York, 1962. We would also like to thank P-E Consulting Group Limited, Egham, Surrey for permission to use their published material relating to HOCUS in chapter 4. We are indebted to the Literary Executor of the late Sir Ronald A. Fisher, F.R.S., to Dr Frank Yates, F.R.S., and to Oliver & Boyd, Edinburgh, for permission to reprint Table VII from their book *Statistical Tables for Biological, Agricultural and Medical Research;* to David Croft and to Macdonald and Evans, London, for permission to reprint Tables A, C, E and F (appendix II) from their book *Applied Statistics for Management Studies;* to Russell Langley and to Pan, London, for permission to reproduce the chart appearing on page 325 of their book *Practical Statistics;* to B. T. Houlden and to English Universities Press, London, for permission to reproduce the formulae on page 108 of their book *Some Techniques of Operational Research;* and to Professor P. G. Moore and to Sir Isaac Pitman and Sons Limited, London, for permission to adapt a decision tree example from pages 118–25 of their book *Basic Operational Research.*

L. R. Carter

April, 1972   E. Huzan

Chapter 1

Introduction to the Principles of Simulation

This chapter illustrates the principles of business simulation by a simply worked example. Various aspects of simulation arising from this example are then elaborated in the subsequent chapters. Before commencing the example, though, it is necessary to explain what is meant by the term simulation and to introduce the idea of random numbers.

SIMULATION

To simulate, in general usage, means simply to represent artificially, i.e. simulated leather, a flight simulator etc. Not every characteristic is represented, but only details that are of interest. If simulated leather was an exact copy of leather in *every* respect, it would in fact be real leather.

Simulation requires then that a representation be made. This representation can be called a model and may be a physical model, as in the case of a plant layout, it may be an analogue, as in the case of the flight simulator, or it may be solely mathematical. We are concerned with mathematical models of a particular kind, ones that entail the use of random numbers to introduce into the model the variabilities of the real world.

There are various reasons why simulation proves such a useful technique; these may be summarised as:

(1) The technique allows changes to be made in the model and their effects to be assessed without the necessity of actually implementing them. This prevents changes being made without foreknowledge of the consequences. This is true of models as a whole and hence simulation models.

(2) It is usually much quicker to simulate a period than to allow it to expire in reality. For instance, three alternatives each requiring a month to assess in reality might be simulated in a matter of hours. Not all models allow

one to speed up time, but simulation models can be constructed to have this capability.

(3) A further reason for using simulation, and possibly its most unique feature, is that the variables involved in the model do not have to conform to established frequency distributions, and no assumptions need be made in the relationships between the variables in the model.

The significance of mathematical modelling in business and the relationship of simulation to other techniques is developed in chapter 2.

RANDOM NUMBERS

Monte Carlo simulation uses random numbers to generate changes in the model. The term Monte Carlo arises from the idea of generating the random numbers by successive spins of a roulette wheel. In practice, this method is likely to be time consuming, instead, for manual simulations, tables of random numbers are consulted (see appendix 16), while for computer simulations the computer is programmed to generate its own numbers by means of a subroutine.

The tables of random numbers found in most books are composed of two digit numbers in the range 00 to 99. Tables of five-digit numbers would range from 00000 to 99999 etc. The number of digits is of no significance, as if too many digits are given the number can be truncated, alternatively, if too few digits are presented, successive numbers can be run together to give the required number of digits. The important feature of tables of random numbers is that each digit has an equal chance of appearing at any place in the table. A table of random numbers is given in appendix 16.

The manner in which random numbers are used in simulation will become evident as a simple example is explained and developed. In practice, this example would quite likely be part of a much larger problem.

SIMULATION EXAMPLE

A new version of plant is to be introduced comprising two basic units, a motor and a gear unit. These two units have been in use in the plant for some years but they have not previously been used together. This means that the failure patterns of the motor and gear unit are known and it is now necessary to establish the failure pattern of the combination. The plant manager wants this information so that he can establish the best planned maintenance intervals and the manpower requirements. He wants this information now and cannot afford to wait a year or so until actual data have been collected.

14

Simulation can be used to transform the independent failure patterns of the motor and gear unit into a failure pattern for the combined unit. It is this aspect of the problem which will be dealt with below.

The failure patterns of the two units are shown in figures 1.1 and 1.2, these have been drawn from past records.

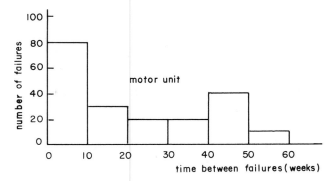

Figure 1.1   Histogram of motor unit failure

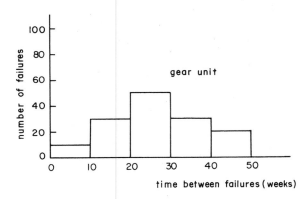

Figure 1.2   Histogram of gear unit failure

The information contained in figures 1.1 and 1.2 is presented in tabular form in the first two columns of table 1.1 and 1.2. In these tables the data have been grouped in ten-week intervals, i.e. 0 to 10, 10 to 20 etc. These intervals will be identified by their mid-point value, i.e. 5, 15, 25 etc.

Random numbers have to be allocated to each unit in turn such that the proportion of numbers allocated is the same as the proportion of units failing in any particular interval. To do this the frequencies are converted into

15

percentage frequencies. This step is given in column 3 of table 1.1, for the motor unit.

The next step is to allocate the 100 random numbers, 00 to 99 inclusive, in proportion to the percentage frequency. Referring to column 4 of table 1.1, the first 40 numbers, i.e. 00 to 39, represent failures at five-weekly intervals and so on.

Table 1.1   Frequency table of motor unit failure

Motor unit

Weeks between failures	Frequency	Frequency per cent	Random numbers
5	80	40	00–39
15	30	15	40–54
25	20	10	55–64
35	20	10	65–74
45	40	20	75–94
55	10	5	95–99

Table 1.2   Frequency table of gear unit failure

Gear unit

Weeks between failures	Frequency	Frequency per cent	Random numbers
5	10	7	00–06
15	30	20	07–26
25	50	33	27–59
35	40	27	60–86
45	20	13	87–99

The two tables with random numbers allocated can now be used to simulate the failure intervals of a combined unit. Each random number read from a table of random numbers represents a 'weeks between failures' period for either the motor or the gear unit according to which table (1.1 or 1.2) it is applied.

Let the first random number picked from a table of numbers be 20, then referring to the motor unit table 1.1, this number is among the 00–39 group and therefore represents a motor that runs for five weeks before failing. A second random number is picked from the tables, say 17, and this number is applied in table 1.2. This represents a gear unit that runs for 15 weeks before failing.

Under these circumstances a combined motor and gear unit would therefore run for the shorter of these two periods, namely five weeks. To simulate the failures of the combined unit the above procedure is repeated. In short, two random numbers are picked and applied to the motor table and gear table respectively. The running periods of each unit is found from the

Table 1.3   Simulation worksheet for combined units

Simulation data				
Motor unit		*Gear unit*		*Combined unit*
Random number	*Running period*	*Random number*	*Running period*	*Running period*
20	5	17	15	5
74	35	49	25	25
94	45	70	35	35
22	5	15	15	5
93	45	29	25	25
45	15	04	5	5
44	15	91	45	15
16	5	23	15	5
04	5	50	25	5
32	5	70	35	5
03	5	64	35	5
62	25	49	25	25
61	25	00	5	5
95	55	97	45	45
37	15	99	45	15

table, and the shorter period of the two is taken to be the running period of the combined unit. A portion of the simulation is given in table 1.3. The simulation for the purpose of this exercise was continued until 100 failures of the combined unit had occurred.

The data simulated for the combined unit in table 1.3 can be used to give a frequency table as shown in table 1.4, which in turn can be depicted as a failure pattern as in figure 1.3.

Having obtained the above failure pattern, the manager is in a position to plan the maintenance periods and manpower for the combined unit just as effectively as he plans for the existing units. The precise use of the simulation is not our immediate concern, rather, the illustration of the Monte Carlo simulation method. Also certain practical issues in carrying out the simulation have been ignored. These issues, such as the collection of initial data, the development of the necessary steps etc. are discussed in chapter 4. A short comment on the length of the simulation should be made.

Table 1.4   Simulated frequency table of combined units

Combined unit	
Weeks between failures	*Frequency*
5	43
15	26
25	17
35	9
45	5
55	0

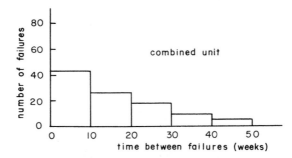

Figure 1.3   Histogram of combined unit failure

The length of the simulation depends upon the desired accuracy sought in assessing the results. Each simulated failure can be regarded as one sample from an infinite population of such periods, and hence the length of the simulation is governed by the sample size required. An alternative and more practical approach, which may be appropriate, is to calculate the cumulative average of whatever statistic is of interest. As the simulation progresses, this cumulative average will settle down to a steady value; when this occurs there is no need to continue the simulation. An example of this is given below by calculating the cumulative average running period of the combined unit from the data simulated in table 1.3.

The results as presented in table 1.5 rapidly settle down to around 15 ± 2 approximately, if the calculations are continued the cumulative average at the end of 100 simulated periods is 15.6. This method of determining when to curtail a simulation may not be possible if the objective is to assess the largest, or smallest value that might occur, as in that context an average value is of no interest. Also some simulation models may generate cycles (as in industrial dynamics), and it is important to distinguish between a value 'settling down' and a value approaching the crest or trough of a cycle.

Table 1.5   Calculation of cumulative average running time

Combined unit running period	Cumulative running period	Number of failed units	Cumulative average running period
5	5	1	5.0
25	30	2	15.0
35	65	3	21.6
5	70	4	17.5
25	95	5	19.0
5	100	6	16.6
15	115	7	16.5
5	120	8	15.0
5	125	9	13.9
5	130	10	13.0
5	135	11	12.3
25	160	12	13.3
5	165	13	12.7
45	210	14	15.0
15	225	15	15.0

The above example is so simple that the outcome might be calculated theoretically, Nevertheless a FORTRAN program (COMF) (see appendix 2) has been provided so that readers may extend the simulation if interested. However, in practice, the complexity of simulation studies precludes a theoretical analysis and usually warrants using a computer. To help facilitate the writing of simulation programs, special languages have been devised such as CSL, see chapter 6. Quite a lot of useful work can be done using an ordinary scientific programming language such as FORTRAN, see chapter 5.

Chapter 2

The Place of Simulation in Management Science and Operational Research

The manager today works in a rapidly changing situation in which he has little time to acquire rule-of-thumb experience. With no experience of a new problem and being only too conscious of the uncertainty in the situation, he is tempted to 'take chances' and play hunches. The development of Operational Research (O.R.) has provided management with the ability to analyse situations with the rigour of mathematics. This, together with the speed of computers, has brought to management a scientific basis only previously found in physics, biology and chemistry. To appreciate the context of this development it is useful to consider the main schools of management thought.

APPROACHES TO MANAGEMENT

The Human Relations School

This is perhaps the oldest school of management. Problems of motivation and leadership are emphasised on the grounds that 'management is the art of getting things done through people'. Leaders from time immemorial have recognised the importance of this aspect of management, whether managing a business, an army, or a government.

The Empiricalist School

This school believes in learning through experience. 'He who does not learn from the past, is doomed to repeat his failures'. The thesis is that one can learn from the experience of others, so that by examining the experience of successful managers it is hoped that the key to their effectiveness can be deduced. There is particular emphasis on case studies in this school.

The Financial School

The commercial aspects of management gave rise, at an early stage, to the development of accountancy procedures (such as double entry book-keeping in the fifteenth century). Developments such as cost accounting have led to a school of management that controls a business by financial manoeuvres. The significance of this school is that:

(1) it was the first to develop generalised methods in business;
(2) it was the first to place emphasis on quantitative methods.

The Scientific Management School

This school, traditionally associated with F. W. Taylor, is primarily concerned with production and the efficiency of men and machines. It believes that by analysing a process, particularly in detail, a better method can be found, and that, with objective work measurement, control can be effectively exercised. The distinction between O.R. and work study will be amplified later.

The Mathematical Model School

Logical processes are expressed mathematically in order to build up a model of a situation. Manipulation of the model then reveals relationships that can guide the manager in his actions. This represents an attempt to generalise the situation through symbolism. This school is often the one called operational research.

The Decision Theory School

This school, which is very close to the mathematical model school, believes that the primary activity of a manager is to make decisions. The investigation of the decision-making process will lead to a deeper understanding by management. It is more important to make the right decision than to use scientific management to implement a poor decision efficiently. This school is also identified with operational research. O.R. in this context is not restricted to mathematical methods, but covers any method of making better decisions.

The emergence of O.R. as a powerful tool of management does not mean that other schools of management have been superseded, but rather that they have been complemented. Unfortunately people tend to align themselves with one or other as though they were political parties. Management is still an art however and always will be, for art is the skilful application of a body of knowledge.

THE DEVELOPMENT OF O.R.

Decisions concerning any problem can be based on intuition, established management principles or various management techniques. Over the past years, increasing emphasis has been placed on management techniques, and the use of mathematical models has been developed to aid decision making. This approach is called operations research in the USA and operational research in the UK.

In its early days it had little to do with business management, but was developed in the armed services during World War II. Traditionally problems of war had been solved by trained officers, but the last war brought many new and complex problems, such as 'with limited radar equipment, how could you best protect Britain from enemy bombing raids?' To answer such problems, teams of scientists were formed to develop techniques which, it was later found, could also be applied to industry.

The term 'operational research' was coined, as mentioned above, to cover the research activity being undertaken in the operational areas of the armed services. Research teams formed for this purpose were composed of individuals from different disciplines. This provided some unexpected advantages as physicists, chemists, and mathematicians found that their knowledge could be used in other areas. For example, the delays in unloading supplies were found to be similar to the delays previously studied by electronic engineers in telephone networks.

Today it is recognised that queueing theory (a technique of O.R.) can be applied to a queue in any system. The queue might be material waiting to be drawn from stock; it might be machines waiting for attention by setters or the maintenance department; it might be jobs waiting to be processed; or it might be people waiting for promotion. In short, a queue of anything—men, materials, machines or money—in any type of system will exhibit similar characteristics.

In time, short cuts and standard procedures were developed that allowed the techniques to be applied to quite small problems. Computers helped spread the use of standard techniques by allowing very large problems to be solved economically and also by the development of packaged programs for small problems that would not have otherwise warranted individual attention.

THE BASIC CONCEPTS OF O.R.

The ability to abstract the essence of a situation so that it can be scientifically examined depends upon a basic concept of O.R.—the model.

Experimentation is the basis of all scientific work and O.R. is no exception. But how do you experiment with an administrative system? The answer is to build a model—not a physical model but a mathematical model. For example, a mathematical model could be built from the following simple situation.

A distribution company is to store and distribute two products, Crunchnuts and Wigwams. Space in the warehouse is limited to 160 000 m³. One hundred Crunchnuts occupies 20 m³ and 100 Wigwams occupies 80 m³. If the warehouse decides to handle Crunchnuts it will require 6 man-hours to pass 10 000 through the warehouse and 60 lorry-km to distribute. Wigwams require 5 man-hours to handle 10 000 and 20 lorry-km to distribute. The warehouse has 150 man-hours handling capacity per week and 1 200 lorry-km available per week.

To obtain a contract the warehouse must handle at least 50 000 Crunchnuts and 80 000 Wigwams per week. The profit margin on Crunchnuts is £10 per 100 and on Wigwams, £20 per 100.

To build a mathematical model of the above situation we have to resort to algebra.

If the number of Crunchnuts handled is x and the number of Wigwams handled is y, then a mathematical model representing the above situation would look like the following equations:

$$\frac{10}{100}x + \frac{20}{100}y = \quad \text{profit, to be maximised subject to:}$$

$$\frac{20}{100}x + \frac{80}{100}y \leqslant \quad 160\ 000$$

$$\frac{6}{10\ 000}x + \frac{5}{10\ 000}y \leqslant \quad 150$$

$$\frac{60}{10\ 000}x + \frac{20}{10\ 000}y \leqslant \quad 1\ 200$$

$$x \geqslant \quad 50\ 000$$

$$y \geqslant \quad 80\ 000$$

where $\leqslant$ means 'less than or equal to' and $\geqslant$ means 'greater than or equal to'

This model can be examined using linear programming methods. However the intention here is to illustrate how a business situation can be expressed in mathematical terms. Once the situation is viewed as a mathematical model it is easy to see how changes can be made to the model and their effect assessed without changing the actual situation. For instance, consider the space expressions.

The existing situation entails that for x units of Crunchnuts, $20/100$ m³ of space is required, similarly for Wigwams, $80/100$ m³ of space is required. Thus the total space required is

$$\frac{20}{100}x + \frac{80}{100}y,$$

but there is only $160\,000 \text{ m}^3$ available, hence this figure must not be exceeded, or mathematically,

$$\frac{20}{100}x + \frac{80}{100}y \leqslant 160\,000$$

This is a statement of the present situation, and on this basis an answer can be found. In addition though, it is possible to work out the effect of having more space available. Suppose an additional $40\,000 \text{ m}^3$ can be obtained, the expression can be readily changed to:

$$\frac{20}{100}x + \frac{80}{100}y \leqslant 200\,000$$

Likewise if the application of work study could reduce the time to handle the Crunchnuts to 3 man-hours per 10 000, then the corresponding expression becomes:

$$\frac{3}{10\,000}x + \frac{5}{10\,000}y \leqslant 150$$

These changes and many more can readily be incorporated into the mathematical model without implementing them in practice. On the basis of the improvements or not in the model's answer, it is then possible to decide whether to implement any of the experimental changes.

A further concept that needs mentioning, in addition to experimentation and model building, is the measure of effectiveness. When a model of the situation has been built and the factors are being experimentally varied, it is necessary to be able to decide when an improvement has been achieved. Some measure, termed the measure of effectiveness, has to be established. In the above model, this measure was taken to be profit, so that, the equation,

$$\frac{10}{100}x + \frac{20}{100}y = \text{profit}$$

would be used as measure of the effectiveness of alternative possible combinations of x and y.

The measure of effectiveness does not have to be profit, it can be any criteria the management care to use, return of capital, plant utilization, customer service, etc.

USE OF MODELS IN BUSINESS

The warehousing model considered above illustrates certain uses and advantages in having available a model of the situation under study. Other uses include measuring the relationship between variables. This is similar to a controlled experiment in science where the effect of altering one variable, in systematic steps, is observed and may be plotted graphically. Thus an inventory model might be examined to obtain the relationship between stockholding and customer service, see figure 8.15.

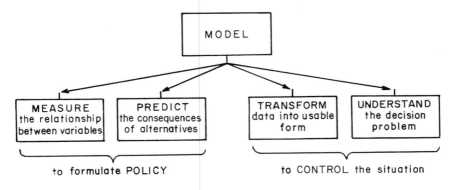

Figure 2.1   Uses of models in operational research

A second use of the model is to predict the consequences of alternative policies. Here the model is not being changed by degrees, but quite specific and possibly unrelated alternatives are applied to the model. An extra loading bay may be added in a distribution model for instance, or in a marketing model the advertising media may be switched.

In both the above uses the model is being used to assess possibilities; in the general management sense they are concerned with establishing policies so that plans may be developed. Planning is closely associated with controlling, and models may help in exercising control from two aspects.

Firstly data may not arise in a form that is convenient to use. A model could help transform data into a more usable form. For example, the orders received by a dispatch department might be expressed initially in monetary

25

terms, while for vehicle scheduling the orders need to be converted to van loads. A simple model might enable a relationship between monetary value and load to be established, i.e. a particular vehicle may be found to be capable of containing £1 400 of goods. This relationship, once established, may be used by the dispatchers to compile loads quickly.

The second aspect that may help in the control of a situation is the 'understanding' model building brings into a situation. The action of building, or of attempting to build a model, necessitates cause and effect to be examined very closely. Factors inherent in the situation are recognised and, in the jargon of O.R., the controllable and uncontrollable variables identified. These uses of models in business are shown diagrammatically in figure 2.1.

APPLICATIONS OF O.R.

The ability to inter-relate numerous factors has led to O.R. being applied to most fields of business. There is no industry or function of management to which O.R. cannot be applied but, naturally, large companies have been in the forefront with applications.

Companies with mixing or blending problems, whether they be mixing chemicals, blending oils or food products can use linear programming methods to find the most economic combination of ingredients. Problems involving alternative ways of moving materials can be solved by similar methods. Large grocery chains have many ways of distributing their goods among warehouses, and the best vehicle routeing can be established by the use of O.R. methods. The railways have an identical problem in deciding how best to move their rolling stock around the network to meet the changing demand at each depot.

The principles of inventory control can be applied to a wide range of problems. O.R. can be used to determine the best policy in stocking blood, where there is a limited shelf life. Other hospital problems examined, using O.R. methods, have been the appointments system in outpatients departments to compare relative consultant patient waiting times and service.

Steel companies have used O.R. to help devise the best shutdown and overhaul procedures. Large-scale projects in the construction industry are being increasingly controlled by the critical path methods of O.R.

In addition to the production and distribution problems cited above, O.R. can also be applied to the marketing and financial function, the allocation of money and planning of advertising campaigns for example. The strategies to adopt in bidding for contracts can be examined using O.R. methods and are, in fact, used by some oil companies in bidding for exploration rights. Investment trusts can use O.R. to determine the allocation of money among funds. Numerous further examples can be found by reading the situations vacant columns for O.R. workers where the projects currently being undertaken are often mentioned.

THE RELATIONSHIP OF O.R. TO STATISTICS AND WORK STUDY

It has already been mentioned that in O.R. a mixed team is used, but apart from this it is possible to confuse O.R. with other disciplines such as statistics and work study. The distinction is sometimes a fine one but, nevertheless, the following comparisons may help to give a better understanding of O.R.

O.R. frequently makes use of statistical methods, particularly techniques based upon probability theory, but it is not restricted to statistical methods. This is because a statistician is primarily concerned with the relationship between numbers, while to the O.R. worker this is a means to an end. The O.R. worker is concerned with understanding the system in order to control it. A particular fine distinction exists between statistics and O.R. where simulation is concerned. In this book, simulation is considered as falling within the sphere of O.R. simply on the grounds that most O.R. books cover simulation, but very few standard statistical works mention the technique.

The distinction between O.R. and work study is also extremely blurred for both are trying to improve the efficiency of the company. Work study officers usually apply standard methods and techniques to their projects and therefore work within the limitations of these methods. O.R. people develop, by way of the model, methods to suit the particular problem on hand. If a standard method is suitable, well and good, but if not, a new one is devised.

When techniques developed in O.R. have wide application, there is no reason why these standard techniques cannot be adopted by other disciplines such as work study or accountants. The point is that O.R. is operational *research*. Other management disciplines have a body of knowledge which is applied daily by their practitioners and their research is done outside of the day-to-day applications of their knowledge. O.R. workers though are all research workers, every project is a research project.

O.R. projects require the gathering of data and often these data can be obtained via the work study section. For this reason, and others of administrative convenience, some firms have set up management services departments, which comprise work study, O & M, O.R., statistics and systems analysis.

RESUME OF O.R. METHODS AND TECHNIQUES

The main areas of O.R. that have led to standardisation or 'cook-book' methods of solutions are outlined below, together with a comment on the relevance of simulation.

Linear Programming

The technique of linear programming (l.p.) enables one to select the most effective combination from many possible alternatives, thus the Crunchnuts-Wigwams problem, which is one of choosing the best combination of merchandise, can be solved by l.p. methods. Problems involving the best allocation of resources, be they men, materials, machines and money, or any mixture of these resources, can often be described by an l.p. model.

A condition, that the relationship in the model must be linear, might appear unduly restrictive at first sight, but straight-line relationships can often be assumed in practice over small ranges of data. The general procedure in l.p. starts with a feasible solution and systematically improves the solution until an optimum is reached. Depending on the nature of the problem, one of three basic methods is appropriate: the assignment method, the transportation method and the simplex method. Computer packages are readily available for the simplex method, which is a general method capable of solving any l.p. The transportation method is also available as it is inconvenient to translate a straightforward transportation problem into a simplex format, but the assignment method, being a particular case of the transportation problem, can be solved readily with a transportation package.

Linear programming forms part of the larger field of mathematical programming which also comprises quadratic programming, parametric programming, dynamic programming etc.

Simulation and l.p. tend to be regarded as two quite separate techniques. However, it is possible for l.p. sub-problems to exist in a large simulation model. For example, if a production planning and scheduling system were being simulated, the load for each particular day or week would have to be established. The orders might be met by cutting material from a stock size, giving rise to a sub-problem of cutting to minimise material wastage. This type of sub-problem is a well known l.p. problem termed trim-loss (some computer manufacturers have an l.p. package specifically for this trim-loss problem).

Inventory Control

Inventory control in O.R. is concerned with stocks of any resource so that various aspects of the theory can be applied to stocks of money (investment problems), stocks of people (personnel, training and manpower planning problems), stocks of plant (maintenance and replacement problems) and the obvious area of stocks of materials.

The general approach is to establish the costs involved in obtaining, holding and running out of stocks together with considerations of the variability of demand, so as to arrive at a policy judged to be economic relative to the risks involved. The risks largely arise from variability of demand and variability of lead times. This means that stock control systems rely on establishing a good method of forecasting to reduce the risks involved.

In practice, stock control situations do not lend themselves to direct application of the theory because of the many assumptions built into the formulae. Simulation is often the only way of assessing the behaviour of alternative inventory policies in practice.

Forecasting Techniques

Forecasting techniques have developed a long way from the traditional moving averages and linear regression methods. It is recognised that no forecast will be perfect and that forecast errors occur. The errors are examined statistically and are used as a correction factor in the next forecast. Thus any change in the basic pattern of figures, while giving rise initially to a larger error, is used in the subsequent forecasts so that the forecasting system adapts itself to these changing conditions.

The setting up of an adaptive forecasting system can entail extensive simulation to find the values of the parameters that will lead to the smallest forecasting errors. The majority of forecasting applications are directed towards stock control; more details will be provided in chapter 8.

Forecasting is closely allied to prediction, where the objective is to assess the future without the advantage of a past time series. The strategies to adopt in bidding for contracts for instance cannot be based upon past bids for the same contract.

Queueing Theory

Queueing theory studies the results of arrivals requiring service from some resource. When the arrival rate and service rate do not exactly correspond, queues are likely to develop or the service facility is idle. The formulae developed allow one to calculate the facility idle time, average waiting time, queue length etc. for various conditions. The main parameters considered are, the frequency distribution of arrivals, the frequency distribution of service rate, the number of service channels and queue discipline.

Unfortunately, there are so many combinations of frequency distributions and other parameters that it is very often found impossible to use existing formulae. The usual way of solving queueing problems in practice is simulation, so much so that many text-books place their coverage of simulation in their chapter on queueing. Once again, because of its practical importance a separate chapter (7) deals with the solution of queueing problems by simulation.

Replacement Theory

Replacement techniques generally cover three types of situation, namely, where there is deterioration, obsolescence or failure.

Problems of deterioration In these types of problems, the mounting maintenance or running costs cause one to consider when to cut losses and invest in a new resource (figure 2.2).

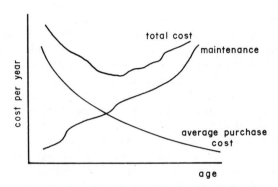

Figure 2.2   Cost factors of deteriorating plant

The cost factors that conflict are the depreciation and the running costs.

The correct approach is to find the replacement period that minimises the average total cost per year.

Problems of obsolescence These problems are often of a broad nature involving top management policy. The correct policy to follow is the one that optimises the company's strategy.

With problems involving straight comparisons between existing resources and alternatives, the choice should be based on a comparison of the minimum average costs per year.

If a change in resource is indicated, the timing of the change also needs consideration. The existing cost per year should be compared with the expected average cost per year of the proposed resource, and the change made when the average cost is the lower of the two.

Problems of failure When items are subject to failure, the policy to choose should be the one that minimises the expected costs. This involves considering what is likely to happen, based on the probability of failures.

In this type of problem, the question of stocks of spares arises and therefore the problem can be considered as a probabilistic inventory control problem. The cost of ordering, stocking, and shortages are therefore relevant. This last type of problem, involving distributions of component life, is ideally suited to simulation. The simple simulation example in chapter 1 might be part of a replacement problem.

Critical Path Analysis

Critical path analysis is a technique that shows diagrammatically the steps (termed activities) and the inter-relationships involved in carrying out a project. Analysis of the network of activities on a time basis allows management to assess the consequences of delays and helps in deciding the required remedial action. In its simplest form, critical path analysis is a planning and control tool of functional managers. The technique may be elaborated to include resource allocation and hence linear programming, and also to develop probabilistic project durations.

As a network represents a proposed plan, it may be regarded as a model for simulation purposes, thus the effects of different weather conditions in a construction project may be simulated by reference to a network.

Routing Techniques

Routing techniques are one of the rapidly developing areas in O.R. A typical routing problem involves visiting each of several locations once, starting from and finishing at a particular location (e.g. a warehouse), in such a way that the total distance travelled is minimised. Optimal algorithms exist for this type of problem and are being increasingly applied, owing to the availability of computer packages. There is scope for simulation in this area as the 'best' solution might change from tour to tour. Simulation allows near 'optimal' solutions to be compared to establish a possible standard route.

SUMMARY

This chapter has indicated the relationship of simulation to other O.R. techniques.

In many instances, the straightforward application of a suitable O.R. technique will lead to an optimal solution, and this is therefore to be preferred to simulation. When, however, it is not possible to solve the problem mathematically, then simulation may be used. Thus simulation is capable of yielding results where other methods cannot be used.

The results obtained from simulation can be regarded as statistical estimates. In this context, the accuracy of the results depend on several factors such as:

(*a*) the viability and accuracy of the input data;
(*b*) the assumptions made in the structure of the model;
(*c*) the exhaustive validation of the model;
(*d*) the sample size (i.e. length of run).

A carefully designed simulation can provide results of sufficient accuracy for many practical situations.

Chapter 3

A Review of Some Statistical Concepts

The building of simulation models might require the application of a wide range of statistical knowledge. Particular areas of statistics are associated with different areas of application, e.g. Weibull distributions with maintenance and reliability models. The more specialised areas of statistics will be dealt with as the need arises in subsequent chapters. This chapter is intended to be a review of some basic concepts that need to be known. Those readers, who until now have found the usual coin tossing and dice rolling examples to have little relevance to business life, should find in this chapter a guide to the areas that they need to revise.

PROBABILITY

The probability of an event occurring can be defined as the relative frequency with which this event occurs in the long run.

i.e.
$$P(E) = \frac{\text{number of times } E \text{ occurred}}{\text{total number of occurrences}}$$

where $P(E)$ means 'the probability of E' and is a compound symbol [$P(E)$ does *not* imply P times E as in other areas of algebraic relation].

The minimum and maximum values for $P(E)$, from the above definition, are 0 and 1, and it also follows that the probability of E *not* occurring, written $P(\bar{E})$, is the difference between $P(E)$ and 1, or

$$P(E) + P(\bar{E}) = 1$$

An example of the above relationships and the practical implications might be based upon a newspaper statement saying that of the 120 000 people who flew from London Airport, 42 000 flew on British airlines.

Hence the probability that a passenger at London Airport is 'flying British' is given by

$$P(\text{British airline}) = \frac{42\ 000}{120\ 000} = 0.35$$

and
$$P(\text{non-British airline}) = \frac{78\ 000}{120\ 000} = 0.65$$

which can also be found from,

$$P(\text{British airline}) + P(\text{non-British airline}) = 1$$
i.e. $\quad P(\text{non-British airline}) = 1 - 0.35 = 0.65$

These probabilities relate to the chance that anyone in the original 120 000 passengers would be flying British or not. The probabilities are inapplicable to passengers at Rome or any other airport, furthermore, they may be inapplicable to other passengers (beyond the 120 000) at London Airport. The validity of applying probabilities to further passengers at London Airport depends on whether 120 000 original 'readings' constitutes a valid sample of a larger group. If the results are applied to a subsequent situation the question of trends, seasonal patterns etc. enters the picture.

Thus even the deceptively simple ideas of probability have to be applied very cautiously in practice.

When the probability of more than one event is to be considered, it becomes necessary to know how to manipulate the probabilities arithmetically to arrive at an overall probability. This requires us to consider whether the events are mutually exclusive. Suppose for example, that we had a more detailed analysis of 370 000 passengers at London Airport, as shown in table 3.1.

Table 3.1   Passenger distribution (× 1 000)

Flight	First Class	Tourist	Charter	Total
BEA	10	40	30	80
BOAC	20	50	—	70
Other British airlines	—	40	60	100
Non-British	40	70	10	120
Total	70	200	100	370

We may want to find the probabilities of the following situations:

(a) that a passenger is flying with BEA,

(b) that a passenger is flying tourist with BEA,

(c) that all four passengers arriving in a taxi are flying BOAC (assuming they are strangers who joined just to get a taxi),

(d) that a passenger is flying first class or tourist with a non-British airline.

To answer these and many similar questions some of the 'laws' of probability are involved. The notation to be used is:

$$P(A) \qquad \text{meaning the probability that an event } A \text{ occurs}$$
$$P(A + B) \qquad \text{meaning the probability that events } A \text{ or } B \text{ occurs}$$
$$P(AB) \qquad \text{meaning the probability that both } A \text{ and } B \text{ occur}$$
$$P(A \mid B) \qquad \text{meaning the probability that } A \text{ occurs } given \text{ that } B \text{ occurs.}$$

Then it can be shown that:

$$P(A + B) \quad = P(A) + P(B) \tag{3.1}$$
$$P(AB) \quad = P(A) \times P(B) \tag{3.2}$$

also

$$P(AB) \quad = P(A \mid B) P(B) \tag{3.3}$$

We can now answer the four questions about the flying habits of passengers.

(a) Probability of flying with BEA = 80/370 = 0.216

(b) Probability of flying tourist with BEA = 40/370 = 0.108

An alternative approach could be from equation 3.3,

$$P \text{ (tourist with BEA)} = P \text{ (BEA given tourist booking)} \times P \text{ (tourist)}$$

$$= \frac{40}{200} \times \frac{200}{370} = 0.108$$

or

$$P \text{ (tourist with BEA)} = P \text{ (tourist given BEA)} \times P \text{ (BEA)}$$

$$= \frac{40}{80} \times \frac{80}{370} = 0.108$$

The method chosen in practice will depend on which figures are more readily available.

(c) Probability that all four passengers fly with BOAC, from equation 3.2,

$$= P \text{ (first flies BOAC)} \times P \text{ (second flies BOAC)} \times P \text{ (third flies BOAC)}$$
$$\times P \text{ (fourth flies BOAC)}$$

$$\frac{70}{370} \times \frac{70}{370} \times \frac{70}{370} \times \frac{70}{370} = 0.00128$$

(d) Probability, from equation 3.1,

$$= P \text{ (first class with non-British)} + P \text{ (tourist with non-British)}$$

$$= \frac{40}{370} + \frac{70}{370} = \frac{110}{370} = 0.297$$

Once again this answer may be obtained along simular lines to the alternative in question (b), i.e.

$$P \text{ (first class or tourist with non-British)}$$
$$= P \text{ (first class with non-British)} + P \text{ (tourist with non-British)}$$
$$= P \text{ (first class given non-British)} \times P \text{ (non-British)}$$
$$+ P \text{ (tourist given non-British)} \times P \text{ (non-British)}$$
$$= \left(\frac{40}{120} \times \frac{120}{370} \right) + \left(\frac{70}{120} \times \frac{120}{370} \right) = \frac{40}{370} + \frac{70}{370} = \frac{110}{370} = 0.297$$

EXPECTATION

Expected value is an arithmetic average calculated by taking into account the respective probabilities of alternative outcomes and their 'value'.

i.e.   Expected value = $V_A P(A) + V_B P(B) + \ldots V_n P(n)$
where V_n = value of event n occurring

For example, in the airport passenger problem, if BOAC gets an average profit of £25 for first class bookings and £15 for tourist class, the expected value (i.e. profit in this case) to BOAC of one passenger passing through London Airport is

$$£25 \times \frac{20}{370} + £15 \times \frac{50}{370} = £3.38$$

Thus, if 2 800 passengers pass through the airport per week then BOAC on average will make 2 800 × £3.38 = £9 459 profit per week. Another way of examining the figures would be to calculate the expected value of a definite BOAC booking,

i.e. $£25 \times \frac{20}{70} + £15 \times \frac{50}{70} = £17.86$

Thus BOAC would make £17.86 average profit on every booking they receive.

FREQUENCY DISTRIBUTIONS

Frequency distributions arise wherever data of a variable are classified by the magnitude of that variable. Thus the weekly demand for replacement electric motors might be recorded for, say, twenty weeks and be as shown in table 3.2.

Table 3.2   Weekly demand for electric motors

Week	1	2	3	4	5	6	7	8	9	10	11	12	13	14	15	16	17	18	19	20
Demand	1	2	0	3	1	2	2	0	3	1	2	0	1	0	1	1	0	3	1	4

If these data are consolidated to show how frequently a particular demand occurs, the result is a frequency table (table 3.3).

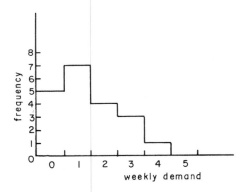

Figure 3.1   Frequency distribution of weekly demand

Table 3.3   Frequency table of weekly demand

Weekly demand	Frequency
0	5
1	7
2	4
3	3
4	1

This frequency table can be plotted graphically to illustrate how the data are distributed over the range encountered. A graphical representation of the

37

frequency table is termed a frequency distribution (figure 3.1) and gives an immediate indication of the smallest value, the largest value, the range, the most frequently occurring value (modal value), whether the distribution is symmetrical etc.

The assessment of data in terms of a frequency distribution is often fruitful because under certain conditions particular frequency distributions arise. This is useful from two standpoints, if an expected distribution is found it suggests the conditions have been interpreted correctly; if data are found to follow a 'known' distribution, light may be thrown on the underlying conditions and from this the mathematical properties of the 'known' distribution may enable the analysis of the data to be extended.

The 'known' distributions are too numerous to describe in this introductory work, for any distribution is likely to be encountered in Monte Carlo simulation, depending on the application area. This chapter, intended for the newcomer to statistics, will outline four basic frequency distributions, the binomial, the Poisson, the normal and the exponential.

The Binomial Frequency Distribution

The word 'binomial' means 'consisting of two classes' and is a convenient term to use for situations in which there are only two possible outcomes. A simple example of this is coin tossing as the outcome must be either head or tail. The term has wider significance if a group of things can be divided into two classes. Thus, all the output from a machine could be divided into good or defective. All housewives can be divided into those who use instant coffee and those who do not.

It is common practice in discussing situations of this kind to call one of the possible outcomes a *success* and the other a *failure*. The assignment is arbitrary, heads can be regarded as a success and tails a failure in coin tossing or vice versa. Whatever the assignment, it must be adhered to throughout a problem.

The mathematics of the binomial situation were first worked out by Bernoulli in the eighteenth century. The basic assumption made is that there is no pattern of successes or failures.

Thus successes or failures are likely to occur with the same frequency throughout a sequence of occurrences. A process that meets these conditions is known as a Bernoulli process.

> If p is the probability of a *success*
> and q is the probability of a *failure*

then the probabilities of various outcomes occurring in n trials are given by the terms of the *binomial formula* :

$$p^n + \frac{n}{1} p^{n-1}q + \frac{n(n-1)}{2 \times 1} p^{n-2}q^2 + \frac{n(n-1)(n-2)}{3 \times 2 \times 1} p^{n-3}q^3 + \ldots q^n$$

which arises from expanding the expression $(p + q)^n$.

In many applications we need to know the probability of a specified number of successes. This specified number can be given the symbol r.

The use of the symbol r allows the formula to be manipulated so that, given r, the probability of r occurring can be calculated direct. This formula is:

$$P(r) = \frac{n!}{r! \, (n-r)!} p^r q^{n-r}$$

where $P(r)$ is the probability of r successes.

Note: ! means factorial   i.e. $3! = 3 \times 2 \times 1 = 6$

also $0! = 1$

A simple application of the above formulae would be in the following situation. A car manufacturer receives a batch of sparking plugs containing 10 per cent defective and does not inspect them prior to use. They are used in four cylinder engines, which will just about start on three cylinders but not on two or one cylinder. What proportion of cars will not start at the end of the assembly line?

Here, $p = 0.1$ (a defective plug) and $n = 4$ (cylinders) and we are required to find:

$$P(2 \text{ defective plugs}) + P(3 \text{ defective plugs}) + P(4 \text{ defective plugs}).$$

It is easier to calculate instead:

$$1 - [P(0 \text{ defective plugs}) + P(1 \text{ defective plug})]$$

for which we need to substitute for where $r = 0$ and then 1:

$$P(0 \text{ defective plugs}) = \frac{4 \times 3 \times 2 \times 1}{0! \, (4 \times 3 \times 2 \times 1)} (0.1)^0 (0.9)^4 = 0.6561$$

$$P(1 \text{ defective plug}) = \frac{4 \times 3 \times 2 \times 1}{1! \, (3 \times 2 \times 1)} (0.1)^1 (0.9)^3 = 0.2916$$

Therefore:

$$\text{Probability of not starting} = 1 - [0.6561 + 0.2916] = 0.0523$$

i.e. 5.23 per cent of cars will not start owing to faulty plugs.

The probability of a car having 0, 1, 2, 3 or 4 faulty plugs is given in table 3.4 together with the results graphed as a probability distribution in figure 3.2

(a probability distribution is similar to a frequency distribution but having the frequency scale replaced by a probability scale; the 'shape' remains unchanged).

A binomial frequency distribution, as should be evident from the preceding example and formulae, never goes below zero, always starts at zero and increases in discrete steps of unity, up to the value of n.

Table 3.4   Probability of plug failure

Number of faulty plugs	Probability
0	0.6561
1	0.2916
2	0.0486
3	0.0036
4	0.0001

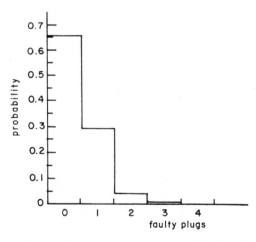

Figure 3.2   Probability distribution of faulty plugs

The Poisson Frequency Distribution

The use of the binomial distribution requires that the proportions of p and q can be stated. In many instances, it is possible to record the number of times an event occurred but impossible to know how many times it *did not* occur. This is particularly true of events that happen in a period of time. Thus the number of people who arrive at a telephone booth can be counted but to speak of the number who don't arrive is meaningless. In this context, n is unknown and presumably very large. Also because n is large, if it were known, the value of p when calculated would be small.

In 1837 Simeon Poisson found how to modify the binomial distribution to suit this situation. The Poisson distribution formula is:

$$P(x) = \frac{a^x e^{-a}}{x!}$$

where $\qquad P(x) =$ the probability of x successes

$\qquad a \quad =$ average or 'expected' number of successes

$\qquad e \quad = 2.7183$, a constant.

This can be regarded as a special case of the binomial where p tends to zero and n tends to infinity.

Consider a retail stores where the average demand for a certain box of chocolates is ten per week. What is the chance of selling twelve in any one week (ignoring seasonal patterns)?

$$x = 12, \quad a = 10$$

$$P(12) = \frac{10^{12} e^{-10}}{12!} = 0.095$$

This type of calculation is tedious and it is possible to refer to tables (see appendix 19) to find $P(x)$ given any value of a, but it is useful to know that successive terms can be calculated as follows:

$$P(0) = e^{-a}$$
$$P(1) = ae^{-a} = a[P(0)]$$
$$P(2) = \frac{a^2}{2} e^{-a} = \frac{a}{2}[P(1)]$$

$$\cdot$$
$$\cdot$$
$$\cdot$$

$$P(5) = \frac{a^5}{5} e^{-a} = \frac{a}{5}[P(4)]$$

i.e. each term can be calculated easily from the preceding term by multiplying by a/x.

Thus in the previous example, the chance of selling fourteen in any one week can be obtained from the previous calculation as follows:

$$P(13) = \frac{10}{13} \times 0.095 = 0.073$$

$$P(14) = \frac{10}{14} \times 0.073 = 0.052$$

In summary then, a Poisson probability distribution is likely to be found where incidents occur at random. The parameter required for the theoretical development of the distribution is the mean. In practice, this is often a mean rate, i.e. demand per week, accidents per square mile per year, number of arrivals per minute etc. Like the binomial, the distribution is discrete and does not go below zero. It has no upper limit however as *n* is infinity, in practice the upper values become so small they can be ignored.

The Normal Frequency Distribution
The binomial and Poisson distributions are examples of discrete distributions. For some situations, the observations made and collected into a frequency distribution may involve measurements—a continuous scale ranging from zero to infinity. A commonly occurring continuous distribution is the normal frequency distribution (see figure 3.3).

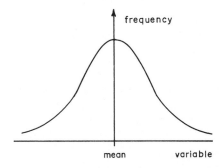

Figure 3.3   The general shape of a normal frequency distribution

The normal frequency distribution occurs when a variable is varying 'at random' about an average value. To specify a particular normal frequency distribution it is necessary to specify a measure termed 'the standard deviation' in addition to specifying the mean. The standard deviation is a measure of the spread of the distribution about the mean and can be estimated from:

$$\text{standard deviation} = \sqrt{\left\{ \frac{1}{n-1} \left[\Sigma fx^2 - \frac{(\Sigma fx)^2}{n} \right] \right\}}$$

where,

n = total number of observations or readings,
x = an individual reading or mid-point of a class interval,
f = frequency with which the particular value of x occurs.

A standard deviation calculated from the above formula is an estimate of the standard deviation because the total number of readings, no matter how large, represent a sample from an infinite number.

By scaling it is possible to relate the properties of any normal curve obtained in practice to one having a mean of zero and a standard deviation of one. The area between any two points on this standardised normal curve can be found from tables (or subroutines). As the total area of a standardised normal curve is unity, areas can be interpreted as probabilities. Suppose, for example, that a company has an average weekly demand of sixty units, the actual variations about this mean of sixty have lead to the standard deviation being calculated as four units. We might wish to know the probability of having to meet a demand in excess of seventy units.

actual situation

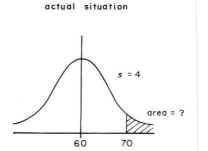

'standardised' situation

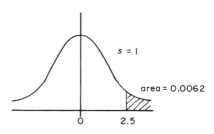

Figure 3.4   Interpretation of area under the normal curve

The deviation, above the mean, $= 70 - 60 = 10$ units where $s = 4$. The pro-rata deviation for a standardised normal curve having $s = 1$, is then, $10/4 = 2.5$ standard deviations.

By reference to normal frequency tables (see appendix 18) it can be found that 0.0062 of the area lies beyond 2.5 standard deviations above the mean. The probability of having a demand in excess of seventy units is similarly 0.0062. This example is illustrated in figure 3.4.

The normal frequency distribution is a widely applicable distribution because, apart from arising in situations that are inherently 'normal', it can be used to approximate binomial distributions (when $n > 50$ and $np > 5$), and Poisson distributions (when $a > 5$). Furthermore, a normal distribution may be obtained when several distributions, other than normal, are combined. This is a consequence of the central limit theorem, details of which may be found in standard statistical textbooks. One such application is in PERT (Programme Evaluation Review Technique, a version of Critical Path Analysis) where, though the individual activity durations are assumed to vary as beta distributions, by application of the central limit theorem, the end event is considered to vary as a normal distribution.

The Exponential Distribution

An exponent is the power to which a number is raised. When this exponent is one of the variables (x) in an expression relating x and y, the equation is of the form:

$$y = a(b)^x$$

where a and b are constants. The shape of such an equation is as shown in figure 3.5.

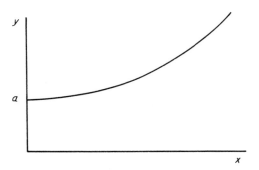

Figure 3.5   An exponential growth curve

This type of relationship exists where the *rate* of increase in y is constant. The rate of increase is often constant in 'growth' situations. For example, the value to which £500 would have grown to (y) over x years if 7 per cent interest is being paid is given by the equation:

$$y = 500 \left(\frac{107}{100}\right)^x$$

With this type of expression a straight line graph is obtained, if y is plotted on a logarithmic scale.

The Negative Exponential Distribution   An exponential distribution that is frequently found in statistical work has the equation

$$y = ae^{-ax} \qquad \text{(where e = 2.71828)}$$

44

and is known as the negative exponential distribution owing to its negative exponent. The general shape of this equation is shown in figure 3.6.

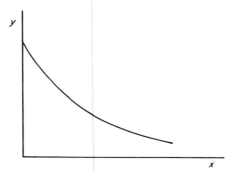

Figure 3.6   A negative exponential curve

If data are following this type of distribution the probability of a value of *x or more* occurring is given by

$$P(x \text{ or more}) = (e)^{-x/M}$$
where M = the mean of the distribution.

Relationship to the Poisson Distribution   It is useful to realise the relationship that can exist between the Poisson and the exponential distributions. This is particularly useful where arrival patterns are being studied for subsequent application of queueing theory or simulation studies.

Consider a situation where the items are arriving at random on a time scale, (that is, the time of arrival of any one particular item is completely independent of any other arrival times). This could be represented diagrammatically as shown in figure 3.7, where the vertical lines represent the points in time at which there is an arrival.

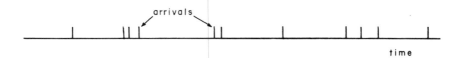

Figure 3.7   A random arrival pattern

If these arrivals are occurring at random, then by grouping the data into equal space time intervals we should obtain a Poisson distribution for the

A Practical Approach to Computer Simulation

number of arrivals per unit time. For example, if the above time scale was divided into, say, 1 hour intervals, the following count of number of arrivals per hourly interval could be made, (see figure 3.8) 1,3,2,1,3 etc.

Figure 3.8   Arrival pattern divided into hourly intervals

The complete data collected in this manner could be presented as a frequency table as shown in table 3.5.

Table 3.5   Frequency distribution of arrivals per hour

Number of arrivals per hour	Frequency
0	4
1	14
2	22
3	23
4	17
5	11
6	8
7	1

This frequency distribution has a mean of approximately three per hour. Substitution of the mean in Poisson formulae will show that this distribution closely follows a Poisson type.

It is also true that if the arrivals are at random then the interval *between* arrivals should follow an exponential distribution. The data would be collected in the manner shown in figure 3.9, resulting in inter-arrival times of 40, 5, 8, 60, 6 min etc.

Figure 3.9   Inter-arrival time pattern

Data from the above could be summarised in a frequency table as shown in table 3.6.

46

Table 3.6   Frequency distribution of inter-arrival times

Interval between arrivals, min	Frequency
0 –	40
10 –	25
20 –	14
30 –	9
40 –	5
50 –	3
60 –	2
70 –	1
80 –	1

The mean of this frequency distribution is approximately 20 min.

Converting the Distributions Data collected and fitted to one of the distributions can readily be converted to the other since:

$$\text{mean of exponential} = \frac{1}{\text{mean of Poisson}}$$

For example:

If the mean number of arrivals per hour is three, the mean of the equivalent exponential is:

$\frac{1}{3}$ hour = 20 min.

Table 3.7   Development of cumulative probability from inter-arrival time

Interval time min	Frequency	Probability	Probability of x or more
0 –	40	0.40	1.00
10 –	25	0.25	0.60
20 –	14	0.14	0.35
30 –	9	0.09	0.21
40 –	5	0.05	0.12
50 –	3	0.03	0.07
60 –	2	0.02	0.04
70 –	1	0.01	0.02
80 –	1	0.01	0.01

Thus the two frequency tables previously given represent the same arrival pattern expressed either in Poisson or exponential terms.

The Use of Semi-Log Paper If data are processed so that the probability of *x or more* is available, this probability can be plotted on a log scale against the value of *x* on a linear scale. If the data are exponentially distributed, a straight line graph will result.

The method is illustrated in table 3.7 and figure 3.10.

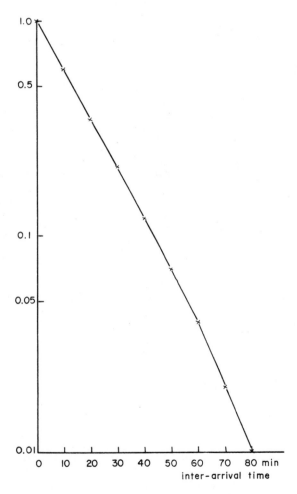

Figure 3.10 Probability of equalling or exceeding inter-arrival time

SIGNIFICANCE TESTING

In practice when data are collected and seem to follow a Poisson, normal or exponential distribution etc., the questions that arise are: 'How closely does it fit the theoretical shape?', 'Are the discrepancies so large that it would be incorrect to assume this theoretical distribution, or are the discrepancies about the magnitude to be expected in this number of readings?'. These types of questions are dealt with in statistics by means of significance tests. There have been many tests of significance developed over the years to meet the needs of differing circumstances, and from these the chi-squared (χ^2) test has been chosen to demonstrate this aspect of statistics.

The χ^2 test compares any three or more groups or classes of data. Thus it can be used to compare any theoretical frequency distribution with an actual distribution, provided that there are three or more class intervals. An example of using the χ^2 to compare collected data with a Poisson distribution would be as follows:

Suppose we wished to check whether the frequency table given previously in table 3.5 is similar to a Poisson distribution. The first step is to calculate the expected results from a Poisson distribution having the same mean. The mean value of the frequency table (table 3.5) is 3.05, and by reference to Poisson tables (see appendix 19) the probabilities of 0, 1, 2, 3, 4, 5, 6 and 7 can be established. These probabilities are then multiplied by the total observations (100) to obtain the expected frequencies if the data were really following a Poisson distribution, see table 3.8.

Table 3.8   Poisson frequency distribution

Probabilities of a Poisson distribution having a mean of 3.05		Expected frequency
0	0.047	4.7
1	0.145	14.5
2	0.220	22.0
3	0.224	22.4
4	0.170	17.0
5	0.105	10.5
6	0.053	5.3
7 (or more)	0.036	3.6

A measure of the 'goodness of fit' can now be obtained by calculating χ^2 from the following expression:

$$\chi^2 = \Sigma \frac{(\text{observed} - \text{expected})^2}{\text{expected}}$$

49

This has been done in table 3.9 and gives a χ^2 value of 3.415.

Table 3.9   Calculation of chi-squared (χ^2)

Observed (O)	Expected (E)	$O - E$	$(O - E)^2$	$\dfrac{(O - E)^2}{E}$
4	4.7	−0.7	0.49	0.104
14	14.5	−0.5	0.25	0.017
22	22.0	0	0	0
23	22.4	0.6	0.36	0.016
17	17.0	0	0	0
11	10.5	0.5	0.25	0.024
8	5.3	2.7	7.29	1.376
1	3.6	−2.6	6.76	1.878

$$Total = \chi^2 = 3.415$$

If the observed figures followed a distribution exactly, the observed and expected figures would be identical, thus $O - E$ would be zero in every case and χ^2 would be zero. As the observed figures depart from the expected, the value of χ^2 increases. χ^2 tables give the probability of certain discrepancies. In order to use χ^2 tables, a parameter termed 'the degrees of freedom' (d.o.f.) has to be established.

d.o.f. = number of classes − (1 x number of restraints imposed)
In the above example,

number of classes   = 8
number of restraints = 2   i.e. expected distribution must
have a mean of 3.05 and total
expected frequency must equal 100.
Therefore d.o.f. 8 − 2 = 6

The formal approach to this example would be that, having obtained the observed values, we think they might have been sampled from a situation that is following a Poisson distribution. We then set up a hypothesis that there is no significant difference between our observed data and a theoretical Poisson. The hypothesis is then tested by calculating χ^2:

if the probability of obtaining the χ^2 value is > 5 per cent there is no significant difference proven;

if the probability of obtaining the χ^2 value is > 1 per cent < 5 per cent the result may be significant, more data should be collected;

if the probability of obtaining the χ^2 value is < 1 per cent the result is highly significant i.e. the hypothesis is unlikely to be true.

In our example, the probability of obtaining $\chi^2 = 3.415$ is much larger than 5 per cent (see appendix 17), so the hypothesis has not been disproved. We can therefore assume that the situation is following a Poisson pattern.

The above example illustrates the general approach to significance testing; the reader is referred to standard statistical books for further detail and other tests. Significance testing may play an important part in building a simulation model. Although input frequency distributions may be handled as unique distributions, the ability to test how closely they conform to theoretical distributions is useful. On the output side of the model it is useful to have a means of testing whether there is a significant difference between the results of two runs so that valid conclusions may be drawn.

Statistics is a large body of knowledge and many other aspects could be touched upon, but this coverage is felt to be sufficient to give the reader an idea as to whether his existing statistical knowledge will suffice. Certain aspects associated with particular applications, such as forecasting techniques with inventory control, will be mentioned in subsequent chapters as necessary.

Chapter 4

Building Simulation Models

TERMS OF REFERENCE

Whenever any project is set up, whether it involves simulation or otherwise, it is essential that the person or team involved is provided with clear terms of reference. The following notes on terms of reference are meant to be a guide to ensuring that no aspect is overlooked, for often projects are 'dropped into one's lap' unexpectedly, or given verbatim, and the onus is on the person undertaking the project to be clear as to what is expected of him. For this reason the following notes are written around the familiar what, why, when, who, where and how procedure, which when applied to a subject usually provides one with a quick but comprehensive view of the matter in hand.

Firstly, 'what?' The issue here is, what is the objective? Usually the objective as stated by one's superiors must be accepted, at least until the investigation shows that the objective was ill conceived. Although therefore the objective when given will not be argued with or queried, it is important to know precisely what the objective is in the eyes of the initiator of the project. The objective should be stated in as a quantifiable manner as possible and should be as specific as possible. This is sound economic sense for broad and vague objectives will lead to equally vague reports having few specific recommendations.

Next is the question, 'why?' This question is meant to uncover the assumptions upon which the study is based. Thus in challenging the objective one hopes to uncover the thinking that has led to the formulation of the objective. For instance, when it is proposed to use O.R. for a project, the proposal to use O.R. can be challenged, why use O.R.? It might be that the answer is that work study for example has been tried but has not yielded the results required. Or alternatively it may be that another firm has used O.R. on a similar situation and has found it extremely useful. A further reason may be that a preliminary survey has been carried out by say the financial department and this was one of its recommendations. Depending upon the nature of the answer to this question 'why', we can therefore uncover the background thinking that led up to the statement of the objective.

Thirdly, 'when?' When is a start to be made and more importantly when are the results required? An optimum solution provided two days late is worthless, a good solution on time is priceless. A project that is going to be used and acted upon must be providing answers to specific management decisions. Management decisions have to be taken at specific points in time, and therefore a project to be of any use must come up with answers by a specified date. An open ended 'look at this and see what you think, at your convenience' approach can only be afforded by a patron of the arts. Of course, a commercial undertaking could act this part for tax loss reasons or to obtain prestige. Another reason might be to place a leading authority under contract thereby preventing him from working for a competitor. The answers to 'when' will indicate the degree of importance attached to the project and the urgency involved. This leads on to the question of resources.

The question of resources comes out in the question 'who?' It should not be forgotten that the effective deployment of staff is in itself a linear programming problem, solutions to which do not automatically lead to 'best' person being allocated to the task. However, assuming equal technical competence between two people they will not produce identical reports. Thus the team leader should not only be chosen on the grounds of technical competence but also in the light of his background. For his part, the team leader needs to know who else will be involved, with whom he is expected to work, who is expected to collaborate closely in the project etc. In extreme cases it is even necessary to make it absolutely clear who is the team leader.

The question of where the study is to be carried out should next be considered. It should be ascertained whether a desk type project is envisaged or an on the spot investigation is proposed. A study of a company's distribution system is likely to yield different projects according to whether it has been conducted from a desk in h.q. or from the cabs of lorries in the company's vehicle fleet. In some cases the question of 'where' raises physical issues, that is the question of ensuring that desks, filing cabinets, phones, etc. are laid on.

The last question is, how will the study be conducted? The person conducting the study will obviously determine the detail, but the initial terms of reference should indicate broadly what is envisaged. For instance, a superficial survey may be in the minds of the originators. It may be the intention that the study is strictly factual and is concerned purely with data collection and analysis as opposed to taking into account as far as possible policy cum political feelings amongst the various parties involved. In other words 'how' provides anticipated guide lines which should ensure that the investigator reports back for further terms of reference if he finds he is straying from the original ones.

To summarise then the following questions provide a framework for a workable set of terms of reference.

What?—the objective
Why?—the challenge
When?—the time factor
Who?—the resources
Where?—the place
How?—the method.

IDENTIFYING RELEVANT FACTORS

The major factors will be highlighted by any theory that surrounds an area of investigation. Thus for an inventory problem the cost of ordering and the cost of holding stock are two basic factors. These factors however will need careful interpretation in a given context. This means that it becomes necessary to discuss the situation with the people involved. Many issues are likely to be raised with this approach; the practitioner's job is to diagnose cause from effect. In some cases, useful leads can be obtained from the experience of people in the field, although on the other hand many factors supposedly influencing the situation will prove to be irrelevant. In interviewing managers of different departments, areas of disagreement should not be written off as examples of internal political bickering. They may well be this now, but their cause may be due to the company having established conflicting departmental objectives.

A technique that may be of use at this stage to broadly inter-relate the alternatives facing management is the use of decision trees.

Decision Trees

Decision trees are a useful way of obtaining an overall or 'birds eye' view of some types of management problem. The tree shows diagrammatically the alternatives open to management in a given situation and, provided all the appropriate data are available, allows management to calculate which decision should be made. Decision trees are relevant to simulation models for two reasons. Firstly, for the birds eye view they give of management problems. The fact that the problem is shown diagrammatically in the form of a tree-like structure helps indicate where simulation may be necessary to quantify the situation. Secondly, approaching the problem via decision trees will often indicate the range of parameters over which a simulation is required. A brief introduction to decision trees is therefore given below and the reader is referred to reference 19 for further details.

Decision trees are a diagrammatic way of showing the relationship between alternative decisions and subsequent events (or outcomes).

The limbs of the tree represent a decision or outcome and are linked by a suitable symbol to illustrate that the branching is due to either alternative decisions being available or that it is due to possible alternative outcomes. A tree is given in figure 4.1 for a simple situation that may face a car owner having difficulty in engaging first gear.

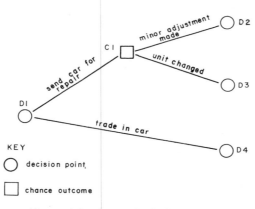

Figure 4.1   A simple decision tree

Although the drawing of a tree is in itself a useful exercise, this representation is also suitable for analysis providing the situation can be quantified. In this example the action of the car owner will be influenced by, the cost of a minor adjustment, the cost of a unit change and the relative chance of one of these on the one hand and on the other hand the cost of trading in the car.

  the cost of a minor adjustment will be £8
and the cost of a replacement unit will be £40,
  the 'chance' of having to replace the unit is judged to be 50:50,
and the cost of trading in the car is £30
then this information can be added to the decision tree as shown in figure 4.2.

An analysis of the data with respect to the tree can then be carried out by working from the tips of each branch progressively down the tree (i.e. from

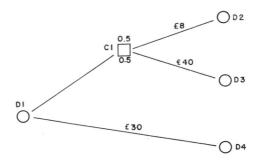

Figure 4.2   The decision tree quantified

right to left). In performing this analysis the data at a merge point (node) are treated one of two ways:

(1) If the merge point is at a chance outcome, the expected value of the two merging limbs are calculated

i.e. at C1 in the example,
expected value = (0.5 × 8) + (0.5 × 40) = £24.

This value is then brought forward down the common branch.

(2) If the merge point is a decision point, the branch having the 'best' value will be chosen and therefore this value is brought forward. i.e. at D1 in the example there is a choice between £24 which has been brought down from C1 and £30 which has been brought down the other limb. In this case, we are trying to minimise our expenditure and so the value £24 will be chosen which by implication means we chose to follow the D1–C1 limb rather than D1–D4.

This is the essence of analysing decision trees. In practice, there might be some problems in determining the appropriate tree to use.

In this example, it is possible to adopt a slightly different approach of sending the car for inspection and in the light of the findings have the necessary repairs carried out or trade the car in. This would result in a different tree as shown in the following figure, 4.3.

The analysis of this tree would then be:

at D2 choose the cheaper limb i.e. £8
at D3 choose the cheaper limb i.e. £30
at C1 calculate the expectation from the cost of the two decisions D2 and D3, i.e. (0.5 × 8) + (0.5 × 30) = £19.
at D1 choose the cheaper limb i.e. £19 rather than £30.

56

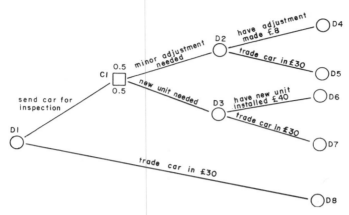

Figure 4.3   An alternative decision tree

In summary, the decisions can be summarised as:

Send car for inspection, if an adjustment is needed have it made, if a new unit is needed trade car in instead.

A slightly more complicated example is illustrated by Moore (reference 19) and is reproduced here in modified form.

The Flexible Coupling Company   The FCC is expanding its factory and needs to decide initially whether to build a small extension, (at a cost of £20 000) or a larger unit at a cost of £70 000. It is felt that there is a 80 per cent chance that the demand for FCC's products will be 'high' in the next two years. At the end of two years certain contracts expire and there is only a 75 per cent chance of the 'high' demand continuing.

Continuing 'high' demand will yield a present value of £100 000. An initial 'high' demand followed by 'low' demand would yield £20 000, while a constant 'low' demand yields £10 000. If they do not expand and the high demand continues the market has a present value of £40 000.

If FCC build small initially they can expand in 18 months time at a cost of £60 000.

The decision tree for the above situation, together with the calculated values at various points, is shown in figure 4.4. From this it will be seen that the decision 'build small' should be made, and even if the market happens to be initially high no further expansion should be considered.

In the examples given the payback values are assumed to be known. Simulation can be used to establish the probability distribution of income in projects. This type of application is dealt with in chapter 9 and illustrated by the programs PRAC and PRAS in appendices 8 and 9.

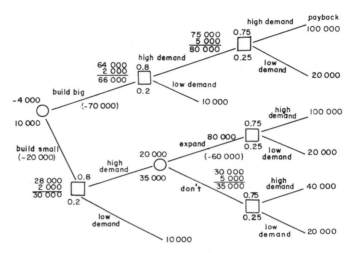

Figure 4.4   Decision tree for the Flexible Coupling Co.

Statistical Aspects

From the mass of supposed factors and issues thrown up by the initial interviews, the practitioner needs to identify the relevant factors, i.e. those that appear to have some influence or bearing upon the situation being studied. The factors needing attention fall into three types, those that are 'obviously' relevant as acknowledged by the body of theory, those that are claimed to be correlated in some way to others, and lastly those factors which are claimed just to be non-random.

The factors that are obviously involved should be defined and the data collected in a form dictated by the theory involved. Those factors that are claimed to be correlated in some way need careful examination to ascertain whether there is in fact correlation and also to determine the cause from effect. The method of establishing simple correlation is explained in chapter 8 where forecasting techniques are discussed. Evidence of correlation is useful in so far as it may allow a simple form of data collection; that is, we collect data on (*a*) rather than (*b*) and knowing the correlation between (*a*) and (*b*) we can transform the data into (*b*) values. Evidence of correlation may also help simplify a model or it may cut out a stage of simulation. Finally, there is the question of testing for randomness in a run of data. A run test provides a simple way of examining a sequence of figures to establish whether the order is significant.

Run Tests The data for a run test must be presented in two classes. Male/female, or yes/no situations are already in this form. If the data are numeric, the values are classified as being either below the median or above (including equal to) the median.

The procedure involved in conducting a run test is best described by reference to an example. Suppose twenty-three orders for either Crunchnuts or Wigwams were received within a month. If the first eleven orders were all for Crunchnuts and the remaining orders were only for Wigwams then the sequence of orders would appear to be non-random and should be explainable in other terms. However, consider the sequence of orders as shown in table 4.1, are these data non-random?

Table 4.1   Sequence of orders received

C	W	C	C	W	W	W	C	W	C	C	C	W	C	C	W	W	C	C	W	W	W	W

C = Crunchnuts   W = Wigwams

It may be that the warehouse manager can 'see' that the orders for Wigwams always occur at the end of the month. The first step in conducting a run test is to group similar results together while still preserving a sequence as shown in table 4.2. Each group 'or cluster' represents a run of similar results and in the example here there are twelve such clusters or runs of similar results.

Table 4.2   Orders grouped into clusters

C	W	CC	WWW	C	W	CCC	W	CC	WW	CC	WWWW

The next step is to note the number of results in each class. That is, out of the twenty-three results there are eleven Crunchnuts and twelve Wigwams. The number of results in each class can be designated n_1, n_2, while the total number of runs can be designated r.

If there are too many or too few runs, then the null hypothesis that the sample is random is not correct. To determine what is meant by too many or too few runs, it is necessary to consult r tables as given in appendix 21. For a given combination of n_1 and n_2, the r table gives the upper and lower values of r to be expected from a random sample. In this case, where n_1 = 11 and

$n_2 = 12$, there is only a 5 per cent chance of r laying outside the range 7 to 18. As the calculated value of r is 12, it is between these limits and there is therefore no proof that the data in table 4.1 are non-random. Further examples of run tests can be found in reference 17.

Sample Size Errors   A further aspect of data collection should be borne in mind at this stage, that is that all the data collected represent but samples of the populations. All the parameters developed from the sample data are only estimates of the true population parameters. Obviously, the larger the sample the more accurate will be the estimate of the population parameter, but unfortunately the accuracy of sampling does not increase linearly with the size of the sample. The accuracy of a sample varies with the square of the sample size, thus, to double the accuracy of a sample, it is necessary to take a sample 4 times as large. A useful formula for use in this area is a formula which is termed the standard error of the sampling distribution of a percentage. This is usually written as:

$$SE = \sqrt{\left\{ \frac{P(100 - P)}{n} \right\}}$$

where,

SE = standard error
P = percentage occurrence
n = size of sample

We can be 95 per cent confident that the true percentage of occurrence lies within ±1.96 standard errors from the mean. For ease of calculation 1.96 is usually rounded off to 2. Thus we can be 95 per cent confident that the true percentage of occurrence lies between:

$$\pm 2 \sqrt{\frac{P(100 - P)}{n}} \tag{4.1}$$

The use of the above formula can be illustrated by reference to the data in table 4.1. Having ascertained that the run of Crunchnuts and Wigwams appears random, we might next consider simulating such a pattern by sampling random numbers allocated in the proportions of Crunchnuts and Wigwams, as given in table 4.1. That is Crunchnuts occur in eleven out of twent-three occasions, i.e. 47.8 per cent. However, table 4.1 contains only twenty-three readings, and therefore we cannot be sure that the figure of 47.8 per cent is representative of the true proportions of Crunchnuts to Wigwams. The use of equation 4.1 allows us to calculate the 95 per cent confidence limits around the 47.8 per cent chance of occurrence. In this case $P = 47.8$ and $n = 23$, substituting the limits can be calculated as,

$$L = \pm 2 \sqrt{\left\{ \frac{47.8(100 - 47.8)}{23} \right\}}$$

$$= \pm 2 \sqrt{\left\{ \frac{47.8 \times 52.2}{23} \right\}}$$

$$= \pm 20.8$$

These limits are rather large for practical purposes, for we can only be 95 per cent confident that the proportion of Crunchnuts lies between 27 per cent and 68.6 per cent, obviously there are not enough data in table 4.1 to give us a useful simulation. However, we may work back from a desired degree of accuracy to establish the sample size required, thus if we wish to know the percentage occurrence of Crunchnuts within ±2 per cent then the substitution would be as follows:

$$2 = 2 \sqrt{\left\{ \frac{47.8(100 - 47.8)}{n} \right\}}$$

i.e.
$$n = \frac{2^2(47.8 \times 52.2)}{2^2}$$

$$= 2\,500 \text{ approximately}$$

The answer of 2 500 readings is the statistical answer, whether it is feasible is another matter. At the rate of approximately twenty five orders per month, a sample of 2 500 represents approaching 9 years worth of data. Even if it were possible to go back 9 years to collect this number of readings, in practice it would be unwise for it is extremely unlikely that data 9 years old would be at all representative of the situation today. In these types of circumstances the practitioner will have to go back as far as he dares to get as large a sample as possible and then calculate the error involved from say 3 years' figures. The errors so calculated may form the basis of sensitivity runs made on the final model once it is constructed, thus, to go back to the original set of twenty three readings, if these were the only results available, the simulation of the orders received should also be carried out for a 27 per cent occurrence of Crunchnuts and a 68 per cent occurrence of Crunchnuts, and the value of the model judged in the light of the stability of the answers obtained.

CONSTRUCTING THE INTER-RELATIONSHIPS

As various influencing factors are discovered, their relationships are gradually assembled, like a jigsaw, to give the complete model. Initially, it is useful to think in terms of developing a manual simulation model, for if it cannot be simulated manually it cannot be effectively programmed. Obviously, in developing a manual simulation at this stage one is not interested in accuracy of results and therefore the drawback of manual simulation is largely avoided. It is only necessary to be able to follow completely through the model with one set of randomly generated figures for every alternative available to check there are no dead ends and that the steps taken are reasonable. The form that the model might take depends upon the application, and examples of various applications and simulation methods will be found in subsequent chapters. However, there are two approaches to modelling that are not illustrated in subsequent chapters but deserve mention. The first of these approaches is particularly appropriate to queueing type situations which lend themselves to an entity-state description. This approach was developed by P.E. Consulting Group and goes by the name of HOCUS[13]. Another approach to modelling which is pertinent to management control systems generally has been developed by Jay Forrester and is termed industrial dynamics (reference 12). In industrial dynamics the management system is represented by rates of flow, of material, money, etc., between different levels, i.e. stocks. A brief description of these two approaches to simulation modelling follows.

HOCUS

HOCUS stands for 'hand or computer universal simulator'. It brings a new power to simulation by providing a simple model-building language in flow diagram form. This enables simulation studies to be carried out as a team effort by non-specialist staff, and at the same time allows the results to be widely understood and accepted within an organisation.

A HOCUS model is set up in three stages:

(1) An activity diagram is prepared of the situation to be modelled. This is an adaptation of the familiar process flow diagram, showing how the relations of the various resources change with progression of time.

(2) This activity diagram then becomes the 'playing board' for a hand simulation. Discs moved around the board according to the rules of the particular diagram represent the changing state of the model. At this stage, any errors in formulation or logic quickly come to light and can be corrected on the diagram. It is also easy for the model-builders as they watch the

process to appreciate more precisely the interactions of the resources being used.

(3) The completed model is prepared for computer running simply by copying the diagram entries onto punched cards. The standard HOCUS program then enables the long-term operation of the model to be studied in a few minutes of computer time. Statistics may be collected and runs repeated at will, either under operator control on computers with conversational facilities or under automatic control on batch machines.

HOCUS acts as a common language between line manager and specialist, ensuring effective communication. Using HOCUS, both sides come to grips with the problem to be solved—they do not get bogged down with the problem-solving technique.

HOCUS has six main advantages:

(1) Anyone can use it to build simulation models.

(2) Models are tested quickly by paper and pencil.

(3) No special computer programs have to be written. The standard HOCUS program can be used whenever use of a computer is warranted.

(4) Results are available within hours, not weeks.

(5) Line managers help to build the models and thus understand the results.

(6) Because HOCUS is simple to learn and use, expertise can be gained within hours.

In addition, it has been installed on a wide range of computers, including IBM 360/30+, ICL 1903+, IBM 1130, Burroughs 3500, CDC 6600, GE-265, Univac 1108 and PDP 10.

A simple example A problem to which HOCUS was particularly applicable arose during the design of a warehouse site. Storage requirements were such that the space allowed for traffic around the site entrance and unloading area appeared small. The management was worried that this area would become seriously congested and thus impair the smooth operation of the warehouse.

To build the warehouse first and later have to rebuild it to ease congestion, would have been a disaster. So management decided to simulate normal operation using HOCUS. The warehouse designer produced a model, using the actual schedules of vehicles which would service the warehouse.

The model consisted of the HOCUS activity diagram shown in figure 4.5, which includes the life cycle and linkage of each entity within the transport arrival and departure system.

This HOCUS activity diagram showing the life cycle and linkage of each

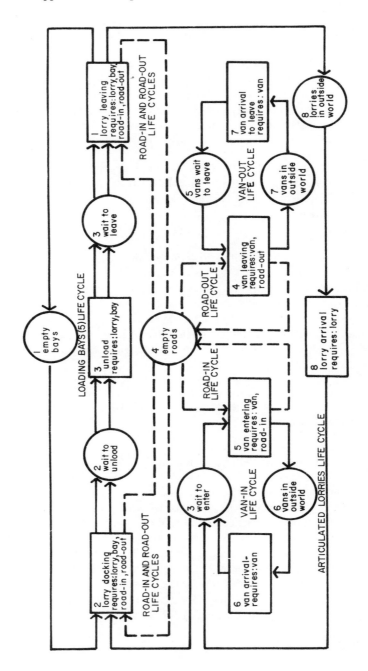

Figure 4.5 A HOCUS activity diagram

entity, was prepared from the definition of entities and discrete states, as follows:

Entities	Discrete states
Articulated lorry	Arrival, wait to dock, docking, wait to unload, unload, wait to leave, leave, outside world.
Loading bay	Empty, lorry docking, waiting to unload, unload, wait to leave, lorry leaving.
Vans-in	Outside world, arrival, wait to enter, enter.
Vans-out	Arrive to leave, wait to leave, leave, outside world.
Road-in	(1) Empty, lorry docking.
	(2) Empty, lorry leaving.
	(3) Empty, van entering.
Road-out	(1) Empty, lorry docking.
	(2) Empty, lorry leaving.
	(3) Empty, van leaving.

The entities, Road-in and Road-out, have several life cycles.

The model was produced in half a day and was checked and run in a further half day. When 'played' by those concerned, it quickly demonstrated

(1) that with the proposed design no congestion would occur at any time during the day;

(2) that for the vehicle schedule proposed, only two main loading bays would be needed, with a third as a standby.

The use of HOCUS thus enabled the design problem to be posed and the answer received in *one day*. It saved further costly work on site layout re-design and construction, and in particular enabled the need for a fourth and a fifth bay to be questioned at an early stage. Finally, it enabled all concerned to see exactly what would happen, when, and how under operational conditions.

Industrial Dynamics

'Industrial dynamics is a way of studying the behaviour of industrial assistants to show how policies, decisions, structure and delay are interrelated to influence growth and stability'. This statement by the originator of the term 'industrial dynamics', Jay Forrester, briefly defines the term. The results of such research carried out at MIT since 1956 have been published (see reference 12) and initially a computer compilar 'DYNAMO' was written for an IBM 1620, but is available now on other machines.

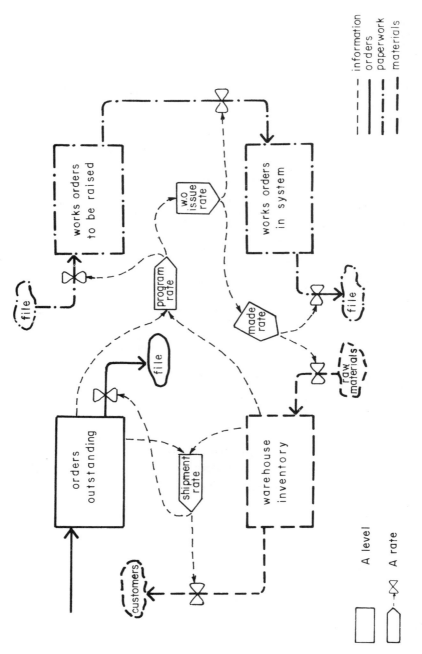

Figure 4.6   A simple industrial dynamics system

The analysis of industrial policies and decisions, whether for marketing, stock control, production, etc, in the past have been based on an unrelated collection of techniques. Industrial dynamics offers a standard codified way of describing the relationships involved in terms of money, material, paperwork, personnel and information flows. The dynamic aspect of industrial dynamics stems from the fact that, by stating a situation in suitable terms, the effects of a decision taken today can be traced forward in time and its repercussions noted.

A situation can be represented in industrial dynamic terms initially by means of a chart drawn in control systems terms. A simple example of an industrial dynamic system is shown in figure 4.6. This diagram shows a simple system where orders received are initially outstanding until they are met. The level of orders outstanding will influence the rate at which paperwork is raised within the organisation which in turn influences the rate at which the works orders are issued. The manufacturing rate, which is influenced by the rate at which works orders are issued, governs the rate at which works orders leave the system and corresponding inventory is brought into the warehouse. The level of finished warehouse inventory influences the rate of shipment which in turn affects the level of orders outstanding. Figure 4.6 is a concise way of showing their relationships and feedback loops using the minimum of symbols. It may be written in DYNAMO or any conventional scientific type language. The writing of the program requires two types of statement to be developed. One set of statements will show how the various rates in the system are related to the levels in the system. The other set of statements will show how the levels in the system are related to the rates in the system. The program is initialised at suitable parameters and then the rates are calculated for the existing levels. After this the levels are revised in the light of the rates. On a second pass through the program, new rates are calculated from the revised levels and then new levels calculated from these revised rates. The above description simplifies the procedure somewhat but gives a general idea. It is extremely easy to write the program in FORTRAN, the advantage of using DYNAMO being the availability of special functions and special output routines.

An industrial dynamics model is very useful for showing the inherent stability or otherwise of a system, for example, for a given set of parameters the system shown in figure 4.6 gave a very unstable pattern of work in progress (see figure 4.7) even though the rate of orders received remained constant.

An example of one set of relationships can be described by reference to the level of works orders in the system shown in figure 4.6.

The level of works orders (say FORTRAN variable name, WOK) now can be calculated from the previous level of works orders (variable name, WOJ) plus the difference between the rate that works orders are being issued at present (PIRJK) and the rate of manufacture (PMRJK) times the time interval (DT),

i.e. $\quad$ `WOK = WOJ + DT *(PIRJK - PMRJK)`

Having computed the new level, WOK, all other levels would be computed before proceeding to the calculation of the new rates. Thus if the new work

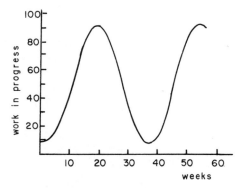

Figure 4.7 Fluctuations in work in progress generated from a constant rate of orders

order issue rate is simply the previous program rate (PPRJK) then

$\quad$ `PIRKL = PPRJK`

(Notice the use of JK and KL at the end of the variable names. K is now, J is the previous point in time and L the next point in time. Thus present levels end in K, previous levels end in J, while present rates end in JK and future rates in KL.)

We have now calculated the present levels and the future rates over the next increment in time.

To effect this advance in time, all K levels are made J levels and all KL rates made JK rates

i.e. $\quad$ `WOJ = WOK`

etc. for all levels
and,

$\quad$ `PIRJK = PIRKL`

etc. for all rates.

68

The program then loops back to the beginning to represent an advance of DT. Starting levels, rates and the incremental value DT are prescribed parameters read in at the beginning of the run.

VALIDATION OF THE MODEL

When a suitable model has been written as a computer program, it is essential to carry out extensive test runs. This is particularly difficult with simulation models as the results obtained cannot easily be checked by simple arithmetic. In the ultimate, a simulation program is accepted as being correct only because all the cross checking carried out has failed to show the model as being incorrect. With careful thought, many aspects of simulation programs can be checked by the construction of special input data. For example, in queueing type problems the arrival rates and service rates can be made constant and multiples of each other. Usually, this allows the effects of these particular figures to be calculated and the computer answers checked against these. Thus if a service rate was fixed at six per hour i.e. 10 min average and the arrival rate was fixed twelve per hour with two servers, providing the initial conditions are suitable, no queue should be built up and no waiting should be incurred. Furthermore, the utilisation of the servers should be 100 per cent. The number of arrivals for any particular length of simulation run can be calculated exactly. In this way, several aspects of the program can be checked, but a certain amount of ingenuity is required to devise a thorough series of tests. In some situations, the plotting of results obtained from a series of runs can be a help in confirming that the program is behaving satisfactorily. When several runs are made over a range of values, the results when plotted usually provide smoothed curves. Any sudden changes e.g. slope should be fully accounted for in the context of the program, if they cannot be explained they may point to a fault in programming logic, for instance, the result of over-looking the consequences of a particular combination of parameters. This can be illustrated by reference to the following simple stock control simulation program.

Checking a Stock Control Program

The program was designed to simulate demand, this demand being withdrawn from stock if available. Any demand not met was written off and would contribute to a service level of below 100 per cent. The range of inventory policies simulated were for each combination of order quantities from 20 up to 100 in steps of 10 and re-order levels (r.o.l.s) from 5 up to 60 in steps of 5. In each simulation the lead time was three periods. A listing of the relevant part of the program is given in figure 4.8. The program simulates the demand in line 32.

If the demand is less than the net stock, the cumulative issues to the customer are increased by the demand amount (see line 38). Also the net stock level is reduced by the demand value, as in line 37. However, if the demand is greater than the net stock level, the cumulative amount issued to the customers is

```
19              FOR OQ=20,100,10
20                WRITE(2,2)
21                WRITE(2,3)
22                FOR ROL=5,60,5
23                  TD=0
24                  TC=0
25                  LI=3
26                  N=80
27                  AVN=0
28                  FOR WK=1,200
29                    IF(LI)4,5,4
30        5           N=N+OQ
31                    LI=3
32        4           D=SAMPLE(1,DEMAND,STREAM)
33                    IF(N-D)6,6,7
34        6           TC=TC+N
35                    N=0
36                    GO TO 8
37        7           N=N-D
38                    TC=TC+D
39        8           TD=TD+D
40                    AVN=AVN+N
41                    IF(N-ROL)9,9,10
42        9           LI=LI-1
43       10           DUMMY
44                  SERVICE=TC*100/TD
45                  AVN=AVN/200.
46                  WRITE(2,11)OQ,ROL,SERVICE,AVN
47       11 FORMAT(1H ,12X,I3,11X,I2,F13.1,F13.2)
48                  DUMMY
49                EXIT
50                END
```

Figure 4.8   Portion of stock control program

increased by only the net stock level, and the net stock level now becomes zero (see lines 34 and 35). The cumulative amount demanded is increased by the latest demand value in line 39 and a variable, termed AVN, is increased by the net issued. The variable AVN will subsequently be divided by the length of the simulation, in line 45, to give the average value of net stock. After deducting the appropriate amount from the stock level a test is then made, in line 41, to see whether the net stock level is now below the re-order level. If it is, then a count, LI is reduced by 1. The value of LI is tested near the beginning of the run in line 29. If it is zero then this signifies the delivery of the appropriate order quantity and therefore in line 30 the net stock level is increased by the order quantity. Immediately following this, the count, LI, is reset to the value 3 ready for any subsequent countdown that may be required as the re-order level is broken. This explains the major part of the simulation, and, as it turns out, the error. One set of results for an order quantity of 20 and various re-order levels ranging from 5 to 60 are shown in figure 4.9. Careful examination of these results should show

```
INVENTORY POLICIES

    ORDER QUANTITY      R.O.L.      SERVICE      AV.  STOCK
         20               5          42.0         2.65
         20              10          43.0         3.05
         20              15          47.0         3.31
         20              20          52.0         3.37
         20              25          49.0         2.93
         20              30          49.0         3.20
         20              35          46.0         2.71
         20              40          49.0         3.19
         20              45          49.0         3.30
         20              50          50.0         4.24
         20              55          49.0         3.68
         20              60          47.0         3.31
```

Figure 4.9   Output for an order quantity of twenty

that there is something wrong, however the plotting of these results will certainly show that something is wrong. The results have been plotted in figure 4.10. Inventory theory would lead us to expect an exponential type graph of average stock plotted against percentage service level for a given range of inventory policies. That is a high level of service such as 98 per cent should be obtainable if the stock level is high enough, and as the stock level is reduced the percentage service level falls off rapidly in an exponential manner. The results obtained and plotted in figure 4.10 though show a series of plots clustered around 40–50 per cent service with apparently no way of achieving higher service levels. Something is incorrect in the program for the combinations of order quantity and re-order level simulated should give a fair spread of points from 100 per cent service level downwards.

On closer examination of the program, it should become apparent that the stock balance has been calculated in terms of the number in the stores as opposed to the number in the system. That is, once the re-order level has been broken, the quantity in the system should be increased by the order quantity immediately. If this is not done, then next time round the number in stock will still be below the re-order level and a further order will be placed and orders will continue to be placed until a quantity is delivered to bring the stock level above the re-order level. The first thing then is to create in the program the concept of an actual stock level as held by the stores, and a

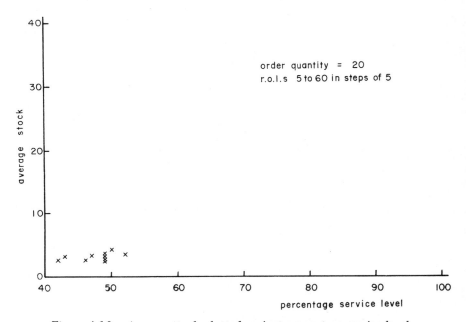

Figure 4.10   Average stock plotted against percentage service level

provisioned stock level being composed of items actually in the stores and quantities already ordered and in the pipeline. Once it is realised that the orders in the pipeline must be taken into account, it then becomes clear that for each order placed there must be a suitable countdown system otherwise the program will prevent ordering at more frequent intervals than the prescribed three weeks lead time. The results of making such amendments gives the results shown in figure 4.11 and the graph shown in figure 4.12. The graph now is following the pattern that one would anticipate from a knowledge of inventory theory. The fact that the graph is not a smooth curve is due to a short simulation. The correct version of this program (STAN) is described in a later chapter on inventory control and a full listing is given in appendix 13.

INVENTORY POLICIES

ORDER QUANTITY	R.O.L.	SERVICE	AV. STOCK
20	5	40.0	2.93
20	10	44.0	2.86
20	15	46.0	2.86
20	20	70.0	4.78
20	25	77.0	6.19
20	30	79.0	7.12
20	35	85.0	7.48
20	40	92.0	12.67
20	45	98.0	15.38
20	50	99.0	18.56
20	55	99.0	23.69
20	60	100.0	29.15

Figure 4.11   Revised output for an order quantity of twenty

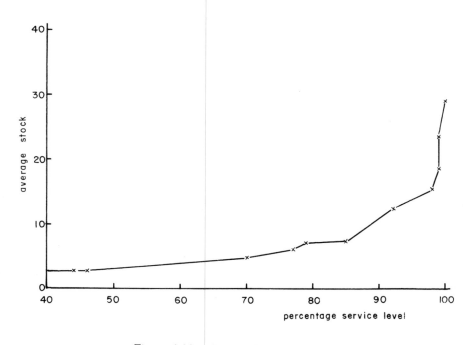

Figure 4.12   Graph of revised output

This simple example serves to illustrate how errors in writing simulation programs could arise. The original program was logical in itself but did not represent a real situation. Any stock clerk is only too well aware of the need for a provisioned stock system as it may be termed, but a systems analyst brought up on the theory may not recognise the need for these practical refinements.

Apart from any statistical tests that can be made upon the simulation program, the only other check is to simulate the existing situation and cross check the output against known results obtained in practice. In order to do this, it may be necessary to program extra output that is not required once the simulation model has been validated. In queueing models, the number of servers, the arrival patterns and service patterns should initially be set to those already in existence. The results can then be checked against the real situation from as many points of view as possible. The simulation of an inventory model should give the existing level of service and average stock levels when the present parameters are used. Any discrepancies may point to further factors that have been overlooked but need incorporating into the model.

THE IDEAL SIMULATION PROGRAM

In writing various simulation programs, depending upon the objective, certain aspects are concentrated on while other aspects may be overlooked until the run has been made. If an extensive simulation program is to be written, it would be useful to bear in mind the following points, treating them as a checklist.

(1) Most programs will have at the beginning an initialisation stage. Should any of these parameters be read in as variables at run time thereby increasing the long term flexibility of the program?

(2) Should routine options be incorporated in the program to be requested by means of parameter card? Options such as:

(a) ignoring results over a stipulated 'running in' period,
(b) printing out simulated variables in the form of standard histogram formats, or graphs,
(c) printing out diagnostics.

(3) Should the programming be elaborated to incorporate variable and automatic incrementing to speed up the simulation where possible but to produce fine detail where necessary?

(4) Should the program be constantly monitoring the variability in various criteria? The mean and standard deviation to date being printed out every x simulations.

(5) Should the program be dumped onto storage media prior to the end of the run so that if the run is to be extended it can continue from this point.

(6) Should a series of error messages be developed to be printed out whenever variables either go outside anticipated limits or exhibit apparently impossible characteristics?

The above points are not meant to be either exhaustive or original, but they cover aspects of programming that are likely to be ignored in practice. Once the program is operational, it may then prove rather difficult to go back and alter the program to accommodate some of the above features. The writing of a simulation program involves a large amount of effort and resources, and although it is initiated usually to solve one particular problem, possibilities to give the program increased flexibility should not be overlooked.

SUMMARY

Plan the study. Obtain specific terms of reference around the what, why, when, who, where and how concept.

Decision trees. They may help give a birds eye view and indicate the range of parameters involved.

Diagnose the factors. Look further than symptoms. Use all the tools of statistics to check out any suggested hypothesis.

Construct a suitable model. The nature of the problem often indicates the type of model. Simulate a few readings manually.

Validate the model. Cross check the theoretical output against the actual results from as many angles as possible. If all cross checking agrees you have only not disproved the model but it may still be wrong.

Chapter 5

The Use of Fortran for Computer Simulation Studies

THE USE OF COMPUTERS FOR SIMULATION

In even the simplest simulation problems, similar calculations need to be carried out many times to give a reasonable length simulation. Although it is possible to solve these using random number tables, pencil and paper, it is usually quicker and more accurate to use a computer first of all to generate random numbers and then to perform the repetitive calculations. Much longer simulations can be attempted in a relatively short time, and alternative policies can easily be tested by substituting new data and running the same computer program again. For more complex simulation projects it is even more essential to use a computer as it may not be possible to carry out the necessary calculations manually in the required time.

Special purpose programming languages have been designed to aid the translation of the mathematical model into a computer program, and one such language (CSL) will be described in chapter 6. However, for many simulation problems, the use of a conventional scientific programming language is sufficient. The language outlined in this chapter has been chosen because it is 'universal', that is most modern computers have a FORTRAN compiler (a computer program to translate the FORTRAN program into the computer's own machine code). The basic facilities provided are similar for most FORTRAN compilers. Unfortunately, a completely universal Standard FORTRAN does not exist at present, although the NCC Standard FORTRAN Programming Manual[26] attempts to define a standard subset of the two existing published standards[23,30].

The version of FORTRAN used in this book is ICL Basic FORTRAN[2], and can be used on any ICL 1900 computer with a minimum core store of 8K words. The following notes are not intended as a complete guide to FORTRAN programming but illustrate the main features of the language in sufficient detail for the reader to appreciate the simulation programs written in FORTRAN which are found in appendices 1-7, and perhaps to attempt some simple FORTRAN programming for simulation problems. To this end several useful hints on writing and correcting programs (based on the authors' experience) have been included.

INTRODUCTION TO FORTRAN

FORTRAN (FORmula TRANslator) was developed by International Business Machines Corporation in 1956 to provide scientists and engineers with an easy to write programming language for mathematical formulae. It is a high-level language in that one FORTRAN statement may be equivalent to several machine code instructions.

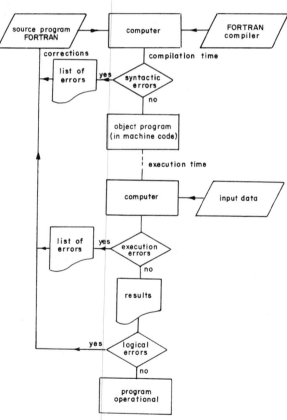

Figure 5.1   The FORTRAN system

77

A FORTRAN program consists of a series of statements of four different types:

(1) Arithmetic statements—these specify the arithmetic operations to be performed.

(2) Input/output statements—these read a data card or block from paper tape or magnetic tape, print a line of results, punch a card of results, write a block on paper tape or magnetic tape.

Statements 1 and 2 are executed in the order in which they are written.

(3) Control statements—these alter the sequence in which the instructions are obeyed.

(4) Specification statements—these are non-executable; they provide the compiler with information about the nature of the constants and variables used in the program, and information required to allocate locations in store for certain variables and arrays (lists and tables).

All the statements that specify the procedures used in solving a problem are together called the source program. When the source program has been written and punched into cards or paper tape, it is converted by a FORTRAN Compiler into an object program in machine code. A schematic diagram of the FORTRAN system is shown in figure 5.1. This will be explained in greater detail later in this chapter when the detection and correction of errors is discussed.

THE FORTRAN CODING FORM

A FORTRAN program is written normally on a FORTRAN coding form (figure 5.2). The information on each line is punched into a single card or paper tape block.

The numbers shown above the first line of the coding form stand for the card columns or character positions on paper tape into which the information on the form will be punched. The first field on the form, columns 1–5, contains the statement number, if any; this may be any unsigned number between 1 and 9999. Column 1 is used also to indicate a comment card; if column 1 contains a C, FORTRAN does not process the information on the line, but only prints it on a listing of the program.

Column 6 is used to indicate a continuation line. If a statement is too long to go on one line, it may be continued on up to five continuation lines, and column 6 must be punched with a character other than zero or space. The first card of a continued statement will still have a zero or blank in column 6. The statement itself is punched in columns 7–72, but need not begin in

FORTRAN STATEMENT — IDENTIFICATION AND SEQUENCE No.

```
C EXAMPLES OF ARITHMETIC STATEMENTS          E.H.  5.2.0
  IRT=IRT+MIN                                 E.H.  5.3.0
  IREP=IREP+1                                 E.H.  5.4.0
  COST=650.0/ATBF                             E.H.  5.5.0
C EXAMPLES OF INPUT/OUTPUT STATEMENTS
  READ(1,1)L,LF
  WRITE(2,103)IREP,IRT,ATBF,COST
C EXAMPLES OF CONTROL STATEMENTS
  IF(I-3),30,30,31
  GO TO 60
C EXAMPLE OF SPECIFICATION STATEMENT
  DIMENSION L(8),LF(8)
```

Figure 5.2 A FORTRAN coding form with examples

column 7. Blanks in this field are ignored except within headings. Columns 73–80 are not processed by FORTRAN but will be printed on the compiler listing and may be used for card or program identification.

BASIC DEFINITIONS IN FORTRAN

The numeric data that can be used in FORTRAN will be considered first and then the various types of instructions or statements which need to be written in the program to access and manipulate the data.

Constants and Variables

Two forms of data may be used—constants and variables. A constant is any number used in a computation without change from one execution of the program to the next. Constants may be either fixed-point, that is ordinary integers (whole numbers) without a decimal point, or floating-point (real) where the number is treated as a decimal number times a power of 10. Both types of constants must be within a range depending on the computer and may be positive or negative; the number is taken to be positive if unsigned.

Fixed-point numbers : 0, 100, −1, +2435
Floating-point numbers : 100., 0.7, −0.05

Reference needs to be made to computer storage locations which hold different values for different executions of the program or at different stages within the program; this is achieved by the use of variables. A variable is thus a symbolic representation of a quantity that may assume different values, and variable names are devised by the programmer according to certain rules. These will vary depending on the computer to be used. The following limitations will allow the program to be run on most computers:

A variable name consists of 1–5 alphanumeric characters (A through Z and O through 9, not special characters e.g. = + * , . ( ) ' /). The first character must be alphabetic and indicates the type of variable corresponding to the type of data the variable represents (i.e. fixed or floating-point).

(1) If the first character of the variable name is I, J, K, L, M or N, the variable is a fixed-point (integer) variable.
   e.g. IRN1, LIFE, MIN, J.
(2) If the first character of the variable name is *not* I, J, K, L, M or N, i.e. A through H and O through Z, the variable is a floating-point (real) variable.
   e.g. ATBF, COST, SUM, X.

Arithmetic Statements

Arithmetic operations to be performed are specified in arithmetic statements which consist of a variable name on the l.h.s. (left-hand side) of an equals sign and an arithmetic expression on the r.h.s. (right-hand side), as shown in the following example from program (CAPF), appendix 1.

line 50   IORDS = IORDS - 1

An arithmetic statement is an order to evaluate the expression on the r.h.s. and give that value to the variable named on the l.h.s. The effect of the preceding statement, therefore, is to replace the contents of location IORDS by one less than its previous value. The variable name IORDS has been chosen to be meaningful (it represents number of orders), however, since the name must represent an integer it has to start with a character from the set I through N.

Again certain rules must be observed by the programmer when writing expressions. The following list will allow programs to be run on most modern machines and are more restrictive than necessary in many cases, for instance rule 5 does not apply for FORTRAN IV compilers on larger machines. Reference should be made to the appropriate manufacturer's manual for detailed language specifications.

(1) Two symbols of operation must not appear next to each other. A*−B is not valid, A*(−B) is valid.

(2) Within brackets standard functions are evaluated first, then the hierarchy of operations in an expression is as follows:

(i) ( ) inner brackets are worked out first, the next innermost second etc.

(ii) ** exponentiation (raising to the power).

(iii) * multiplication and division from left to right.

(iv) + − addition and subtraction.

(3) Brackets must be used to indicate groupings just as in ordinary mathematical notation.

(4) Any expression may be raised to a positive or negative fixed-point (integer) quantity, only floating-point (real) expressions may be raised to a floating-point power. A negative value raised to a real power will result in a run time error.

(5) Fixed and floating-point quantities must not be mixed in the same expression; however, fixed-point quantities may appear in floating-point expressions as exponents and subscripts.

(6) Brackets only indicate groupings; they never imply multiplication.

An illustration of rules (2), (3) and (6) is given in the same program.

line 105   X = A + (B - A)*R

If the brackets were removed the expression on the r.h.s. would be equivalent to A + B − AR (since * is higher in hierarchy than −) which gives a quite different result and emphasises that care must be taken in the placing of brackets. However, excessive use of brackets should be avoided as these can lead to errors due to brackets being missed off in writing or punching the program.

It is possible to convert from floating point to integer values by assignment in an arithmetic statement as shown in program (CAPF),

line 46   MTIME = TIME

or by using standard functions (illustrated later). In the previous statement the floating point value located in TIME is accessed, the decimal places are truncated, and the integral part is stored in location MTIME; TIME will continue to hold the original unchanged real value.

Standard Functions
Several standard functions are available in Basic FORTRAN as listed in table 5.1. These are used in an arithmetic expression by writing the name of the

Table 5.1   Basic FORTRAN standard functions

Function	Definition	Number of arguments	Type of arguments	Type of function	Name
Exponential	e^a	1	R	R	EXP
Natural logarithm	$\log_e(a)$	1	R	R	ALOG
Trigonometric sine	$\sin(a)$	1	R	R	SIN
Trigonometric cosine	$\cos(a)$	1	R	R	COS
Arctangent	$\tan^{-1}(a)$	1	R	R	ATAN
Hyperbolic tangent	$\tanh(a)$	1	R	R	TANH
Square root	$+(a)^{1/2}$	1	R	R	SQRT
Absolute value	$\lvert a \rvert$	1	R	R	ABS
			I	I	IABS
Float	INTEGER converted to REAL	1	I	R	FLOAT
Fix	REAL converted to INTEGER	1	R	I	IFIX
Transfer of sign	$\lvert a \rvert$ multiplied by sign of a_2	2	R	R	SIGN
			I	I	ISIGN

function with the argument (quantity to be operated on which may be any expression of the type specified in the table) in brackets, e.g. IFIX(TIME) would enable the integral part of TIME to be used in an expression. However, less computer time is used if the integral value is assigned to an integer variable once, as shown previously, rather than using IFIX(TIME) several times.

Input of Data

It is necessary to distinguish quite clearly between program statements (punched into paper tape or cards) and data which are also punched but are not read into the computer until called for by the translated FORTRAN program, i.e. machine code program at execution time. Statements need to be written in the FORTRAN source program which call for data to be read in.

An example of such an input statement is shown in program (SIMQ), appendix 6.

line 58   READ(1,3) N,IEND

This statement initiates the reading of a new record, i.e. the next record available in the device is specified by the first number in the brackets and which refers to line 3 in the program listing:

line 3   INPUT 1 = CRO   (device 1 is card reader zero).

The second number in brackets in the READ statement refers to the associated FORMAT statement which states in what format the data values are punched:

line 59   3   FORMAT(2I4)

The combined effect of the READ and associated FORMAT statements is to read in data values into the locations named in the list after the READ brackets according to the specified formats. If in the example given the data card was punched as follows:

Col. 1   Col. 8   ∇ indicates space
∇∇∇21000

then 2 would be read into location N, and 1000 into location IEND (2 channels for 1000 simulations), since two fields of four integers are specified. If the specifications had been (I5,I3) then the values read in would have been 21 and zero.

Other format specifications are available for reading in floating-point numbers. The reading in of lists and tables (arrays) will be discussed later.

A Practical Approach to Computer Simulation

Output of Results
Results may be output to the line-printer by use of WRITE and associated FORMAT statements. Referring again to program (CAPF):

line 84   `WRITE(6,2) IPC,ITC`

line 85   2   `FORMAT(1H0,I12,I14)`

The combined effect of these statements is to print the contents of locations IPC (plant capacity) and ITC (total cost) on the same line with double spacing between this line and the last one printed. The line spacing is controlled by the first character after the H in the FORMAT statement (0 signifying double spacing). The contents of IPC and ITC will be printed to the left of the fields specified (12 positions allowed for IPC and 14 for ITC). If the numbers are less than the specified field width, spaces are inserted in front of the number.

The format descriptor for printing floating-point numbers is F; this is followed by the total field width (which on output includes positions for the sign and decimal point), a decimal point and the number of decimal places. An example of floating-point specifications is given in program (ELEM), appendix 3.

line 74   `WRITE(2,103) IREP,IRT,ATBF,COST`

line 75   103   `FORMAT(1H0,I8,I17,F14.2,F12.2)`

IREP and IRT are integer variables, ATBF and COST are floating-point variables and therefore need F formats. If the contents of ATBF were 11.256 then this would be printed as ▽▽▽▽▽▽▽▽▽ 11.25, i.e. nine spaces would be inserted before the number and the third decimal place would be truncated.

The list of variables after the WRITE statement brackets must always correspond in order and type to the format descriptors listed within the FORMAT statement brackets; the same applies to the READ statement list.

Printing Headings
WRITE and associated FORMAT statements are also required for printing headings as shown in program (CAPF):

line 14   `WRITE(6,1)`

line 15   1   `FORMAT(29H1▽▽▽▽▽CAPACITY▽▽▽▽▽TOTAL▽COST)`

The number in front of the H must be the exact count of the characters, including spaces, between H and the bracket; the first character after the H this time is 1 and will result in the heading being printed at the top of the next page. There is no list of variables after the WRITE brackets as data is not being printed from specified locations. The output device has been defined as 6 in line 4:

line 4   OUTPUT 6=LP0   (line-printer zero).

Control Statements
So far the statements considered would be obeyed at execution time in the order in which they are written in the program. However, it is often necessary to change the sequence in which the instructions are executed to allow alternative paths in the program to be obeyed according to the result of a test, or to branch back in the program to repeat a set of instructions, or to jump forward in a program to miss out a series of instructions.

Unconditional GO TO
This is a method of transferring control to some statement in the program other than the next one in sequence. The statement is independent of any condition that may exist and a jump to the statement number specified always occurs. An example of jumping back to repeat a sequence of instructions is shown in program (CAPF):

line 100   GO TO 70

This will cause statement number 70 (line 29) to be the next one obeyed followed by the following statements in sequence until another control statement is encountered which could alter the sequence again. It is never possible to obey a GO TO statement followed by the next one in sequence, unless the latter is labelled with the statement number in the GO TO instruction, but this would make the GO TO statement superfluous.

An example of a branch forward is shown in line 94 of the same program:

line 94   GO TO 200

When this statement is obeyed line 95 and 96 are not executed. These can only be obeyed if a jump is made to statement number 304 as shown in the next example.

IF Statement
This instruction allows a jump to be made to two or three different statements in a program as a result of testing a given expression. In line 92 program (CAPF):

line 92   303   IF(I)200,304,305

if I is less than zero (negative), the next statement to be obeyed is the one having the first statement number after the brackets (200), if I is zero 304 is executed or if I is greater than zero (positive), the next instruction to be obeyed is 305, so that one of three different sequences will be executed according to the value of I.

The contents of the brackets in an IF statement may be any valid FORTRAN expression, and two of the statement numbers after the brackets may be the same as in line 91 of program (CAPF):

line 91   302   IF(ITC - IOC)200,200,303

The expression within the brackets is evaluated first, i.e. the contents of IOC (old total cost) are subtracted from ITC (new total cost), and the result is tested for negative, zero or positive value. In this particular instruction, if the result is negative or zero a branch is made to statement number 200, otherwise the next instruction to be executed is 303.

Line 97 of the same program shows an expression with an integer constant:

line 97   200   IF(IPC - 150)400,60,60

and has the effect of terminating the program when the final plant capacity (150) costs have been calculated by jumping to statement number 60 (STOP). When a STOP instruction is encountered the execution of the program is terminated and cannot be re-started.

Subscripted Variables and DIMENSION Statement

It is often necessary to read in and store a list or table of values such as a frequency distribution. By using subscripts it is possible to use just one variable name to represent many quantities. An example of this is shown in lines 21–25 of program (ELEM), appendix 3.

```
line 21            DIMENSION L(8),LF(8)
line 22            READ(1,1)L,LF
line 23       1    FORMAT(16I2)
line 24            WRITE(2,2)L,LF
line 25       2    FORMAT(5H1DATA,16I4)
```

The data to be read in and printed are a frequency distribution of the lives of elements as shown in table 5.2.

The sequence of instructions will read in the values and store them in arrays L (life) and LF (frequency) using lines 22 and 23, and print these using lines 24 and 25.

Table 5.2   Frequency distribution—lives of elements

Life	Frequency
25	7
35	28
45	40
55	60
65	84
75	95
85	98
95	99

Certain information must be given to the FORTRAN compiler when using subscripted variables:

(1) the variables having subscripts,
(2) the number of subscripts for each subscripted variable,
(3) the number of elements in each array, i.e. the maximum size of each subscript.

A DIMENSION statement (line 21) is used to supply this information and appears at the beginning of the program. In the example, eight storage locations have been reserved for the values (L) and eight for the frequencies (LF), and these will be referred to in the program as $L(1)$, $L(2)$, ... $L(8)$ and $LF(1)$, $LF(2)$ ... $LF(8)$, or in general L(integer variable) and LF(integer variable). It is possible for a variable to have more than one subscript and for the subscripts to be integer expressions obeying given rules, but for simplicity only one-dimensional arrays (one subscript, an integer constant or integer variable) will be considered in this book.

The DIMENSION statement is a specification statement which is not obeyed at the execution time of the object program and only provides information for the FORTRAN compiler, e.g. causes storage to be reserved for arrays. Non-subscripted variables have storage allocated automatically when they first appear in the program.

A whole array can be read in or printed out by just listing the variable non-subscripted after the brackets of the READ or WRITE statements as shown in lines 22 and 24. These will need associated FORMAT statements as before. Line 23 specifies a format of 16 integral values of field width 2 and these will appear on the data card as follows:

Col.1.   Col.32
2535455565758595 7 2840 6084959899

The computer accepts the string of numbers and interprets them according to the FORMAT statement. Lines 24 and 25 will cause the data to be printed out on one line at the top of a new page with two extra spaces in front of each number (i.e. three spaces before the 7), and preceded by the words DATA.

The DO statement

The DO statement is a command to execute repeatedly a sequence of statements for a specified number of times. A simple DO statement is illustrated in program (ELEM):

```
line 63        DO 30 J=1,6
line 64    30  LIFE(J)=LIFE(J)-MIN
```

These two statements cause the value of the minimum life (MIN) to be subtracted from each element of the array LIFE in turn, $L(1)$ to $L(6)$, the result being stored as the new value. The first time statement number 30 is executed with $J = 1$. For each succeeding execution, J is increased by one until statement number 30 has been executed with $J = 6$ (the final value), and control then passes to the statement following statement number 30.

An alternative way of writing these statements would be:

```
           J=1
    30     LIFE(J)=LIFE(J)-MIN
           IF(J-6)10,20,20
    10     J=J+1
           GO TO 30
    20     next statement
```

This method, however, requires five statements and therefore is not so efficient as making use of the DO facility.

The initial and final values in a DO statement may be non-subscripted integer variables or unsigned integer constants, as may be the increment (this is written after the final value separated by a comma if not equal to one).

The number after DO always refers to the statement number of the last statement in the DO sequence (range). This last statement must not be another DO, STOP, RETURN, CALL, GO TO or IF; in these cases a dummy statement CONTINUE is used which has the effect of continuing the DO operation. Another use of CONTINUE is when a sequence of statements in the DO range is to be obeyed only according to the result of a test otherwise the DO operation is to be continued such as in program (ELEM):

```
line 191        MIN=LIFE(1)
```

```
line 192          I=1
line 193          DO 22 J=2,6
line 194          IF(LIFE(J)-MIN)21,22,22
line 195    21    MIN=LIFE(J)
line 196          I=J
line 197    22    CONTINUE
```

This sequence of instructions finds the minimum value in the LIFE array so that if a smaller value than MIN (set to the first value in the array in line 191) is found in line 194, this value is put in MIN and I is set to the current value of J, otherwise the next element in LIFE is tested.

Lines 46–47 in program (COMF), appendix 2, illustrate the use of CONTINUE when the last statement to be executed is an IF.

```
line 46           DO 10 I=1,6
line 47           IF(MUNIT(I)-IRN1+1)10,20,20
line 48    10     CONTINUE
```

This example shows also that it is possible to jump out of a DO range according to the result of a test (when the motor-unit frequency, MUNIT(I), is greater or equal to the random number selected plus one, IRN1 + 1), the next instruction to be obeyed is statement number 20, otherwise 10.

If a statement within a DO range causes a jump out of the DO loop, then the value of the controlling variable will remain at its present value until subsequently changed by further instructions. For example, if in the test at line 47 above, the DO loop has been executed four times and on the fifth pass (when the controlling variable I = 5) control passes to statement number 20, then I will be equal to 5 at that stage. However, if a jump is not made out of the DO loop and it is obeyed for the specified number of times (six times in the example) then the value of the controlling variable (I) is indeterminate and may not be used in further instructions unless it is reset to some value.

An example of an implied DO loop is given in the same program:

```
line 19    READ(1,1)(MUNIT(I),I=1,6),(IGUNIT(J),J=1,5),N,IR,IW
```

The part of the statement (MUNIT(I),I=1,6) has the same effect as the DO loop

```
           DO 5 I=1,6
       5   READ(1,1)MUNIT(I)
```

i.e. six values are read into MUNIT(1) to MUNIT(6). Other implied DO loops and single variables may be included in the READ list as in the example.

Subroutines

If a program or sequence of instructions is used more than once, it need only be written once and then reference can be made to it when required. These subprograms (subroutines) may be compiled and tested independently and may be used by different main programs and other subroutines. The variable names used in subroutines are completely independent of those used in the main programs and other subroutines.

It is useful for a large program to be divided up into several subprograms which can be written and tested at different stages. The program (ELEM) will be used to illustrate the use of subroutines and how a simulation program may be developed.

SAMPLE PROGRAM (ELEM)

The main logic of the problem is shown in the form of a flowchart; this should be the first stage in developing a computer program, as the actual coding is then relatively simple. Further details of this exercise are given in chapter 9.

The complete program listing is shown in appendix 3. This includes comments lines explaining the various stages. Relative program statements are listed again next to the flowcharts in figures 5.3 to 5.8 to illustrate the use of a flowchart when coding, and extra explanation is given where necessary.

Main Program

The main program reads in the frequency distribution for the lives of the elements, prints the data and then CALLS the three subroutines for the three policies in turn by means of CALL statements; these give the subroutine name followed by the arguments in brackets. The arguments consist of a list of values to be transferred between the calling program and the subroutine specified. There are other methods of transferring values across, which will not be mentioned in this book.

The subroutine called starts with the word SUBROUTINE followed by the subroutine name and a list of arguments in brackets as shown in the next part of the program.

Subroutine POLICYA

Format statements numbers 100, 101 and 102 are used to print headings at the top of the policy A results page. The format separator/(slash) is used to cause the printer to output a new record, i.e. print on the next line. Two slashes (//) give double spacing. Continuation lines also are illustrated in this example; one convention is to leave column 6 blank for the first FORMAT

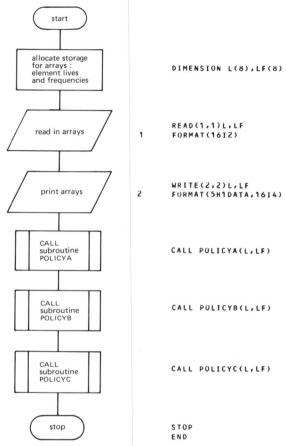

DIMENSION L(8),LF(8)

1   READ(1,1)L,LF
    FORMAT(16I2)

2   WRITE(2,2)L,LF
    FORMAT(5H1DATA,16I4)

CALL POLICYA(L,LF)

CALL POLICYB(L,LF)

CALL POLICYC(L,LF)

STOP
END

Figure 5.3   Program (ELEM)—Main program flowchart

line and then to number succeeding lines of the same FORMAT 1, 2 etc. to the limit specified by the particular compiler being used.

Subroutine POLICYA calls on two other subroutines: SLIFE which samples the life of an element from a frequency distribution obtained from the main program via the calling subroutine, and MLIFE which finds the element having the shortest remaining life. These subroutines are explained next.

Subroutine SLIFE

The subroutine FPMCRV is supplied by the manufacturers (ICL)[25] as a PLAN scientific subroutine and generates a real pseudorandom variate between zero

91

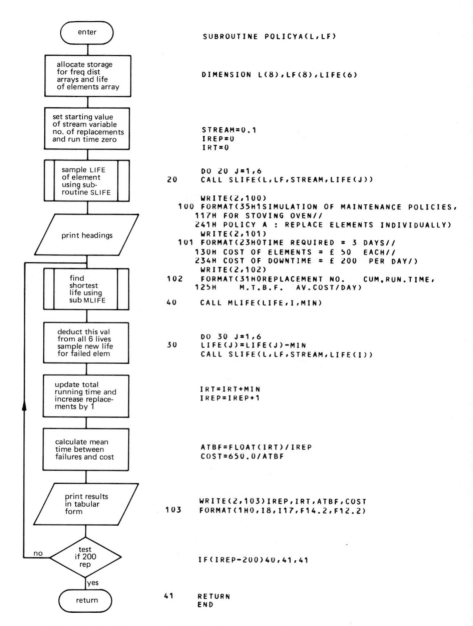

```
                                    SUBROUTINE POLICYA(L,LF)


                                    DIMENSION L(8),LF(8),LIFE(6)




                                    STREAM=0.1
                                    IREP=0
                                    IRT=0

                                    DO 20 J=1,6
                              20    CALL SLIFE(L,LF,STREAM,LIFE(J))

                                    WRITE(2,100)
                             100    FORMAT(35H1SIMULATION OF MAINTENANCE POLICIES,
                                    117H FOR STOVING OVEN//
                                    241H POLICY A : REPLACE ELEMENTS INDIVIDUALLY)
                                    WRITE(2,101)
                             101    FORMAT(23H0TIME REQUIRED = 3 DAYS//
                                    130H COST OF ELEMENTS = £ 50   EACH//
                                    234H COST OF DOWNTIME = £ 200   PER DAY/)
                                    WRITE(2,102)
                             102    FORMAT(31H0REPLACEMENT NO.   CUM.RUN.TIME,
                                    125H    M.T.B.F.   AV.COST/DAY)
                              40    CALL MLIFE(LIFE,I,MIN)


                                    DO 30 J=1,6
                              30    LIFE(J)=LIFE(J)-MIN
                                    CALL SLIFE(L,LF,STREAM,LIFE(I))


                                    IRT=IRT+MIN
                                    IREP=IREP+1



                                    ATBF=FLOAT(IRT)/IREP
                                    COST=650.0/ATBF



                                    WRITE(2,103)IREP,IRT,ATBF,COST
                             103    FORMAT(1H0,I8,I17,F14.2,F12.2)



                                    IF(IREP-200)40,41,41


                              41    RETURN
                                    END
```

Figure 5.4   Program (ELEM)—Subroutine POLICYA flowchart

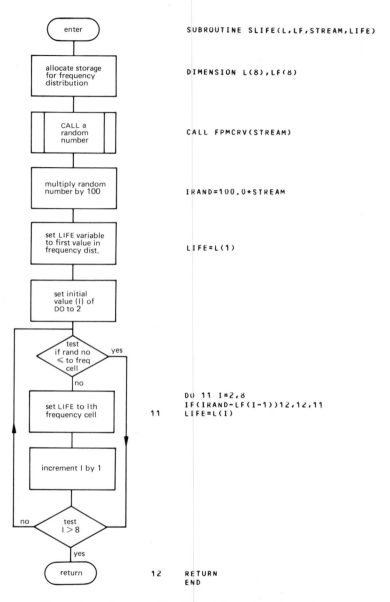

Figure 5.5   Program (ELEM)—Subroutine SLIFE flowchart

and one, using the multiplicative congruential method described by Naylor *et al*[20]. STREAM is a floating point variable set in the user program to a floating-point number between zero and one (but not 0.5), see line 36. At exit STREAM contains the next pseudorandom variate in the series. The method of adding this subroutine to the user program will be explained later in this chapter under Implementation of FORTRAN on ICL 1900 computers.

In the flowchart the DO statement covers three of the boxes: setting the initial value, incrementing and testing. This level of detail is normally not necessary and is shown here for clarification only (figure 5.5).

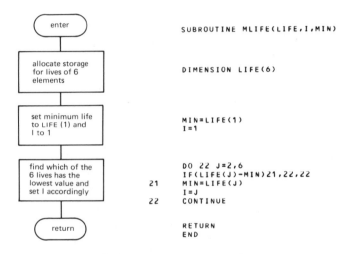

Figure 5.6   Program (ELEM)—Subroutine MLIFE flowchart

The arguments taken across from subroutine POLICYA by means of the CALL SLIFE statement are the frequency distribution, L and LF, (the whole of the arrays is taken across by listing the array names) and the present value of STREAM. The subroutine SLIFE sends back to POLICYA the new value for STREAM and the life of an element LIFE which refers to LIFE(J) in the subroutine POLICYA. In POLICYA LIFE is an array of six elements and in SLIFE LIFE is a single variable; this is possible only because the variable names and array names are independent in the individual subroutines. It would not be permissible to have LIFE as an array and a single variable in one subroutine or main program.

The value of LIFE from subroutine SLIFE is taken back to give a new value to LIFE(J), with the subscript J having the value it had when leaving subroutine POLICYA at the CALL statement. The effect of RETURN at the end of a subroutine is to take the values of the arguments back to the calling subroutine, and the next statement to be obeyed is the one following the CALL statement.

Subroutine MLIFE

In this subroutine, LIFE is used as an array as in the calling subroutine, and must have storage allocated by the DIMENSION statement.

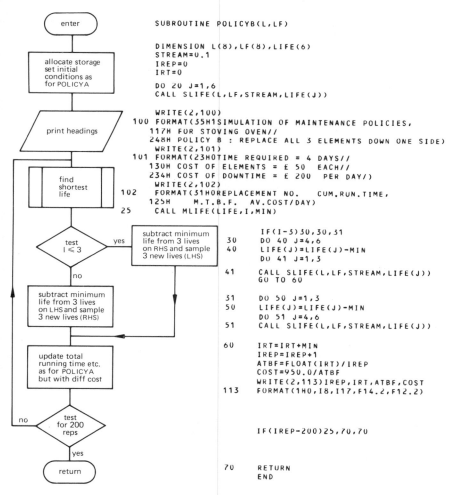

Figure 5.7   Program (ELEM)–Subroutine POLICYB flowchart

A Practical Approach to Computer Simulation

Subroutine POLICYB
The FORMAT statements numbers for the similar WRITE statements in subroutines POLICYA and POLICYB are identical. Again these are independent in the individual subroutines.

Subroutine POLICYC
In the listing (appendix 3), the subroutine SLIFE and MLIFE follow subroutine POLICYC, however, the subroutine may be compiled in any order.

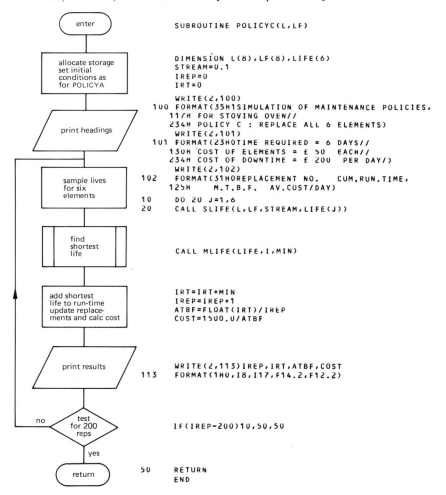

Figure 5.8   Program (ELEM)—Subroutine POLICYC flowchart

DETECTION AND CORRECTION OF ERRORS IN FORTRAN PROGRAMS

There are basically three types of errors that may occur in FORTRAN programs.

(1) Syntactic errors—these are due to disobeying the rules for the FORTRAN compiler used.

e.g. mistakes in spelling commands: REED instead of READ, 1F instead of IF,

punctuation errors (extra commas or full-stop, brackets missing):

        DO 11 I=2,8. , IF(IRAND-LF(I-1)12,12,11;

Statement numbers, continuation indicators or statements in wrong column.

These errors are output by the compiler at compilation time and the program will not be executed until it is completely free from syntactic errors.

(2) Run-time or execution errors—these may be due to several reasons, some of which are:

mistakes in format (integer format descriptors associated with floating point variables and vice versa, H count incorrect);

number calculated is too large to be held in store location giving overflow;

program looping (sequence of instructions being obeyed over and over again without exit being programmed so that the program will never terminate).

These errors must be corrected in the source (FORTRAN) program which needs to be re-compiled and free from syntactic errors before execution.

(3) Logical errors—these may cause errors at execution time; e.g. looping or overflow, but often the program may be run successfully giving completely wrong results. The validity of the final results, therefore, needs to be checked carefully before the program becomes operational. This is especially important in simulation projects where results may look feasible but completely wrong.

One way of checking results is to put extra FORTRAN statements into the program to print results at intermediate stages which can be checked manually. If the intermediate results are satisfactory, the 'diagnostic statements' are removed from the FORTRAN source program which is re-compiled and run with the final data for the required length of run. It may be necessary to have a much shorter run when printing intermediate results as the latter can slow the execution of the program down appreciably.

```
          SUBROUTINE POLICYA(L,LF)                    EH    400
             .
             .
             .
          DO 20 J=1,6                                 EH    442
20        CALL SLIFE(L,LF,STREAM,LIFE(J))             EH    444
          WRITE(2,110)LIFE,STREAM                     EH    445
110       FORMAT(1H0,60X,4H445:,6I5,F9.3)             EH    446
111       FORMAT(1H0,60X,4H481:,6I5,F9.3)             EH    447
             .
             .
             .
40        CALL MLIFE(LIFE,I,MIN)                       EH    480
          WRITE(2,111)I,LIFE(I)                       EH    481
          DO 30 J=1,6                                 EH    485
30        LIFE(J)=LIFE(J)-MIN                          EH    490
          WRITE(2,112)LIFE                            EH    491
          CALL SLIFE(L,LF,STREAM,LIFE(I))             EH    492
          WRITE(2,105)LIFE,STREAM                     EH    495
112       FORMAT(1H0,60X,4H491:,6I5)                  EH    496
105       FORMAT(1H0,60X,4H495:,6I5,F9.3)             EH    497
             .
             .
             .
          SUBROUTINE SLIFE(L,LF,STREAM,LIFE)           EH   3000
             .
             .
             .
          DO 11 I=2,8                                  EH   3110
          IF(IRAND-LF(I-1))12,12,11                   EH   3120
11        LIFE=L(I)                                    EH   3130
12        WRITE(2,100)LIFE,STREAM                      EH   3132
100       FORMAT(1H0,60X,5H3132:,I5,F9.3)             EH   3133
             .
             .
             .
          SUBROUTINE MLIFE(LIFE,I,MIN)                 EH   4000
             .
             .
             .
          DO 22 J=2,6                                  EH   4070
          IF(LIFE(J)-MIN)21,22,22                     EH   4080
21        MIN=LIFE(J)                                  EH   4090
          I=J                                          EH   4100
22        CONTINUE                                     EH   4110
          WRITE(2,100)I,LIFE                           EH   4111
100       FORMAT(1H0,60X,5H4111:,7I5)                 EH   4112
             .
             .
             .
```

Figure 5.9   Program (ELEM)−'Diagnostic' print statements

```
4111:      1     35    65    45    55    45    45
481:       1     35
491:       0     30    10    20    10    10
3132:     35      0.096
495:      35     30    10    20    10    10     0.096


4111:      3     35    30    10    20    10    10
481:       3     10
491:      25     20     0    10     0     0
3132:     75      0.887
495:      25     20    75    10     0     0     0.887


4111:      5     25    20    75    10     0     0
481:       5      0
491:      25     20    75    10     0     0
3132:     55      0.455
495:      25     20    75    10    55     0     0.455


4111:      6     25    20    75    10    55     0
481:       6      0
491:      25     20    75    10    55     0
3132:     65      0.750
495:      25     20    75    10    55    65     0.750
```

Figure 5.10   Program (ELEM)—Intermediate results

Logical errors need to be corrected in the flowchart and source program which is re-complied and executed.

The use of 'diagnostic' print statements is shown in the following part program (ELEM), figure 5.9.

The card sequence numbers (e.g. 445) were used to identify the results which were spaced over to the right-hand side of the print-out (60X in the FORMAT statement gives 60 spaces across the page).

A page of intermediate results for program (ELEM) is reproduced in figure 5.10. This shows the sampling of six lives with the associated value of the stream variable from subroutine SLIFE (card number 3132); the number of the element which has the shortest life, together with the values of all the lives (card number 4111) in subroutine MLIFE; the number of the shortest life and its value in subroutine POLICYA (481) to ensure this has been transferred correctly across the subroutines; the value of the lives after the shortest has been subtracted from all the lives (491) showing the shortest one now set to zero; the new life sampled (3132); and the values of the lives to be used in the next simulation together with the latest value of the STREAM variable (495).

The tabulated results IREP,IRT,ATBF and COST were printed on the left of the print-out and were checked manually against the intermediate results.

This type of check is very easily implemented and ensures accuracy of the final results.

SUMMARY OF PROGRAM DEVELOPMENT

A detailed flowchart is drawn showing the logic of the specified problem. The program is written on coding sheets in the appropriate code, and 'diagnostic' print statements are included so that the accuracy of the results can be checked. The program is punched onto paper-tape or cards and compiled into machine code. When the program is free from syntactic errors it is executed with the appropriate data. Any run-time errors are corrected in the source program which is re-compiled and executed. The results obtained are checked against intermediate results and if these are correct the source program is amended to remove the 'diagnostic' print statements, and the program is compiled and executed with the final data.

It is useful to include statements in the program that will print out the data that are used for any specific run of the program.

STANDARD FREQUENCY DISTRIBUTION—FORTRAN PROGRAMS

Frequently the data to be used in a simulation program follow a standard frequency distribution, and FORTRAN subroutines for these have been published by Naylor *et al.* (reference 20). These subroutines together with tabulations for a 100 generated random values are given in appendix 7, program (SUBF). The use of two of these subroutines UNIFM and NORM are shown in program (CAPF), appendix 1.

The tabulations include the simulated MEAN and STANDARD DEVIATION, and the program written to obtain these will be used to illustrate further facilities in FORTRAN.

FURTHER FACILITIES IN FORTRAN

Nested DO statements
The use of nested DO statements is shown in program (SUBF):

```
line 19              DO 20 J=1,4
line 20              WRITE(2,103)
line 21       103    FORMAT(1H0//)
line 22              DO 20 K=1,5
line 23              DO 30 L=1,5
line 24              CALL UNIFM(1.0,4.0,X(L),STREAM)
line 25       30     WRITE(6)X(L)
line 26       20     WRITE(2,104)(X(I),I=1,5)
```

The tabulations were required in sets of four, five columns across the page with extra spacing between every five rows. The above routine was used to print the values in the specified format and consists of three DO ranges within each other (nested). The range of the first DO is lines 20-26, the second DO lines 23-26, and the third DO lines 24-25.

DO ranges may be wholly nested (as lines 23-25 within lines 22-26), or may terminate at the same statement (as lines 19-26 and 22-26), but must not cross i.e. the second DO statement could not terminate after line 26. For two nested DO ranges, the inner loop is executed first with the initial value of the outer DO and this continues until the inner DO is completed. The following statement in the outer DO, if any, is obeyed next, and then the remaining statements in the outer DO; control now passes to the beginning of the outer DO range and the statements are obeyed with the second outer DO value and so on. This means that the statements in the inner DO range may be repeated several times for each value of the outer DO. Thus, in the example, J is set initially to 1 (line 19), line 20 is obeyed and K is set to 1 (line 22), L is set to 1 (line 23) and lines 24 and 25 are obeyed. This completes one execution of the innermost loop with L taking values 1 to 5 in steps of 1. K is set to 2 next (line 22), L is set back to 1 and execution continues with K equal to 2 and L taking values 1 to 5 in steps of 1. This sequence of instructions is obeyed until it has been carried out with K equal

101

to 5, when J is set to 2 in line 19 and the whole sequence is executed again. This process is summarised in figure 5.11. Lines 24 and 25 are obeyed 100 times to give 100 generated values which are written to magnetic tape.

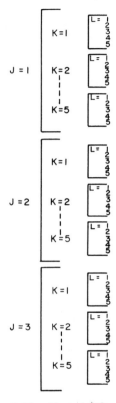

Figure 5.11   Nested DO ranges

USE OF MAGNETIC TAPE

Statements are available in FORTRAN which enable the programmer to write or read from magnetic tape as shown in program (SUBF):

line 25   30   WRITE(6)X(L)

where 6 is the device number for a particular magnetic tape unit and X(L) is the Lth element of array X.

102

The tape is rewound to the beginning using

line 28   REWIND 6

and a subroutine (SDEV) is called which calculates the mean and standard deviation of these 100 simulated values. Within the subroutine, line 117 READ(6)X reads single values from the magnetic tape, and the standard deviation is calculated using the formula:

$$SD = \sqrt{\left\{ \frac{\Sigma(x - m)^2}{n} - \left(\frac{\Sigma(x - m)}{n}\right)^2 \right\}}$$

where

x = the random variables
m = the assumed mean
n = the total number of values

On returning to the main program MASTER SUBF the magnetic tape is rewound again so that the next 100 values can overwrite the old values.

IMPLEMENTATION OF BASIC FORTRAN ON THE ICL 1900 SERIES

ICL 1900 FORTRAN programs are written in segments. The first segment is the program description and this is followed by one and one only MASTER segment (main program) and any number of subroutines (within the storage capacity of the machine) compiled in any order.

All segments are terminated by END, which indicates to the compiler that the end of the segment has been reached. This is not to be comfused with a STOP statement which terminates the program at execution time and which must appear at least once in the program.

Program Description Segment

This names the program, specifies the peripherals and device numbers used in the program and allows the trace package to be incorporated. Thus in program (SUBF) the following statements have the given interpretation:

Statement	Interpretation
line 1 LIST (LP)	list program on line-printer
line 2 SEND TO(MT)	compile onto magnetic tape
line 3 PROGRAM(SUBF)	name program SUBF (4 characters, 1st alphabetic)
line 4 OUTPUT 2,(MONITOR)=LP0	print results and monitor trace on line-printer zero (device 2)

Statement	Interpretation
line 5 CREATE 6=MT0/UNFORMATTED(NUMBERS)	create a magnetic tape labelled NUMBERS which can be written to or read from using magnetic tape unit zero (device 6)
line 6 TRACE	incorporate the trace package to output details of the last 100 statements (Source program) executed including results
line 7 END	

Master Segment
The first statement is MASTER followed by a segment name, consisting of 1 to 5 alphanumeric characters, the first of which must be alphabetic. The first letter of the name has no significance as no type (integer or real) is associated with a MASTER statement.

Subroutine Segment
The first statement is SUBROUTINE followed by a segment name as for the MASTER segment and arguments in brackets for transferring values between segments. The use of arguments can be avoided by using COMMON areas but this will not be dealt with in this introductory treatment. The last statement before END is RETURN which passes control back to the statement following the CALL statement in the calling segment.

Library Subroutines
It is possible to attach groups of subroutines (e.g. FSCE below) from the subroutine library to the source program by means of the following two statements:

line 127   LIBRARY
line 128   READ FROM(MT,-.FSCE)

FINISH
This is the last statement in the whole program and indicates to the compiler that no more statements are to be compiled.

FURTHER EXAMPLES

All the programs are listed below together with references to appropriate chapters in this book which give more details of the theoretical and practical considerations of the actual problems.

Program name	Appendix	Chapter	Application
CAPF	1	9	Plant Capacity
COMF	2	1	Maintenance
ELEM	3	9	Maintenance
FORE	4	8	Forecasting
LOAD	5	9	Production Control
SIMQ	6	7	Queueing

USE OF ON-LINE TERMINALS

Access to a computer may be available via an on-line terminal. This often consists of a teleprinter linked to the computer (which may be many miles away) by a GPO or private telephone line.

A variety of languages (including FORTRAN) can be used on-line depending on the installation; one language that is available currently on several computers is BASIC. This is an easy to learn high-level language, similar in many ways to FORTRAN but with simpler read and print instructions (no formats required) and with some extra facilities. However, simple variable names are restricted to one alphabetic character which may be followed by one digit (giving 286 possible different names); array variable names must consist of one alphabetic character only, giving 26 possible different array names.

One of the main advantages of using on-line facilities is that the user communicates directly with the computer and obtains an immediate response from it. For instance, syntactic errors are returned to the programmer (printed out on the teleprinter) as soon as the program has been translated and the programmer may then type in corrections immediately; these will be inserted in the correct place in the program, so that a syntactic-error-free program may be obtained in a relatively short time. The program itself may be designed to ask the user to type in answers to questions, which allows personnel with no knowledge of a computer language to use a program written by an experienced programmer. This is known as 'conversational programming', and to the user it appears that there is an uninterrupted 'conversation' with the computer. In fact, usually, several users are linked to the computer at the same time, but the requests of each user are processed so quickly that the delay to any user is only a few seconds which is not noticed.

To make a connection between the teleprinter and the computer the user first calls the computer number and is answered by a high-pitched tone. The computer may ask the user to log in with his identification and password which prevents illegal access. When the user has successfully logged in, he may read or type in a program for translation, correction or running, or access any of his programs held in his own library (stored at the central installation usually on disc files), or 'public' library programs. Thus, a manager having use of a computer terminal may phone a number and then test the effect of implementing a policy using an existing program.

Examples of a BASIC program which may be used in this way are given in appendices 8 and 9. These are two versions of the same problem, which use a set of cash flows that have been calculated together with an associated probability for each of three cost categories (LABOUR, OVERHEADS, and INCOME), and from these build up a frequency distribution (histogram) of profitability. One of the programs (PRAS) uses Monte Carlo methods, the other program (PRAC) calculates the profitability mathematically.

To use either of the programs the manager need only know how to establish a connection with the computer, to log in and to obtain the program from the library. By typing in RUN, the first message will be printed on the teleprinter:

```
TYPE 1 TO OBTAIN NOTES ON INPUTTING DATA,
OR 2 IF THESE INSTRUCTIONS ARE NOT
REQUIRED
?
```

i.e. if the user is unfamiliar with the method of inputting data for this program further instructions may be obtained by typing a 1 after the question mark (see lines 230 to 370 of program (PRAS)), however, to save time these instructions may be omitted by typing a 2 after the question mark; the program then skips around the instructions and continues by requesting data, e.g.:

```
LABOUR CASH FLOW(L), 4 VALUES PLEASE

?
```

The user now types in the four cash flows to be held in the array elements $L(1),L(2),L(3)$ and $L(4)$. The next message output on the teleprinter will be:

```
ASSOCIATED FREQUENCIES PLEASE

?
```

106

```
RUN
PRAS


TYPE 1 TO OBTAIN NOTES ON INPUTTING DATA,
OR 2 IF THESE INSTRUCTIONS ARE NOT REQUIRED.

?&2
LABOUR CASH FLOW(L), 4 VALUES PLEASE
?30000,32000,34000,36000
ASSOCIATED FREQUENCIES PLEASE
?10,30,40,20

O'HEAD CASH FLOWS(O), 5 VALUES PLEASE
?14000,16000,18000,20,,,←←←000,22000
ASSOCIATED FREQUENCIES PLEASE
?5,15,50,20,20,
EXTRA INPUT - WARNING ONLY

YOUR FREQUENCIES DO NO ADD UP TO 100, TRY AGAIN
ASSOCIATED FREQUENCIES PLEASE
?5,15,50,20,10

INCOME CASH FLOW(I), 4 VALUES PLEASE
?40000,45000,55000,60000
ASSOCIATED FREQUENCIES PLEASE
?20,25,30,25

NO OF HISTOGRAM CELLS REQUIRED
?50
VALUE OF LOWEST CELL
?-30000
CLASS INTERVALS
?1000
NO OF SIMULATED RUNS REQUIRED
?1000


PROJECT PROFITABILITY ANALYSIS DATA


LABOUR CASH FLOW     30000    32000    34000.      36000.
FREQUENCIES          10       30       40      20

O'HEAD CASH FLOW     14000    16000    18000   20000    22000
FREQUENCIES          5        15       50      20       10

INCOME CASH FLOW     40000.      45000.      55000.      60000.
FREQUENCIES          20       25       30      25

NO OF CELLS, LOWEST, INTERVALS 50          -30000          1000

LENGTH OF RUN 1000
```

} Example of
  incorrect input

Figure 5.12   PRAS input phase

107

A typical input phase showing the computer requests and user responses is shown in figure 5.12. This includes an example of incorrect input where the frequencies did not add up to 100 and caused the computer to request the user to try to input the associated frequencies again, i.e. a check has been written in program (PRAS) which ensures that the frequencies typed in by the user always add up to 100 before the program can be executed. Details of the histogram and the number of simulated runs required also are requested and need to be typed in.

Results for 1 000 simulated runs of program (PRAS) for the data input in figure 5.12 are shown in figure 9.9. A further explanation of these programmed examples of project profitability analysis is given in chapter 9.

The use of computer terminals as illustrated in the preceding examples will become more widespread as computers become more powerful and more data links are established. This will allow the manager with his own computer terminal in his office to use scientific methods (such as simulation) to determine new policies.

Chapter 6

The Use of CSL for Computer Simulation Studies

INTRODUCTION TO GENERAL SIMULATION LANGUAGES

In the previous chapter it was shown how simulation models of business systems may be computerised using a universal scientific programming language (FORTRAN). The actual language had little influence on the structure of the model and similar languages (e.g. ALGOL, PL1) could have been used without changing the structure. However, many modern computers are provided with general simulation languages which not only ease the task of writing a computer program for the system but also aid the user in constructing the model.

A variety of general simulation languages are in existence, and the choice of language in most cases will depend on its availability on the machine being used. A useful summary and comparison of such languages is given by Tocher[28], and by Krasnow and Merikallio[16].

This chapter describes one of the languages implemented on the ICL 1900 series—CSL (Control and Simulation Language).

HISTORICAL NOTES

CSL was originally prepared for IBM computers as a joint project by J. N. Buxton (IBM United Kingdom Ltd.) and J. G. Laski (Esso Petroleum Co.)[4,9]. The language was designed to allow working industrial systems to be simulated on the computer; these programs could be manipulated to test the effect of using alternative methods of controlling the systems. The language was extended at a later stage to enable programs to be written to control real systems.

The second version of CSL was implemented[10] for the IBM 7090/94, and since then versions have been prepared for Horeywell machines[11] and the ICL 1900 series[31].

INTRODUCTION TO CSL

In a CSL program the system is described in mainly static terms by the use of status descriptors (entities). The entities of a simulation model are represented by a series of variable names which have storage allocated to them, and their state as time passes can be changed under the control of logical statements.

Each entity is a member of a class of entities having similar basic properties, and a collection of entities drawn from a particular class is known as a set. A change in the state of an entity can be recorded by moving the entity from one set to another, or by adding it to or removing it from a particular set.

An example of the manipulation of a simulation model in this way is shown in the program (BOWS), appendix 10, which simulates refuelling of aircraft by four bowsers (refuelling lorries). Three classes of entities are defined in this program : 1000 AIRCRAFT, 4 BOWSERS and 4 PARTFILLED.* When an aircraft comes in to be refuelled (i.e. joins the queue), it is placed in the set AIRQUEUE and removed when it has been refuelled. The BOWSER entities are added to a set FREEBOWS when they become available for refuelling. Statements are written in the program which test the contents of the sets to see if there are any aircraft in the queue or if a bowser is available.

In a real system certain changes take place as time passes; this makes it essential for simulation programs to incorporate some form of time-advance mechanism. In CSL, time values are held in time-cells. These have the same properties as other integer cells and can therefore be used in arithmetic and logical statements and in addition have time-advancing properties. Time-cells are defined by the programmer and can exist as separate variables or be associated with entities. Initially and during execution of the program, values are assigned to these time-cells to represent the time at which a change may occur in the model, e.g. time of arrival of next aircraft. To advance time, the time-cell containing the smallest positive value (zero and negative values are ignored) is selected by the time-advance routine; simulation time is advanced by this amount by subtracting the value from all the time-cells making the selected one zero. The time-advance value is added at the same time to a variable called CLOCK (set at zero initially). CLOCK thus represents simulation time and may be used in the program as shown in program (PSIM), appendix 11.

line 160   55 CLOCK GT 840 @ 56

This is a conditional statement allowing alternative paths to be followed in the program according to the result of the test; i.e. if simulation time is greater

*Note: The necessity for a class termed PARTFILLED will be explained later in this chapter.

than 19.00 hours (840 mins) then the end-of-day routine is entered, otherwise time is advanced and the simulation is continued for that day.

The main routines of the program, i.e. the series of actions which change the state of the model whenever specified conditions are satisfied, are known as activities. These routines are entered in turn at zero CLOCK and whenever a time-advance has been made. The activities will be carried out only if the results of certain tests are true.

An example of an activity is shown in program (BOWS):

```
line 71    BEGIN AIRCRAFT ARRIVAL
line 72    T.NEXT EQ 0
  :
  :
line 88      . . . . .
```

The time-cell T.NEXT takes its value initially and during execution of the program by sampling from a frequency distribution and holds the time of arrival of the next aircraft to be refuelled. Initially, it is set to 10 min in the program, i.e. the next aircraft is due to arrive in 10 min. Thus at time zero (first pass through the activities) the test T.NEXT EQ 0, which tests whether the time-value in T.NEXT is zero, results in a jump to the next activity, until 10 min have elapsed when T.NEXT will be zero and the activity BEGIN AIRCRAFT ARRIVAL will be obeyed.

After a complete pass has been made through the activities, the time-cells are scanned and time is advanced as outlined previously. However, since the activities are interlinked, it is possible that the completion of a later activity in the program may allow a previous activity to be obeyed, in which case it is necessary to recycle through the activities without a time-advance by using the RECYCLE statement as shown later in this chapter.

The availability of distribution sampling functions has been mentioned briefly. These make use of a procedure which generates pseudorandom numbers. Distributions may be specified by the programmer, or standard frequency distributions may be used. Another useful facility is the ability to record counts of statistical variables in histograms which can be printed out in a standard form.

CSL programs as implemented on the ICL 1900 series are translated into FORTRAN before being compiled into machine code and executed. A more detailed description of 1900 CSL follows, the order being the same as that of the full description of the language given in the ICL manual[31]. Enough information is given in this chapter for the reader to follow the programs in appendices 10–14.

DATA STRUCTURE

Constants, Variables, Arrays

The forms of data that may be processed by a CSL program are constants, variables and arrays. Constants are written as in FORTRAN programs (see chapter 5). Variable names may consist of up to twenty letters but must not include numeric or special characters; CSL structural words (see end of this chapter) must not be used as variable names. A variable name is made real (floating-point) by defining it in a FLOAT statement at the beginning of the program, otherwise a variable is defined automatically as integer if it has an integer value assigned to it in any statement.

The FLOAT statement simply consists of the word FLOAT followed by the list of variable names (separated by commas) which are required to take floating-point numbers as shown in program (PSIM), appendix 11.

```
line 32     FLOAT AVCOSTPERJOB,CDAYCOST,DCOST,CJOBCOUNT,
line 33    1JOBCOUNT,AMTIME,PATCT
```

Line 33 is a continuation line. In CSL continuation lines follow as in FORTRAN (see chapter 5), except that only two continuation lines are allowed.

Arrays must be defined in the program before they are used with an ARRAY statement, which is similar to the FORTRAN DIMENSION statement (see chapter 5). An array may have up to thirty two dimensions and is defined by listing it in an ARRAY statement with its maximum subscripts (these must be positive integer constants) in brackets. Array elements are accessed by using the array name followed by the appropriate subscripts in brackets. Thus in program (BOWS), appendix 10:

```
line 30     ARRAY ARRIVETIME(2,10),FUELREQ(2,8),ACFILLTIME(4),
line 31    1    ....
line 32    2    ....
```

The time bowser 3 takes to fill a particular aircraft at a certain stage in the program is held in ACFILLTIME(3).

Program (BOWS) will continue to be used for the examples throughout this chapter unless it is stated otherwise.

Classes, Entities, Sets, Attributes

The basic components (entities) of the model are defined in classes at the beginning of the program:

```
line 23     CLASS TIME AIRCRAFT.1000(2) SET AIRQUEUE
```

line 24   CLASS TIME BOWSER.4(1) SET FREEBOWS
line 25   CLASS PARTFILLED.4(1) SET EXT,AV

Each entity belongs to only one class, and is identified by its class name followed by a number (the class index) which indicates its fixed position in the class, so that the fifth aircraft to be refuelled is referred to as AIRCRAFT.5. The class index may be replaced by an integer variable or expression enclosed in brackets:

line 80   AIRCRAFT.J TAIL AIRQUEUE

where in this case J has an initial value of 1 and is incremented by 1 each time the previous statement (J+1) is obeyed.

Subsets of a class are defined as sets, and an entity may be added to or removed from any of the sets defined in its CLASS statement. There are two types of sets: ordered sets and Boolean sets. Boolean sets (BSET), in which entities are held in their class order in fixed positions corresponding to their class indices, are more economical in storage than ordered sets since each possible member of a Boolean set is represented by one bit (binary digit). However, ordered sets are required for queueing systems where an order needs to be established and retained, and entities may only be added to the beginning (HEAD) or end (TAIL) of the set. This is illustrated in the preceding examples where AIRQUEUE was defined as an ordered set (SET) for the CLASS of AIRCRAFT entities (line 23), and in line 80 the Jth aircraft was added to the end of the set AIRQUEUE, i.e. it joined the queue for refuelling.

In the program (BOWS), it was required to store numerical information associated with each aircraft entity—attributes of the entity. The first attribute is the fuel required and the second the 'clocking in time', i.e. the time when the aircraft joined the queue. This information is stored in subscripted variables associated with each entity and is referenced by the entity name followed by the subscript in brackets. Thus in the example, the 1000 AIRCRAFT entities defined in the CLASS statement (line 23) each have two attributes indicated by the 2 in brackets. When an aircraft joins the queue, the elapsed time in the simulation (CLOCK) is recorded in store for this aircraft:

line 81   AIRCRAFT.J(2)=CLOCK

The amount of fuel required is sampled from a frequency distribution which has previously been read in (FUELREQ):

line 82   AIRCRAFT.J(1)=SAMPLE(1,FUELREQ,STREAMB)

The waiting time of the aircraft is calculated at a later stage in the program by subtracting its 'clocking in time' from the present value of CLOCK:

line 155   12 WAIT=CLOCK - AIRCRAFT.M(2)   (see footnote)

Similarly, the four bowsers have been defined as a class of entities with an associated set FREEBOWS, each entity having one attribute which is the amount of fuel it has at any stage. Thus the amount of fuel used by the BOWSER.I (I being 1, 2, 3 or 4) is calculated in line 126:

line 126   BOWSER.I(1)=BOWSER.I(1)-AIRCRAFT.M(1)

i.e. the amount of fuel left in the bowser is its old amount minus the fuel required by the Mth aircraft.

When a bowser contains less than 1 500 gallons of fuel, it is sent to be re-filled and the filling time needs to be calculated, so that the bowser can be added to the FREEBOWS set when it is available again. Time-values therefore need to be associated with the BOWSER entities and this is indicated by including TIME in the CLASS statement (line 24). These values are referenced by the prefix T, preceding the entity name as shown in line 178:

line 178   15 T.BOWSER.I = ACFILLTIME(I) + REFUELTIME(I)

The value of the time-cell at this stage is the time it takes to fill the aircraft (line 124) and the time it takes for the bowser to be re-filled. When this time-value has been reduced to zero by the time-advance routine, it will be free again and can join the FREEBOWS set.

SIMPLE DATA OPERATIONS

Expressions, Arithmetic Statements, Set Act Statements
Expressions may contain, as in FORTRAN, numeric constants, variables, functions, brackets and arithmetic operators. The rules for writing expressions in CSL programs are similar to those for BASIC FORTRAN, except that variables and constants need not be of the same type, the result of a mixed expression being real.

Arithmetic statements are of two types, assignment or incremental. The assignment statement has the form:

variable = expression

CSL statement numbers (such as 12 in line 155) *must* be right-justified in the first five columns i.e. the last digit of the number must be in column 5. This differs from FORTRAN where the statement number may be anywhere in the first five columns.

where the left-hand side may be a variable, time-cell, entity attribute or array element, whose value is replaced by the current value of the expression on the right-hand side.

The incremental statement has the form:

variable ± expression

where the variable on the left-hand side is increased or decreased by the current value of the expression on the right-hand side. The variable and expression must be of the same type.

Examples of incremental arithmetic statements are:

line 163   FILLED+1   adds 1 to to no of aircraft filled;
line 164   CRAFT-1   subtracts 1 from no of aircraft in the queue.

The membership of sets may be changed by adding or removing groups of entities using Set Act statements. Two examples of these are:

line 51   BOWSER LOAD FREEBOWS

this fills the set(s) listed with the entire population of the class to which it belongs preserving its order, so that initially when all the bowsers are free they are held in the order BOWSER.1, BOWSER.2, BOWSER.3, BOWSER.4 in the FREEBOWS set:

line 52   ZERO AIRQUEUE

this statement empties the set (or a number of sets separated by commas), so that initially there are no entities in the set AIRQUEUE.

Several other Set Act statements are available in 1900 CSL and may be found in the ICL manual[31].

SIMPLE TRANSFER STATEMENTS

These are similar to the statements available in FORTRAN (see chapter 5). The GO TO and IF statements are exactly as in FORTRAN, and instead of DO statements FOR statements are available.

The general form of FOR statements is:

FOR . . . . FOR statement
   XXXX
   . . . .   } FOR loop indented
   XXXX
  XXXX   Further program

The statements in the FOR loop are repeated a specified number of times as shown in the following example:

```
line 60     FOR I=1,4
line 61       BOWSER.I(1)=10000
line 62       T.BOWSER.I=-1
line 63       ACFILLTIME(I)=0
line 64       REFUELTIME(I)=0
line 65       TACTIME(I)=0
line 66       TRTIME(I)=0
line 70     ACTIVITIES
```

This part of the program sets up initial conditions for the four bowsers which are filled with 10 000 gallons of fuel and have their time-cells set to −1. All the bowsers are loaded into the FREEBOWS set initially and their time-cells therefore must not be set to zero at this stage or an attempt will be made to add the bowsers again to the FREEBOWS set (see line 99). The aircraft filling time, bowser refuelling time, total aircraft filling time and total bowser refuelling time are set to zero.

The indented statements 60 to 66 will be repeated for I = 1, 2, 3 and 4; control is then transferred to the next non-indented statement, ACTIVITIES. This method of controlling the repetition of the loop is known as Incremental Indexing; an alternative method is Set Indexing, where the number of members in the set controls the repetition, but this will not be dealt with in this book.

The last statement in a FOR loop must not be a transfer or test statement, and in these cases a dummy statement is used as the final statement of the FOR loop, which can be either DUMMY or REPEAT and has a similar effect to that of CONTINUE in a FORTRAN DO statement (see chapter 5).

Nested FOR statements may be used in CSL; these are similar to nested DO statements in FORTRAN. An example is shown in program (SUBC), appendix 14, and should be compared with the nested DO statements example in chapter 5.

```
line 18     FOR J=1,4
line 19       WRITE(2,103)
line 20       FOR K=1,5
line 21         FOR L=1,5
line 22           X(L)=RANDOM(STREAM,4)
line 23           WRITE(6)X(L)
line 24         WRITE(2,104)(X(I),I=1,5)
line 25       DUMMY
line 26     DUMMY
```

Control in a CSL program may also be transferred by means of Arithmetic Test and Set Test statements. The former consist in general of:

$$\text{expression}_1 \text{ relational operator expression}_2 \ n_1 \ @ \ n_2$$

If the test is true the next statement to be obeyed is labelled n_1, if it fails a jump is made to the statement labelled n_2. This test is used often at the beginning of an activity and therefore has been designed to allow the destination clause ($n_1 \ @ \ n_2$) to be omitted, in which case the next statement is obeyed if the test is true, otherwise a jump is made to the beginning of the next activity (the next point in the program at which the word BEGIN appears).

An example is given in line 72 (BOWS):

line 72   T.NEXT EQ 0

If T.NEXT is zero then the next aircraft has arrived and the activity can be obeyed, otherwise the next activity will be attempted.

Either n_1 or n_2 may be omitted, when the rules are as above, so that in lines 85 to 87:

```
line 85      CRAFT GT MAXQ @ 5
line 86      MAXQ = CRAFT
line 87      5 WRITE........
```

MAXQ holds the maximum number of aircraft in the queue at any time, while CRAFT holds the present number in the queue. Line 85 tests whether CRAFT is greater than MAXQ and if it is the next statement is obeyed (n_1 omitted), and the new maximum is placed in MAXQ; if CRAFT is less than or equal to MAXQ then control is transferred to the print statement labelled 5.

Other relational operators are:

```
GE   greater than or equal to
NE   not equal to
LE   less than or equal to
LT   less than.
```

The membership of sets may be tested using Set Test statements. These are similar to Arithmetic Test statements and examples may be found in the ICL manual[31].

COMPLEX CONDITIONAL STATEMENTS

These statements are used for changing the membership of sets and transferring control according to the results of tests. Some of the statements have built in tests (implied tests) as shown in the following examples.

line 80   AIRCRAFT.J TAIL AIRQUEUE

The *J*th aircraft coming in to be refuelled is added to the end (TAIL) of the set AIRQUEUE and the next statement is obeyed, unless it is already a member when in the absence of a destination clause control is transferred to the beginning of the next activity. Similarly, in line 111

line 111   AIRCRAFT.N HEAD AIRQUEUE

the aircraft has not been completely refuelled as the bowser being used has become empty, therefore it is returned to the beginning (HEAD) of the set AIRQUEUE (unless it is already a member of that set).

An entity may be removed from a set by using FROM:

line 118   BOWSER.I FROM FREEBOWS

i.e. if BOWSER.I is a member of the FREEBOWS set I (it is available for refuelling) it is removed from the set and the next statement is obeyed, otherwise control is transferred to the beginning of the next activity.

An entity may be added to the tail of a set without using an implied test by means of TO as in program (PSIM):

line 119   PATROL.I TO PATROLFREE

This statement always adds the specified entity to the end of the set without testing whether it is already a member, so that the statement is executed faster than the TAIL statement.

A number of test statements may be combined to give a single true or false result. These are written as an indented range of statements called a test chain and are used with test chain compound statements. For simplicity these are not described in this book, but the reader is referred to the ICL manual[31].

FIND STATEMENTS

These statements are used to select entities from a set according to the result of a specified test. An example is given in line 117:

line 117   FIND I FREEBOWS FIRST

which selects the first bowser in the FREEBOWS set (if there is at least one member in the set) and assigns the value of the class index of the selected member to the variable name (I in this case). If there are no members in the set, then, in the absence of a destination clause, control is transferred to the beginning of the next activity. If a member has been found then the next statement is obeyed.

Thus, if the membership of the set FREEBOWS at a certain stage when the statement is being executed is BOWSER.4, BOWSER.3, BOWSER.2 in that order, then FIND .... FIRST will result in BOWSER.4 being selected (i.e. I will take the value 4).

An alternative FIND statement FIND I FREEBOWS MIN(I) selects the entity in the set which has the minimum class index value, which in the example is BOWSER.2 (i.e. the third member of the set is chosen and I becomes 2).

FIND statements may also incorporate test chains.

DISTRIBUTION SAMPLING FUNCTIONS

1900 CSL incorporates functions which may be used to sample values from four standard frequency distributions: rectangular, normal, negative exponential and Poisson, or from distributions input by the programmer. Examples of the latter are given in program (BOWS).

Arrays to hold the distributions must first be defined in an ARRAY statement:

line 30   ARRAY ARRIVETIME(2,9),FUELREQ(2,8) ...

The first column of the array contains the total number of observations (check sum) in row 1, and the number of class values observed in row 2. Thus the frequency distribution of interarrival times of aircraft coming in to be refuelled is read in as a 2-dimensional array ARRIVETIME, having two rows and ten columns.

check sum	(nine pairs of values: frequency and class value)							
94	26	20	14	10	8	6	4	3	3
9	5	15	25	35	45	55	65	75	85

Similarly, the fuel required by the aircraft (FUELREQ) is read in as frequency distribution of seven pairs of values.

200	8	16	22	28	34	68	24
7	1000	1250	1500	1750	2000	2250	2500

The CSL READ and FORMAT statements are similar to those used in FORTRAN, the number of continuation lines being restricted to two as stated previously.

```
line 35      READ(1,2)ARRIVETIME,FUELREQ
line 36    2 FORMAT(20I4/16I4)
```

The slash in line 36 associates a new record with the second array FUELREQ, i.e. the first data card of ten pairs of integer values of field width four is read into the **ARRIVETIME** array, and the second data card with eight pairs of values is read into the array FUELREQ.

data card 1

94   9   26   5   20   15   14   25   10   35   8   45   6   55   4   65   3   75   3   8

data card 2

200   7   81000   161250   221500   281750   342000   682250   24500

Having defined the array and read in the frequency distributions, the next procedure is to convert the distributions to cumulative form to enable samples to be taken. This is done by means of a DIST statement as shown in line 46.

```
line 46    DIST ARRIVETIME,FUELREQ
```

The original frequency values are no longer available to the programmer but are stored as cumulative frequencies, i.e.

ARRIVETIME	94	26	46	60	70	78	84	88	91	94
	9	5	15	25	35	45	55	65	75	85

FUELREQ	200	8	24	46	74	108	176	200
	7	1000	1250	1500	1750	2000	2250	2500

Thus **ARRIVETIME**(1,5) will now have a value of 70 instead of 10 and FUELREQ(1,6) will hold 108 instead of 34.

A value is sampled from the appropriate distribution by means of the SAMPLE statement as shown in the following examples.

line 82   AIRCRAFT.J(1) = SAMPLE(1,FUELREQ,STREAMB)
line 83   T.NEXT = SAMPLE(1,ARRIVETIME,STREAMA)

STREAMA and **STREAMB** are the stream variables to be operated on by the random number procedure. Initially, these are set in the program to odd positive numbers:

line 47   STREAMA = 5
line 48   STREAMB = 9

thus ensuring that an independent sequence of random numbers is generated for each separate stream variable.

The current value of the stream variable is operated on by the random number procedure each time the sampling function is accessed and the next value in the stream of pseudorandom numbers is produced, a new value being automatically assigned to the stream variable.

The first number in brackets (line 83), which may be a variable name, indicates the position in the parameter list of the name of the distribution to be sampled. For example:

    T.NEXT = SAMPLE(2,FUELREQ,STREAMB,ARRIVETIME,STREAMA)

would have exactly the same effect as line 83; in each case **ARRIVETIME** is sampled.

The four standard sampling functions are illustrated in program (SUBC), appendix 14. This program is used to print out 100 generated random values from the four frequency distributions with given parameters and also calculates the simulated mean and standard deviation of each of the four sets of values.

Values may be sampled from:

(1) A rectangular or uniform distribution

line 22   X(L) = RANDOM(STREAM,4)

The value assigned to the variable X(L) will be a random number in the range 1 to 4 as specified by the second number in brackets (4); this may be any expression having an integer value. Another example of the use of **RANDOM** might be:

    ORDERS = RANDOM(STREAMA,10)

where there is an equal chance that 1,2,3 ... 10 orders are received daily, the range of the rectangular distribution is 10 (compare with FORTRAN equivalent (CAPF) line 39).

(2) A normal distribution:

line 42   Y(L) = DEVIATE(STREAM,200,1000)

A value is sampled from a normal distribution which has a mean of 1 000 and a standard deviation of 200; again these two parameters may be expressions having integer values. Another example might be:

MTIME = DEVIATE(STREAMB,15,24)

where the frequency distribution for machine hours per order approximates to a normal with a mean of 24 and standard deviation of 15 (see (CAPF) line 45 for the FORTRAN equivalent).

(3) A negative exponential distribution:

line 61   Z(L) = NEGEXP(STREAM,50)

A value is sampled from a negative distribution with a mean of 50 (this may be any expression having an integer value).

(4) A Poisson distribution:

line 79   V(L) = POISSON(STREAM,2.0)

A value is sampled from a Poisson distribution with a mean of 2.0 (the mean may be any expression having a real value).

HISTOGRAMS

In the program (BOWS), the waiting time for each aircraft was calculated as shown in line 155:

line 155   12 WAIT = CLOCK - AIRCRAFT.M(2)

The random variations of these results may be shown conveniently by means of a histogram; this shows the number of times the results fall within specified ranges of values. Statements are available in 1900 CSL which allow histograms to be built up and output in a standard form.

The histogram must be defined at the beginning of the program using a HIST statement as shown in line 49:

line 49   HIST WAITING(14,0,20)

This gives the name WAITING to the histogram and specifies that it has fourteen cells, the first holding entries in the range $-\infty$ to 0. The next twelve cells hold entries in the successive ranges of width 20 and the final cell holds entries from the upper limit of the previous cell (i.e. 241 to $+\infty$).

line 160   13 ADD WAIT,WAITING

has the effect of adding one to the count of the appropriate cell of the histogram. Thus when WAIT is equal to zero, one is added to the first cell count, and if WAIT is equal to 23 then one is added to the third cell count.

The histogram is printed by means of the OUTPUT statement:

line 203   OUTPUT WAITING

The standard form of output prints one line for each value range (cell) of the histogram, specifying the count and range as shown in figure 7.8.

More than one histogram may be defined in the HIST statement as shown in program (PSIM):

line 50   HIST WTIME(25,0,5),GJOBS(20,0,1),JPERDAY(26,0,1),
line 51   1AVJOBCOST(30,0,5)

This defines four histograms of twenty five cells (width 5), twenty cells (width 1), twenty six cells (width 1) and thirty cells (width 5), to hold values for the waiting time of members (WTIME), number of jobs referred to garages (GJOBS), number of jobs per day (JPERDAY) and the average cost per job (AVJOBCOST).

FORTRAN STATEMENTS AND SEGMENTS

1900 CSL programs may contain FORTRAN statements; these are written with an F in column 1 and are copied across unchanged by the CSL Translator (program supplied by ICL) which translates the CSL statements into FORTRAN. An example of this is shown in program (SUBC):

line 27   F   REWIND 6

This is an instruction to rewind the magnetic tape on device 6 and is copied unchanged to the FORTRAN program.

As well as incorporating single FORTRAN statements, CSL programs may include whole segments written in FORTRAN as shown in program (SUBC). The FORTRAN subroutine SDEV, which calculates the mean and standard deviation of a sequence of numbers held on magnetic tape is called up by the main CSL program using a FORTRAN CALL statement:

line 28   F   CALL SDEV(2.5,100,A005,A006)

where A005 and A006 are the translated FORTRAN names of the CSL variables SD (standard deviation) and CMEAN (calculated mean). During translation of the CSL program the CSL variable names are translated into FORTRAN integers I001 ... or reals A001 ... in the order in which they are met, so it is possible to determine the FORTRAN names to be used in FORTRAN subroutines before translation.

COMPILATION AND EXECUTION

The CSL program consisting of segments written in CSL or FORTRAN is presented to the CSL translator for translation into FORTRAN. The translated program then is treated as a normal FORTRAN program and is compiled and executed as usual.

Both the CSL translator and the FORTRAN compiler programs require control statements which specify the type of listing required, source and object program media etc.

CSL translator and FORTRAN compiler control statements

An example of these is given in program (SUBC):

line 1	LISTING(3)	The complete source and object programs are to be listed together with control statements and errors.
line 2	SOURCE(CR,S1)	The source program is input on cards and the source segments are in CSL (S1).
line 3	LABEL(,SUBC,999)	A scratch tape is to be opened and labelled SUBC. This will have a retention period of 999 days.
line 4	OBJECT(MT,SUBC.EH)	The object program is to be output onto magnetic tape labelled SUBC, in subfile EH.

These CSL translator control statements are followed by the CSL segments to be translated, terminated by the statement ENDSUBFILE and on a new line four asterisks in the first four columns. Note these asterisks are not shown in the program listings in the appendices. If there are any FORTRAN segments these are input next, preceded by FORTRAN compiler control statements (see chapter 5). FORTRAN compiler control statements may be inserted at the beginning of the CSL program by putting an asterisk in column 1 (see program (BOWS)).

The next stage is to read the FORTRAN translation of the CSL program from the magnetic tape on which it was compiled using a READ FROM statement as in program (SUBC):

line 99   READ FROM (MT,SUBC.EH)

Next the FORTRAN segment(s) are added:

line 100   SUBROUTINE SDEV(AMEAN,NO,SD,CMEAN)
        .
        .
line 114   END

Special CSL execution routines and FORTRAN standard subroutines and functions are required by the simulation program at run time and need to be incorporated by locating the appropriate subroutine blocks on the library tape as shown in the following statements:

line 115   LIBRARY
line 116   READ FROM (MT,-.SRC2)
line 117   FINISH

indicates end of compilation.

A COMPLETE PROGRAM

The program (BOWS) will be used to illustrate the logic and programming details of a complete CSL program. A special routine is followed if a bowser becomes empty while filling an aircraft, since the aircraft then needs to be returned to the head of the queue for filling to continue by the next available bowser. First the fuel still required by the aircraft is calculated, and the time spent by the bowser filling this aircraft is adjusted. A time-cell associated with this aircraft, T.AIRCRAFT.M, is set to the adjusted filling time. Filling of this aircraft cannot continue until the bowser has completed the partial filling, i.e. when the value of T.AIRCRAFT.M has been reduced to zero, and it is only then that the aircraft is returned to the head of the queue. The PARTFILLED class of entities is used to record the class index of the partially filled aircraft, which is held in its first attribute, the associated sets AV and EXT being used to allow a possible four aircraft class indices to be recorded. A less detailed explanation will be given of certain statements if these have been described previously in the chapter.

A flowchart for the program together with CSL statements follows. It will be noticed that intermediate information is printed at various stages; this is essential to trace the course of the simulation to check on its feasibility. The last statement before END in the program is DUMMY and in this context it causes a time advance and a return to the beginning of the activities for another pass. EXIT terminates execution of the program.

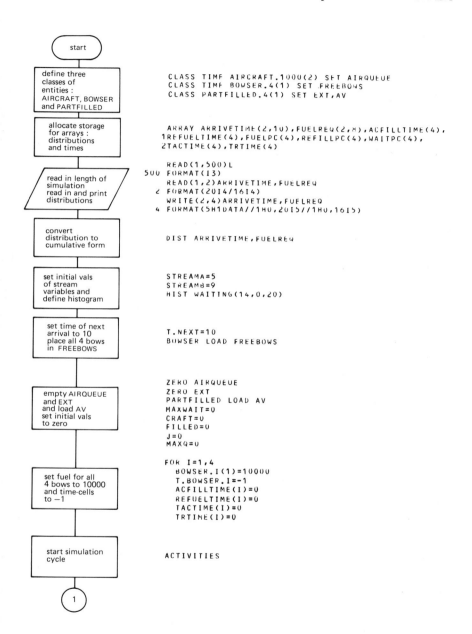

```
                              CLASS TIME AIRCRAFT.1000(2) SET AIRQUEUE
                              CLASS TIME BOWSER.4(1) SET FREEBOWS
                              CLASS PARTFILLED.4(1) SET EXT,AV


                              ARRAY ARRIVETIME(2,10),FUELREQ(2,8),ACFILLTIME(4),
                             1REFUELTIME(4),FUELPC(4),REFILLPC(4),WAITPC(4),
                             2TACTIME(4),TRTIME(4)

                              READ(1,500)L
                          500 FORMAT(I3)
                              READ(1,2)ARRIVETIME,FUELREQ
                            2 FORMAT(2014/16I4)
                              WRITE(2,4)ARRIVETIME,FUELREQ
                            4 FORMAT(5H1DATA//1H0,20I5//1H0,16I5)


                              DIST ARRIVETIME,FUELREQ


                              STREAMA=5
                              STREAMB=9
                              HIST WAITING(14,0,20)


                              T.NEXT=10
                              BOWSER LOAD FREEBOWS



                              ZERO AIRQUEUE
                              ZERO EXT
                              PARTFILLED LOAD AV
                              MAXWAIT=0
                              CRAFT=0
                              FILLED=0
                              J=0
                              MAXQ=0

                              FOR I=1,4
                                BOWSER.I(1)=10000
                                T.BOWSER.I=-1
                                ACFILLTIME(I)=0
                                REFUELTIME(I)=0
                                TACTIME(I)=0
                                TRTIME(I)=0


                              ACTIVITIES
```

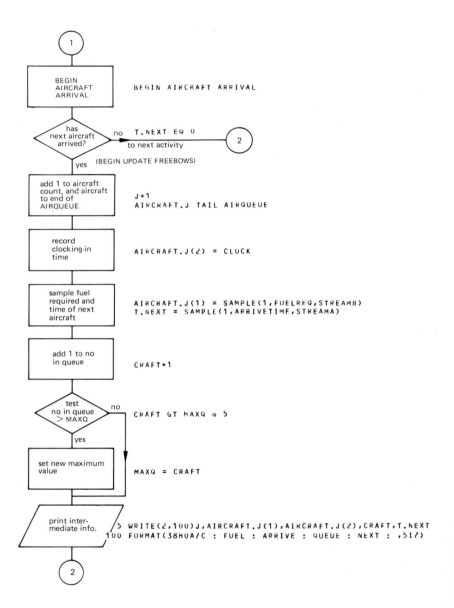

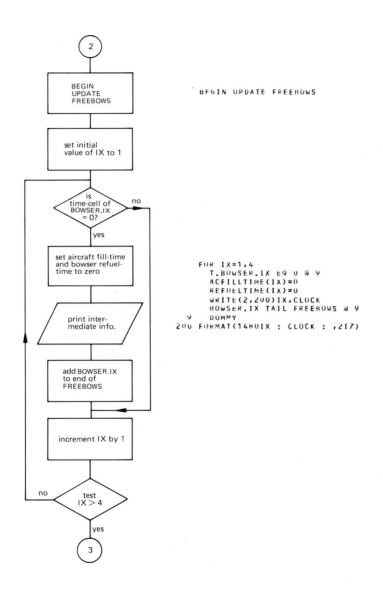

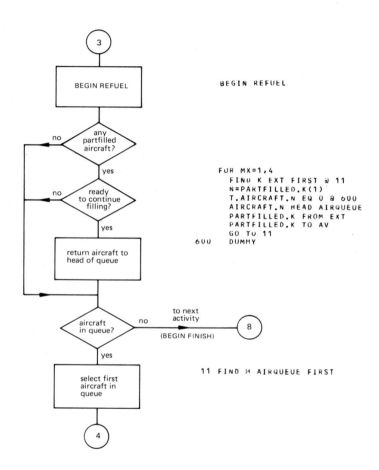

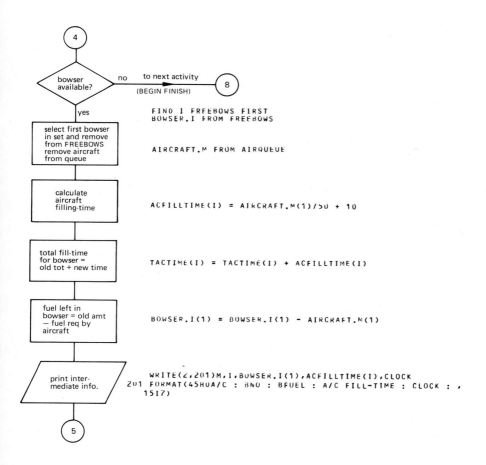

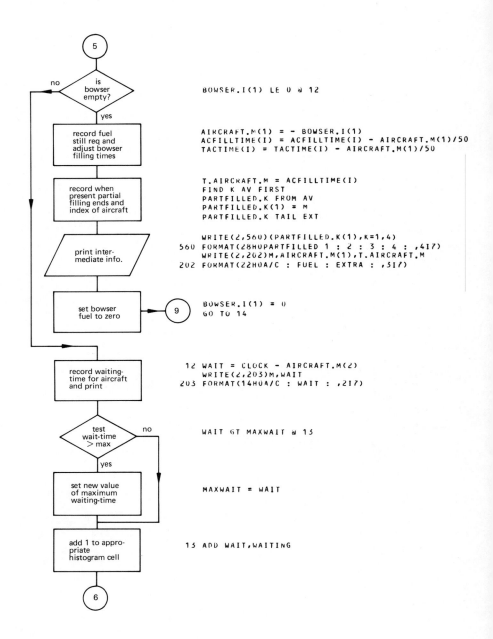

5

is bowser empty? — no

BOWSER.I(1) LE 0 ∂ 12

yes

record fuel still req and adjust bowser filling times

AIRCRAFT.M(1) = - BOWSER.I(1)
ACFILLTIME(I) = ACFILLTIME(I) - AIRCRAFT.M(1)/50
TACTIME(I) = TACTIME(I) - AIRCRAFT.M(1)/50

record when present partial filling ends and index of aircraft

T.AIRCRAFT.M = ACFILLTIME(I)
FIND K AV FIRST
PARTFILLED.K FROM AV
PARTFILLED.K(1) = M
PARTFILLED.K TAIL EXT

print inter-mediate info.

WRITE(2,560)(PARTFILLED.K(1),K=1,4)
560 FORMAT(28HOPARTFILLED 1 : 2 : 3 : 4 : ,4I7)
WRITE(2,202)M,AIRCRAFT.M(1),T.AIRCRAFT.M
202 FORMAT(22HOA/C : FUEL : EXTRA : ,3I7)

set bowser fuel to zero → 9

BOWSER.I(1) = 0
GO TO 14

record waiting-time for aircraft and print

12 WAIT = CLOCK - AIRCRAFT.M(2)
WRITE(2,203)M,WAIT
203 FORMAT(14HOA/C : WAIT : ,2I7)

test wait-time > max — no

WAIT GT MAXWAIT ∂ 15

yes

set new value of maximum waiting-time

MAXWAIT = WAIT

add 1 to appropriate histogram cell

15 ADD WAIT,WAITING

6

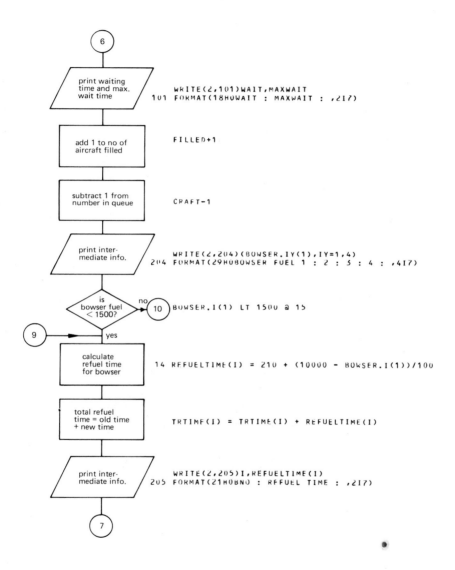

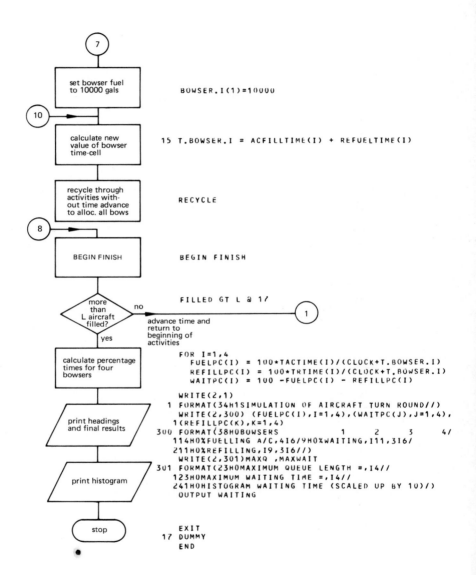

FURTHER CSL EXAMPLES

The following list gives chapter references for the various applications, where further details of the problems are given.

Program name	Appendix	Chapter	Application
BOWS	10	7	Queueing
PSIM	11	7	Queueing
SOMB	12	7	Stock control
STAN	13	8	Inventory control

CSL STRUCTURAL WORDS

None of these words may be used as a name in a CSL program.

ACTIVITIES	ELSE	GT	NIN	SOURCE
ADD	EMPTY		NOTIN	SPLIT
ALL	END	HEAD		START
ANY	ENDSUBFILE	HIST	OBJECT	SUBROUTINE
ARRAY	ENTRY		OR	SUM
	EQ	IF	OUTPUT	SWITCH
BEGIN	EQUALS	IN		
BLOCK	EX	INPUT	POISSON	TAIL
BSET	EXISTS	INTO	PMEND	TAPE
	EXIT		POSTMORTEM	TIME
CALL		LABEL	PRISET	TO
CHAIN	FIND	LAST	PROGRAM	
CHECK	FINISH	LE		UN
CLASS	FIRST	LISTING	QUALIFY	UNIQUE
CLEAR	FLOAT	LOAD		
COMMON	FOR	LOSES	RANDOM	WITHIN
CONVERSE	FORMAT	LT	RANK	WRITE
CONVERT	FROM		READ	
COUNT	FUNCTION	MASTER	RECYCLE	YIELD
		MAX	REPEAT	
DATA	GAINS	MIN	RETURN	ZERO
DEVIATE	GE			ZIBM
DIST	GO	NE	SAMPLE	
DUMMY	GOTO	NEGEXP	SET	

Chapter 7

Queueing Systems

INTRODUCTION

This chapter outlines the basic approach in queueing theory and illustrates the use of some queueing theory formula by reference to a hypothetical example. Owing to the assumptions that are made in developing formula, it is often found that the majority of queueing problems cannot be solved using queueing theory but that simulation has to be used. Initially a simple queueing type problem is illustrated with reference to manual simulation methods. Following this, four computer programs are presented, the first of which is a general queueing program having the arrival rate, service rate, and number of channels fed in as data by the user. The second program, called BOWS, simulates the turnround of aircraft that require refuelling from mobile bowsers. The third program, called PSIM, illustrates a mobile servicing facility that drives to customers as requested and performs some service at the customers location. Finally the program SOMB illustrates the simulation of a repairing and re-issue cycle which forms a closed loop.

QUEUEING THEORY

Many investigations of queueing systems are designed to meet a higher throughput. The superficial approach assumes that if the arrival rate is doubled then the effects can be compensated by halving the service time. For instance, if the arrival rate of lorries is to double then by revising the handling so that they can be unloaded in half the time, the existing number of bays will still be adequate. This simplified view of the situation, although seemingly logical, is not accurate. Statisticians have examined the way arrival rates and service rates influence the formation of queues, and have found that the relationships are by no means simple.

The theory associated with this type of situation has gradually been developed under the general term, 'Queueing Theory' or 'Waiting Line Theory'[6]. One of the earliest researchers into these relationships was Erlang, who examined the arrival rate of telephone calls, the time they took, and how the number of callers waiting varies with the number of lines. The main factors that influence the queueing situation have been found to be: variability of arrivals, variability of service times, the queue discipline, and the number of service stations. These factors will be explained briefly in turn. They will be related to a simple materials handling situation.

Arrivals of material cannot be controlled exactly (excluding flow line production), although there will be an average rate of arrival. The variability in the arrival rate can be observed and examined as a histogram, such as figure 7.1 which shows the arrival rate of cartons for labelling and strapping. The

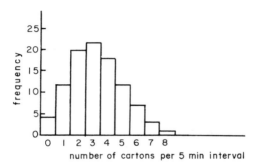

Figure 7.1   A Poisson distribution of arrivals

nature of this histogram partly determines the waiting line formula that will be applicable to the situation. For example a histogram that is found to occur fairly often in practice is a Poisson distribution (see chapter 3). The histogram in figure 7.1 follows a Poisson distribution having a mean of 3.33.

The time materials take to pass through a processing facility is also likely to vary in practice. As with the arrival times, a histogram can be constructed to establish the nature of the variability. Once again simple waiting line theory is based upon the variability of service times following a Poisson distribution. As pointed out in chapter 3, a Poisson arrival rate is related to a negative exponential distribution of inter-arrival times. Thus the type of situation just described is often referred to as one having a Poisson arrival rate and an exponential service time.

Queue discipline is another factor which influences the nature of the queue. Usually a first come-first served discipline is assumed, but other disciplines based upon an order of priorities can exist.

The other main factor is the number of servicing facilities. If there are several service facilities the queue discipline may follow more elaborate rules.

Separate queues may form for each service facility such as happens at the checkout at a supermarket. Alternatively the separate service facilities may draw from a common queue as happens with customers in a barbers.

Queueing Formulae

Queueing formulae must be chosen with due regard to the above factors as there is a miltitude of queueing formulae based upon a variety of assumptions. When a queueing situation is based upon a Poisson arrival rate and an exponential service time, with a single server following first come-first served discipline, then it is termed a 'simple queue'. If,

the mean rate of arrival = a
the mean rate of service = s

then some typical relationships in a simple queue are as follows,

$$\text{utilisation of service facility} = \frac{a}{s} \tag{7.1}$$

$$\text{average number of units in system} = \frac{a}{s-a} \tag{7.2}$$

$$\text{average time a unit is in system} = \frac{1}{s-a} \tag{7.3}$$

$$\text{probability of more than } n \text{ units in queue} = \left(\frac{a}{s}\right)^{n+2} \tag{7.4}$$

There are many other relationships that have been established even for simple queues. For instance, Houlden[14] lists seventeen formulae applicable to a simple queueing situation. However the above four formulae are sufficient to demonstrate the application in this text. Further formulae from Houlden are given in appendix 20.

Example of Application

Consider the problem of designing a roller conveyor system leading to a labelling and strapping operation. The situation is illustrated in figure 7.2. Owing to the inherent variability in the labelling and strapping operation (the service channel) and the variability in the cartons arriving along the conveyor, a queue of cartons is likely to build up on the conveyor. Part of the design problem then is how long must the conveyor be to accommodate the cartons that may build up.

Assuming that data collected to show the arrival rate follow the histogram as shown in figure 7.1, then the mean rate of arrivals is forty cartons per

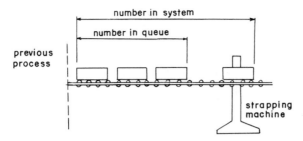

Figure 7.2   Queueing situation at a strapping machine

hour, i.e. from 3.33 cartons per five minute period. Also assume a mean service rate of fifty cartons per hour. Note that the service rate must be higher than the arrival rate otherwise the system will break down completely. By substitution in equation 7.2 above, the average number of cartons in the system can be calculated as shown below;

$$\text{average number of cartons in system} \quad = \frac{a}{s-a} = \frac{40}{50-40} = 4$$

At this point it is as well to point out that the number of cartons in the system means the number in the queue and the carton being serviced (see figure 7.2). To use this result of an average of four cartons in the system to calculate the length of conveyor required is however to perpetrate the superficial approach which queueing theory is designed to overcome. What should be considered is the maximum number of cartons that are likely to build up on the conveyor. The theoretical answer is an infinite number, but a practical answer can be obtained from equation 7.4. Using this formula the probability of there being more than say six, eight, ten, etc. cartons on the conveyor can be found by successive substitution. For example, The probability of more than 5 cartons in queue is given by

$$= \left(\frac{40}{50}\right)^7 = 0.21$$

The calculation has been done over a range of values for n and plotted in a graph as shown in figure 7.3. From this graph, the number of cartons to be allowed for according to the acceptable risk, can be read. Management often work to a 95 per cent of assurance which in these terms would mean accepting a 5 per cent chance that the conveyor would not be long enough. This is equivalent to a probability of 0.05, and from the graph it can be read that the conveyor should cater for eleven cartons. Thus if the cartons are 18 in long, a conveyor 17 ft long is required, say three 6 ft lengths.

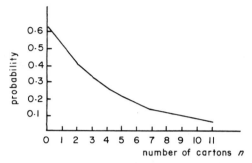

Figure 7.3   Probability of exceeding n cartons in queue

The above example shows how waiting line theory can be applied to the design of a simple handling system. It also illustrates how easy it would be to underestimate the requirements if simple averages were relied upon. However, to use even this simple theory has necessitated several assumptions. One assumption which is often not appropriate in practice is that the arrival rate is consistently withdrawn from the same Poisson distribution. That is to say that the rate of arrivals does not vary over the course of the working day. In practice, even quite simple queueing situations are often simulated, as it is frequently necessary to take into account a variable arrival rate over a working day to invoke priority rules. To illustrate how a simple queueing situation having a variable arrival rate can be manually simulated; a dispatching problem will now be examined.

A DISPATCH PROBLEM

The Bleach Products Co. started many years ago as a small 'back garden' firm selling bottled bleach to local retail outlets. Sales and output have increased consistently over the years and the company now has a factory of 10 000 ft^2 in the south-east London area, employing approximately fifty people in the factory and dispatch section.

The process is essentially bottle filling. Bleach is supplied and stored in a tank in the roof of the factory and pumped to the filling machines as required. A recent change from glass to plastic bottles has drastically increased the production capacity. When glass bottles had been used a bottle washing machine was required, this had now been removed freeing space for a further filling machine. Another consequence of changing to plastic bottles is that wooden returnable crates are no longer needed, again freeing more space, but more important, allowing sales to be made over a much greater area. The possibilities of exporting is also being considered.

The consequence of the above changes is that the loading and dispatch of lorries is becoming a bottleneck. When glass bottles were being used it was found that two loading bays sufficed to cope with the turn-round of lorries; in fact there were four loading bays built into the factory but due to the pressure of space, the other two had been used to store part of the factory's output.

On changing to plastic bottles and increasing the output, it was apparent that management would have to consider making changes in the dispatch section.

At present vehicles turn up for loading any time from 07.00 to 16.00 hours. Some of the vehicles are on contract hire by the company and some are sent by the purchasers of bleach, consequently the capacity of the vans might range from 1 to 6 tons. The vehicles do not arrive at a constant rate over the day but tend to arrive mainly early in the day or after 14.00 hours.

Management are considering the possibility of owning their own lorries but before undertaking a detailed cost study they wish to know the effects on overtime (after 16.00 hours) and van waiting time of opening up the other loading bays. To this end data have been collected of lorry loading over a typical week (see appendix 15). There is no seasonal pattern and the data supplied are representative of normal output (for the sake of the illustration the sample has been kept small).

An analysis of the data will show that there are two aspects of the situation in particular that need suitable treatment. The first is that the arrival of lorries shows a pattern over the day with a peak in the morning falling off during the lunch period and peaking in the early part of the afternoon. The second aspect of the situation is that an analysis of the loading times for the lorries show that the loading time varies over a considerable range. These two aspects will be discussed in turn.

Simulating the Arrival Pattern
The first problem is how to generate a representative arrival pattern. Two methods will be described that have been used in short manual simulation runs and appear to work reasonably well. The first method is to treat the development of an arrival time as a two stage process, selecting a random number to represent the number of lorries arriving within any particular hourly period, and then selecting further random numbers for each lorry to represent the minutes past the hour at which the individual lorries arrive. This

means that the data have to be analysed in two ways to give, (*a*) the average number of arrivals for each hour of the day, and (*b*) a histogram of arrivals expressed as minutes past the hour. The results of treating the data supplied in this manner is shown in figure 7.4. The actual number of lorries arriving within any particular hourly period is assumed to vary as a Poisson distribution where the mean of the Poisson is the average number that varies from hour to hour.

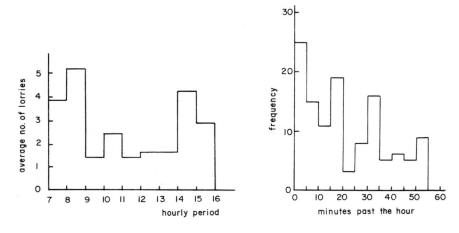

Figure 7.4   Arrival pattern of lorries

For example to simulate the arrival of lorries between 7.00 and 8.00, firstly a Poisson distribution having a mean of 3.8 is sampled. Say the outcome is 2. This means two lorries have arrived sometime between 7.00 and 8.00. The next stage is to sample twice (once for each lorry) from the distribution of minutes past the hour. If the minutes past the hour are 05 and 20 then the lorries turned up at 7.05 and 7.20. A similar procedure is then carried out to simulate the next hour and so on throughout the day.

The second method is to use a cumulative arrival time graph. This graph is drawn by taking all the lorry arrival times and arranging them in order of occurrence. These times are then plotted against the cumulative number of lorries in the data. The results of this approach with the data given are shown in figure 7.5. Thus from this graph it can be seen that at 7.0 a.m. no lorries had arrived and by 16.00 hours all 122 lorries were accounted for.

This graph automatically reflects the peaks and troughs of lorry arrivals over the course of the day. To use this type of graph to simulate lorry arrival times it is necessary to scale the cumulative number of lorries to run from 00 to 99 (if two-digit random numbers are to be used). It is convenient when plotting these graphs to plot in a scale that is appropriate to the original data, thus in this example the maximum entry on the cumulative number of lorries scale is made at 122.

To scale this over a range of 100 uniform intervals it is necessary to set up a second scale at a convenient angle to the first in the following manner. As 122 is twenty two units above 100, (which will be the maximum of the

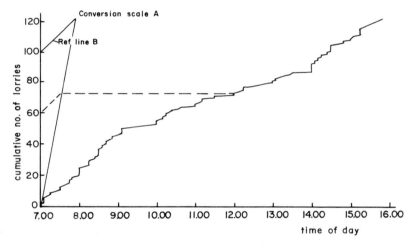

Figure 7.5   Cumulative graph of lorry arrivals

random number scale) then the second conversion scale (marked conversion scale A) is set up so that its maximum point, level with 122, is eleven units to the right at 122. This means when the tip of the scale is joined to 100 on the cumulative number of lorries scale the connecting line is at 45°. The slope of this line is immaterial in theory but it is convenient to set the conversion scale up at such an angle that the connecting line (B) can easily be set up. To use this arrangement when a random number is chosen it is first of all found on the original cumulative number of lorries scale, and will therefore lie somewhere between 0 and 100. A line is then drawn from this position parallel to line B, to the conversion scale A. This has the action of scaling up the random numbers chosen by the proportion of 100:122. The graph in figure 7.5 illustrates how a random number 60 is scaled up as described and then carried horizontally across the graph to yield a lorry arrival at 12.00 hours. This then is the way that a particular arrival time can be simulated

143

whereby any inherent arrival patterns will be automatically introduced into the times generated.

The remaining issue is to determine how many random numbers, and thereby lorries, are to be chosen to arrive within any one day. This graph has to be used in conjunction with a frequency distribution of the number of lorries arriving per day. The appropriate distribution for the data given is shown in table 7.1, where it can be seen that in this instance there is a 20 per cent chance of twenty three lorries, a 20 per cent chance of twenty four lorries, and lastly a 60 per cent chance of twenty five lorries. The first random number chosen in this method is therefore applied to the distribution shown in table 7.1, i.e. random number 43 would represent twenty five lorries arriving. Twenty five further random numbers would then be chosen and applied to the graph as previously described. This would yield twenty five arrival times which then need to be sorted into order of occurrence.

Table 7.1   Distribution of lorries per day

Number	Frequency	Per cent frequency	Allocated numbers
23	1	20	00–19
24	1	20	20–39
25	3	60	40–99
Total	5	100	

Simulating the Loading Times

The second aspect of the situation is the lorry loading times. Examination of the loading times will show that there is some correlation between loading time and load size, although there are some inexplicable readings. For instance in day 2, the lorry that arrives at 7.30 requires 2 tons to be loaded. The loading started at 7.35 but finished at 9.35! A total time of 120 min. However, the majority of the loading times are in the region of from 20 to 40 min. It is thus necessary to decide how to regard the data where the loading time appears unusually long, or short. The manner in which such readings are dealt with depends on the objective in performing the simulation. The unusually long loading time could be an error in data collection, in which case this reading should be excluded from further considerations. On the other hand it may transpire that this reading is genuine although not typical. If this is the case from the point of view of the simulation the reading should be taken into account, although from the point of view of management it raises other issues. Genuine readings of this nature indicate erratic loading times and point to bad management control of the loading operations. The reason may be due to bad production control causing a material shortage at the loading bay end of the system, or it may be due to defective and unreliable handling equipment, or it may be due to bad paper work systems causing the loading vans to wait for further instructions. Whatever the actual reason there is scope for the application of work study. Several courses of action are now open to the management;

(1) Call off the simulation study until the system being examined has been made more efficient, otherwise the simulation will be based on unrealistic data.

(2) Continue the simulation study with the data exactly as collected, thereby reproducing the inefficiencies of the existing situation faithfully.

(3) Elaborate the situation to include simulations based not only upon the existing state of affairs but upon supposed improvements.

The third course of action is preferable for in this way it would be possible to judge the scope and potential savings arising from any work study investigation. The cost of any such proposed investigation could then be evaluated against the indicated potential savings.

One method of simulating the loading times from the finally agreed data would be to collate the load sizes into a frequency table and allocate random numbers in these proportions. In addition, the loading times will be collated by load size and similarly built into a frequency table, one table for each load size, with associated random numbers. This is illustrated in tables 7.2 and 7.3 respectively.

Table 7.2   Distribution of load sizes

Load	Frequency	Per cent frequency	Allocated random numbers
1	19	15.6	00–15
2	31	25.4	16–40
3	30	24.6	41–65
4	11	9.0	66–74
5	21	17.2	75–91
6	10	8.2	92–99

Two points should be made with respect to table 7.3. Firstly, in practice a much larger sample of data would be collected, the table here is based upon only eleven readings. Secondly the percentage frequency values have been

Table 7.3   Distribution of 4-ton loading times

Load time (mins)	Frequency	Per cent frequency	Allocated random numbers
5	1	9	00–08
10	1	9	09–17
15	–	–	
20	2	18	18–35
25	–	–	
30	2	18	36–53
35	1	9	54–62
40	3	27	63–89
45	1	9	90–98

rounded off and only add up to 99 instead of 100 per cent. This means that only ninety nine random numbers are allocated, i.e. 00 to 98 inclusive. If the random number 99 is sampled during a simulation, in this context it has no meaning and a further number would be sampled.

Thus by picking a random number and applying it to the distribution load sizes a particular load size can be simulated. A second random number is then picked and applied to the appropriate distribution of loading times, e.g if the first random number selected is 68 then from table 7.2 a load of 4 tons has been simulated. A second random number is now picked, say 81 and applied to the distribution of loading times for a 4-ton load, see table 7.3. From this it will be seen that a loading time of 40 min has been simulated. The above method then, makes the simulation of loading times a two stage process, first the size of load is simulated and second the loading time associated with that sized load is simulated. However, unless it is necessary for other reasons to know the size of the load, it is unnecessary to simulate loading times in such an elaborate fashion.

If all the loading times, irrespective of load size, were built into one frequency table of loading times, as shown in table 7.4, then random selections made from this table would automatically include the correct mix of load sizes.

In terms of the pure queueing aspects, provided a loading time of, say, 30 min, is simulated in the right proportions, it is irrelevant whether this 30 min is due to a 4-ton load or a 3-ton load for example. Assuming this method gives as good results as the previous method described, then considerations outside of simulation techniques would determine which method ought to be adopted. The first method is more elaborate and therefore possibly more time consuming, but on the other hand yields greater information, whereas the second method is possibly more direct and therefore 'efficient'. If one of the objectives behind the simulation study is to deliberately alter the load sizes by for example standardising on 4 ton vans, then the first method must be used to provide the necessary detail. Only close collaboration between management, who should determine the objectives of the simulation study, and the model builders can yield effective simulation studies.

Table 7.4   Distribution of consolidated loading times

Minutes	Frequency	Percentage x 10	Allocated numbers
5	3	25	000–024
10	7	57	025–081
15	11	90	082–171
20	22	180	172–351
25	11	90	352–441
30	16	131	442–572
35	10	82	573–654
40	14	115	655–769
45	8	66	770–835
50	6	49	836–884
55	5	41	885–925
60	2	16	926–941
65	2	16	942–957
70	2	16	958–973
75	1	8	974–981
105	1	8	982–989
135	1	8	990–997
Total	122	998	

Outline of Manual Method
An outline of steps we might use to simulate this situation is then as follows:

(1) Pick a random number, say 53

(2) Apply to the *Distribution of lorries per day* table, i.e. 53 means twenty five lorries

(3) Pick twenty five random numbers and arrange in ascending order, i.e.
     07, 09, 15, 18, 26, 32, 33, 39, 39, etc

(4) Apply these numbers to the *Lorry arrival time graph* to obtain twenty five arrival times

(5) For *each* lorry pick a random number and apply to the *Distribution of loading times* to establish a loading time for each lorry

(6) Enter the arrival time and loading time of each lorry on the work sheet and complete as indicated in table 7.5.

A Practical Approach to Computer Simulation

The work sheet as shown in table 7.5 is virtually self-explanatory, but a few entries have been made to illustrate the way they are made. Initially the cumulative load, i.e. forward load, on bay 1 and bay 2 is set at the start time of 7.00 hours. As a result of picking something like twenty five random numbers and arranging them in ascending order it has been ascertained that the first lorry arrives at 7.05 and the simulated loading time for this lorry is 25 min. This lorry is seen by bay 1 and therefore the cumulative load on bay 1 now goes forward to the arrival time 7.05 plus loading time 25 min i.e. to 7.30. The bay came into use at 7.05, therefore the bay was initially idle for 5 min and this entry is made in the appropriate column.

Table 7.5   Manual work sheet for dispatch problem

Arrive time	Loading time	Waiting time	Bay 1 Cum. load	Idle	Bay 2 Cum. load	Idle
			7.00		7.00	
7.05	25		7.30	5		
7.15	30				7.45	15
7.55	20		8.15	25		
8.00	50				8.50	15
8.10	45	5	9.00			
8.30	10	20			9.00	

The second lorry arrives at 7.15 and requires a loading time of 30 min. At 7.15 the situation portrayed on the work sheet is that bay 1 is in use (until 7.30), but bay 2 has been available since 7.00 hours, therefore the second lorry is seen by bay 2. As the lorry came in at 7.15 and requires 30 min loading, bay 2 will now be occupied until 7.45; the idle time for bay 2 is from 7.00 to the arrival of the lorry at 7.15, i.e. 15 min. The third lorry that turns up is similarly dealt with by bay 1 giving a forward load on bay 1 to 8.15, and the fourth lorry is seen by bay 2 forward loading it to 8.50. When the fifth lorry arrives at 8.10, requiring a load time of 45 min, both bays are occupied. Bay 1 will become free at 8.15 and bay 2 will become free at 8.50, therefore bay 1 will take this fifth lorry that arrived at 8.10, thereby causing a wait of 5 min for that lorry. The forward load for bay 1 is now updated from the time it became available, 8.15, to 45 min later, i.e. 9.00. In the last entry shown in table 7.5 the lorry arrives at 8.30 but bay 2 will not be available until 8.50 therefore the lorry waits 20 min, lorry loading starts at 8.50 and requires ten minutes loading, thereby occupying bay 2 until 9.00.

148

This type of manual simulation is easy to reproduce on a computer. Basically for each column on the work sheet a variable name is created and is consistently updated as and when necessary.

An example of a general program to simulate queueing situations has been written in FORTRAN.

A GENERAL QUEUEING SIMULATION PROGRAM (SIMQ)

The input to SIMQ consists of an inter-arrival time frequency distribution and a service time distribution. Both these distributions have ten class intervals and the frequencies inputted are the individual frequencies of occurrence, the program subsequently cumulates the frequencies. In addition, the number of channels is inputted and the total length of the simulation run expressed as elapsed time. The number of channels is restricted to a maximum of ten but there is no limit on the length of the simulation.

Output from SIMQ

The output obtained from SIMQ is shown in figure 7.6. A complete list of such output is printed after every 50 units of elapsed time. This allows graphs to be drawn of the fluctuation in results as the simulation progresses. Thus the first line of output quotes the number of channels as inputted as N and the elapsed time as L. The next two lines print out the mean arrival rate and the mean service rate of the data which can conveniently be compared to the subsequent two lines which give the mean arrival rate and mean service rate as generated by the simulation program. The number of channels being simulated is printed out again so that the lay user does not have to worry about the meaning of N. Following this, various aspects of the simulation to date are then given. The first of these is the actual elapsed time at the moment of printout. This normally exceeds the value for L quoted at the head of the printing out by a small amount. The total number serviced by this elapsed time is then printed followed by the total waiting time. The average waiting time, of those that waited, is then given, followed by the maximum waiting time encountered so far. The total channel idle time is then printed followed by its value expressed as a percentage thereby representing the utilisation.

The output at each 50 unit increase contains a certain amount of information that remains constant, for example the mean arrival rate and service rate of the data. However, it was designed with the intention that any page of output could be taken and be self-contained. There are elaborations that could be introduced into the output for instance, the fluctuations in the average waiting time could be monitored and the program terminated when the fluctuations were within a specified proportion of the mean. If this

```
SIMULATION OF QUEUEING      N = 2  L = 2050

MEAN ARRIVAL RATE (DATA) =  0.595

MEAN SERVICE RATE (DATA) =  0.877

MEAN ARRIVAL RATE (GENERATED) =  0.591

MEAN SERVICE RATE (GENERATED) =  0.905

NO OF CHANNELS=  2

ELAPSED TIME=2050.50

TOTAL SERVICED= 1211

TOTAL WAITING TIME=  92.50

AVERAGE WAITING TIME=   0.08

MAXIMUM WAITING TIME=   3.00

TOTAL CHANNEL IDLE TIME=2763.00

%CHANNEL UTILISATION=  32.63
```

Figure 7.6   Typical output from SIMQ

approach was adopted it may not be necessary to output the situation every 50 units. Alternatively, the output of the variables could be plotted by means of suitable sub-routines thereby showing the fluctuations due to the simulation in a concise manner.

Description of Program

A listing of SIMQ is given in Appendix 6. Line 15 sets up a series of arrays for storing up to ten values. The figure ten has been chosen in an arbitrary

150

manner; it would be easy to amend the program so that the arrays were larger, but if the arrays in practice associated with the arrival and service time distributions were smaller than ten intervals, it would be a simple matter to create further intervals to bring the total number to ten, these extra intervals having an associated frequency of zero. The data are read in at line 19 and immediately printed out at line 21. This is to ensure that if the output is subsequently examined it is obvious which data the simulation was based upon. A further check is built into every page of output as already described by having the mean of the data printed, although this would not distinguish between experiments where the mean had been kept the same but different standard deviations used. Lines 29 to 47 cover a series of initialisation stages, including the calculation of the mean arrival rate and service rate from the data inputted. After converting the frequencies as read in to cumulative frequencies over lines 51 and 53, the final set of data are read in, i.e. the number of channels to be used in the queueing situation and the total elapsed time to be simulated. Lines 59 and 60 'zeroise' the elapsed time of a suitable number of channels. From line 65 to 71 an inter-arrival time is simulated and added to the cumulative arrival time to date. Lines 75 to 81 then cause each channel elapsed time to be examined and the channel with the minimum elapsed time to be identified as channel J. One of two situations can now arise: either the elapsed time of the channel is less than the cumulative arrival time, in which case the channel is available and the difference represents channel idle time, or the channel elapsed time is greater than the cumulative arrival time in which case the arrival has to wait by an amount equal to the difference. A test to cover this situation is made in line 89, and from this either channel idle time is cumulated or waiting time is cumulated in a series of statements down to line 97. Whatever the result of the above test that arrival is now being seen by a channel, the number seen is therefore updated by one as given in line 101. From line 105 to 113 a service time is then simulated and added to the appropriate channel elapsed time. If the cumulative arrival time is a factor of fifty, then a table of results to date is printed as already described and shown in figure 7.6. If not the program loops back to line 65 to generate another arrival time. Lines 117 to 135 cause a page of output to be printed, and following this line 140 tests for the end of the simulation. If it is not the end of the simulation a variable, L is increased by fifty so that a further page of output is obtained after an elapsed time of fifty units.

Monitoring Simulation

In simulating queueing situations it is often important to obtain a feel of the 'ebb and flow' of the queue. When a manual simulation is undertaken this feel is obtained automatically as the calculations proceed. For example, in one manual simulation of the data used in SIMQ for one channel, it was obvious that only chance prevented a queue of more than four building up. This feel of a situation is harder to obtain from a computer simulation. The only way is to output the state of affairs on each pass through the program, however this is likely to lead to an extremely large volume of output which would probably not be studied in practice. The method used in the program SIMQ seems a reasonable compromise, that is a summary is produced every, say, fifty cycles through the program. A low figure such as fifty has been suggested deliberately to accentuate short term cycles where the total length

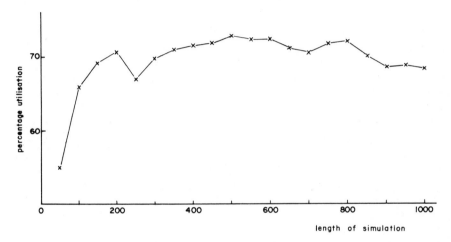

Figure 7.7   Graph of channel utilisation from monitored output

of the simulation is something like 1 000 or more cycles. A graph of channel utilisation for a single channel simulation up to a total elapsed time of 1 000 units is shown in figure 7.7.

This graph illustrates how the percentage channel utilisation figure has settled down to around 66 per cent, but short term cycles nevertheless persist. This type of result is typical of queueing problems, as once a queue develops there is a tendency for it to persist until a long inter-arrival time is encountered which allows the queue to be exhausted. From then on, because the rate of service is greater on average than the rate of arrival, the channel is likely to cope for some time until the run of figures result in several short inter-arrival times occurring in succession which have the effect of building up a queue once again.

152

SIMULATION PROGRAM OF REFUELLING AIRCRAFT (BOWS)

When a queueing situation is more elaborate than the 'simple queue', special purpose-built programs usually have to be written. An example of such a program is BOWS, the listing of which is given in appendix 10. This program has already been used to illustrate an application of CSL in chapter 6. The program simulates the turnround of aircraft as they are refuelled by bowsers which in turn have to leave the airfield for refuelling. In this case the data used are purely hypothetical. Aircraft on landing at the airport require refuelling and are attended to by one of four bowsers. Each bowser can contain 10 000 gallons of fuel and this fuel can be pumped into the aircraft at the rate of 50 gallons per minute. The amount of fuel required by the aircraft varies, and the frequency distribution of fuel required forms one part of the input data. In addition to the fuel pumping time, the bowser will require 10 min for the connection and removal of the fuel hose. The inter-arrival times of aircraft form another set of data which are provided as input.

This situation is a queueing problem where aircraft form the arrivals and bowsers form the service channels. However, there is one complication in this queueing problem, that is the bowsers must return to the bulk storage tanks when their fuel falls to less than 1 500 gallons. The time taken by the bowser to return is determined by the amount of fuel that needs to be replaced to bring the total back up to 10 000 gallons, (this is replaced at the rate of 100 gallons per minute), and a fixed travelling time of 210 min. To allow integer working, these values are the true values scaled up by 10. The program simulates the situation using a first-come first-served priority rule for the aircraft. The rule for selecting the appropriate bowser has been explained in chapter 6.

Output from BOWS

A sample of output obtained from this program is shown in figure 7.8.

In this case, the output gives the proportion of time spent by each channel in refuelling, waiting and refilling. The maximum number in the queue also is printed, together with the maximum waiting time encountered during the run of the program. Finally, a histogram of waiting time is presented to assist in the assessment of variations in waiting time. This type of output could be obtained from the previous situation described under SIMQ, alternatively the output obtained in SIMQ could similarly be outputted for this program. However, the intention is to illustrate the different types of information that may be relevant to queueing situations. As this is a hypothetical situation no mention has been made as to the objective in the simulation study. In practice, it may be that the waiting time of the aircraft is of paramount

```
SIMULATION OF AIRCRAFT TURN ROUND


BOWSERS              1      2      3      4

%FUELLING A/C       44     38     38     37

%WAITING             7     15     13     16

%REFILLING          49     47     49     47


MAXIMUM QUEUE LENGTH =    9

MAXIMUM WAITING TIME = 247

HISTOGRAM WAITING TIME (SCALED UP BY 10)

COUNT              RANGE
  31                 TO        0
   4           1 TO          20
   5          21 TO          40
   1          41 TO          60
   4          61 TO          80
  16          81 TO         100
  15         101 TO         120
   9         121 TO         140
   6         141 TO         160
   6         161 TO         180
   3         181 TO         200
   0         201 TO         220
   0         221 TO         240
   1         241 TO
NORMAL EXIT
```

Figure 7.8   Typical output from BOWS

importance, if these were service aircraft the turnround time may be of strategic importance. It is for this type of objective that one would require a histogram of waiting time, whereas in a normal queueing situation an average waiting time may suffice. There are several alterations that could be introduced into the simulation to assess their effect on, say, the turnround time of the aircraft. The bowsers at present start off completely full and then go away for refilling when they run down below a common level of 1500 gallons. The effect of this is that initially the aircraft are serviced without much waiting, but after a time all four bowsers are getting low on fuel and at this stage there is a chance that the aircraft may have to wait for considerable periods owing to the fact that most bowsers are away refilling. Thus the pattern that emerges during the simulation of one day's operations shows a very good turnround of aircraft initially with little waiting time, followed by a spate of queueing which ultimately sorts itself out as four bowsers come into operation again. An alternative policy that might be simulated to judge its effects would be to deliberately send bowsers back for refuelling regardless of their fuel state but with respect to some sort of schedule. Other policies that might be considered are moving the bulk storage tanks closer so that the time to refill the bowsers, which is made up predominantly of travelling time, is considerably reduced. Alternatively, various bowser queue disciplines could be tried out, for instance the first bowser could service as many aircraft as possible thereby requiring refilling rather quickly while the fourth bowser is acting as standby for when the first bowser is away, when the first bowser returns it in turn acts as standby while the fourth bowser takes as many aircraft as possible.

SIMULATION PROGRAM OF TWO MOBILE PATROLS (PSIM)

This program simulates the operation of two mobile patrols. They come on duty at 08.00 hours and normally work until 20.00 hours each day. The work load does not vary with the time of day or the season. Once they have set out to a job they will complete it regardless of how late they finish. However, they only receive calls up 19.00 hours and will accept them only if they can set out to them before 19.30 hours. All calls not dealt with at the end of the day are passed to garages.

When a call is received, if both patrols are free, the one having the shortest drive time attends to the job. If only one patrol is free he takes the job. When both patrols are engaged the job waits accordingly. The cost of operating a patrol is £1 per hour.

The basic data available are, the intervals between calls for assistance, the times taken to drive to jobs, and the times taken at the scene of the breakdown. These three sets of data have been converted into frequency distributions and formed the input to the program. The program simulates the operation of two patrols over a period of 350 days.

Output from PSIM

The output obtained from PSIM is shown in figures 7.9(a) to (d). First some statement of basic values is given, the number of patrols, the length of

```
SIMULATION OF MOBILE SERVICING PATROLS

NO OF PATROLS = 2

TOTAL SIMULATED PERIOD(DAYS) = 350

TOTAL SERVICED =    3538

AVERAGE SERVICED PER DAY =   10
```

HISTOGRAM JOBS/DAY

COUNT	RANGE	
0	TO	0
0	1 TO	1
0	2 TO	2
0	3 TO	3
2	4 TO	4
6	5 TO	5
12	6 TO	6
34	7 TO	7
49	8 TO	8
47	9 TO	9
49	10 TO	10
56	11 TO	11
33	12 TO	12
25	13 TO	13
16	14 TO	14
15	15 TO	15
3	16 TO	16
3	17 TO	17
0	18 TO	18
0	19 TO	19
0	20 TO	20
0	21 TO	21
0	22 TO	22
0	23 TO	23
0	24 TO	24
0	25 TO	

(a)

HISTOGRAM GARAGE JOBS

COUNT	RANGE	
14	TO	0
84	1 TO	1
89	2 TO	2
79	3 TO	3
46	4 TO	4
24	5 TO	5
13	6 TO	6
0	7 TO	7
1	8 TO	8
0	9 TO	9
0	10 TO	10
0	11 TO	11
0	12 TO	12
0	13 TO	13
0	14 TO	14
0	15 TO	15
0	16 TO	16
0	17 TO	17
0	18 TO	18
0	19 TO	

(b)

TOTAL WAITING TIME = 77985

AVERAGE WAITING TIME = 22

MAXIMUM WAITING TIME = 65

TOTAL PATROL IDLE TIME = 323920

PATROL UTILISATION PERCENT = 29.89

TOTAL COST OF JOBS = 155014.00

AVERAGE COST PER JOB = 43.81

HISTOGRAM WAITING TIME

COUNT	RANGE	
0	TO	0
310	1 TO	5
524	6 TO	10
404	11 TO	15
720	16 TO	20
478	21 TO	25
511	26 TO	30
271	31 TO	35
163	36 TO	40
104	41 TO	45
37	46 TO	50
9	51 TO	55
6	56 TO	60
1	61 TO	65
0	66 TO	70
0	71 TO	75
0	76 TO	80
0	81 TO	85
0	86 TO	90
0	91 TO	95
0	96 TO	100
0	101 TO	105
0	106 TO	110
0	111 TO	115
0	116 TO	

HISTOGRAM AVERAGE JOBCOST

COUNT	RANGE	
0	TO	0
0	1 TO	5
0	6 TO	10
0	11 TO	15
0	16 TO	20
1	21 TO	25
20	26 TO	30
41	31 TO	35
81	36 TO	40
57	41 TO	45
47	46 TO	50
44	51 TO	55
5	56 TO	60
34	61 TO	65
0	66 TO	70
12	71 TO	75
0	76 TO	80
0	81 TO	85
6	86 TO	90
0	91 TO	95
0	96 TO	100
0	101 TO	105
2	106 TO	110
0	111 TO	115
0	116 TO	120
0	121 TO	125
0	126 TO	130
0	131 TO	135
0	136 TO	140
0	141 TO	

NORMAL EXIT

(c)

(d)

Figure 7.9   Typical output from PSIM

simulation, the total number serviced, the average service per day. Then follows two histograms, one of the jobs per day and the other of the number of garage jobs. Details of waiting and idle time are then outputted. The output consists of, total waiting time, average waiting time, and maximum waiting time, the patrol idle time and the resulting percentage utilisation. A histogram of waiting time is also produced. Finally, some details of costs are given, the total cost incurred, and the average cost per job, followed by a histogram of average patrol costs (the average being the daily average).

Description of Program

A general listing of PSIM is given in appendix 11. The program has been written in CSL. Lines 30 to 35 are devoted to specify the classes and sets to be used, the size of the arrays to be used and floating some of the variables involved in the program to make them non-integer. Lines 40 to 43 read in the three distributions involved in the simulation, namely, inter-call time, driving time, and job time and then write these out on the line printer for reference purposes. Line 44 then heads up the next sheet to give some general details of the simulation as it is proceeding the format of this WRITE statement being given in lines 45 and 46. The first item outputted in this WRITE statement is the day. The reason for outputting the results day by day is to monitor the simulation run so that one can ascertain that the computer has not gone into a loop at some stage but is proceeding up to day 350 in a satisfactory manner. Lines 50 to 61 are concerned with initialising various aspects of the simulation, while lines 66 to 81 are concerned with initialising conditions at the start of each days simulation. The ACTIVITIES statement begins at line 82 where the program begins by ascertaining that the time to the next call is equal to zero (in line 84). If the time to the next call has been reduced to zero another call is due to be simulated, however, if the total elapsed time has reached 20.00 hours (i.e. 840 minutes from the start) then no further calls are to be attended to. A test to this effect is made in line 85, if no further calls are to be received then the execution of the program passes to the statement labelled 70 which is the beginning of the next section and falls on line 106 in the listing. The action of the program over lines 90 to 93 is to sample the next inter-call time, increase the number of calls received by one, place that caller at the end of a MEMWAITING set and attach the CLOCK time to the time cell associated with this member.

The next lines from 94 to 98 ascertain whether any patrols are now free, if so they are added to the tail of a PATROLFREE set. Lines 106 and 107 find the first member waiting, if there is a member waiting, and check that he called before 659 min from the start. If the call was received after this time the program jumps to line 150 where the garage count is increased by one and the member is assumed to be serviced by the garage. Assuming the member will be serviced by the patrol then line 108 finds the first patrol free; if there is no patrol free then the program jumps to the end thereby causing the CLOCK to increment by the smallest positive time-cell. Assuming a patrol is free, the drive time for this patrol is sampled in line 109. Line 110 removes the first patrol in the set PATROLFREE set. Line 111 finds the next free patrol, if there is one, if so the drive time is again sampled and in line 113 the lower of the two drive times is found. If the second patrol proves to have the shortest drive time then in line 118 the second patrol is removed from the PATROLFREE set and the first patrol is replaced in the PATROLFREE set.

At line 124 the situation is that the patrol having the shortest drive time has been removed from the PATROLFREE set. This line calculates the member's waiting time as being the CLOCK time plus the drive time less the time at which the member first called. The next step in line 129 is to check the arrival time of the patrol by adding the drive time to the CLOCK time; if this arrival time (ARTIME) is equal to 690 or greater than 690 min from the start then the program jumps to line 50 where the member is added in as a garage job. However, if the arrival time is less than 690 min from the start then the member will be seen by the patrol previously identified. Line 131 cumulates the total members' waiting time and lines 132 and 133 enables the longest waiting time to be carried forward. In line 134 the waiting time is added to the waiting time histogram.

The next section of the program starting at 139 is concerned with working out the effects of servicing this member's call. The job time is sampled and the total patrol time is found by adding the drive time to the job time just sampled. In line 141 the total patrol time to date is calculated. In line 142 the number of jobs serviced is increased by one. Then in line 143 to 145 the extra time worked beyond 660 min from the start is cumulated on each pass through this section of the program. The member, having been serviced, is removed from the member waiting set in line 151. Line 152 contains the RECYCLE statement which causes further passes through the activities without a time advance until there are no members waiting, or until both patrols have been allocated. In these instances the RECYCLE statement is bypassed by jumping to lines 160 and 215 respectively. Line 160 tests whether it is the end of the day (19.00 hours). If not, a jump is made to line 215. The DUMMY statement in line 215 causes time to be advanced and a new pass through the activities. At the end of the day lines 161 to 171 update various histograms and cumulative values. In line 171 a summary of that day's operations is printed out.

The first of the values printed in this line is the day count; this enables the program to be monitored during run time to check the validity of the

159

program. The total number of days simulated is checked at line 174; if the 350 days have been completed then the finish routine is commenced. The statements from line 179 to 213 are concerned with printing out summaries of the simulation in terms of histograms etc. as previously described, and in addition a histogram of waiting time is produced.

Finally, some details of costs are given, the total cost incurred and the average cost per job, followed by a histogram of average patrol costs (the average being the daily average). These outputs have already been mentioned and typical results are shown in figures 7.9(a) to (d).

SIMULATION PROGRAM OF A REPAIRING AND RE-ISSUE CYCLE (SOMB)

The program SOMB simulates a maintenance bay situation. The type of situation simulated is a closed loop system whereby items being maintained are processed through workshops and then put into stock, to be withdrawn subsequently as a replacement to a unit which has broken down in service and has been sent to the workshops. A queueing situation exists in the workshop area and one aspect of the problem is to determine the number of servicing bays to be provided, but closely connected to this is the stockholding situation. The slower the turnround of items in the workshops the larger the stockholding of units in the system needs to be, conversely a quick throughput in the workshops allows a reduction of total numbers of units in the system. This type of situation is illustrated by reference to a supposed aircraft maintenance situation.

Due to the nature of the work or due to an overload, units are passed from the hangars to the workshops. Providing there is a stockholding, a replacement unit can be made immediately available to the hangars. The repaired unit is

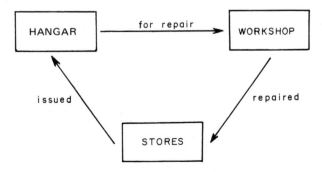

Figure 7.10   Repair, re-issue cycle

subsequently taken into stock from the workshops. This is illustrated diagrammatically in figure 7.10.

The frequency of a shortage will be determined by the number of units in the system and also by the nature of the delays in the workshops. In this problem, as in the other queueing type problems, the two main variables that need to be sampled are the inter-arrival time of units for repair into the workshops, and the time required for repair in the workshops. The consequences of the units passing through the workshops and of queues occasionally developing will be reflected in the fluctuations of stock levels in the stores. Thus if there is a queue of three units in the workshops and there are two maintenance bays, then the implications are that there are a total of five units being processed through the workshops which in turn means that the stock level in the stores has been reduced by five units at this point in time. If there were no units at all in the workshops then the stock level would have reached its maximum value as determined by the total number of units in the system less the units in service on the aircraft.

Output from SOMB

The maximum number of units that are likely to be in the workshops at any one time represents the maximum stockholding that is necessary. A simulation, therefore, that monitors the number in the system in the workshops will yield useful information as to the stock fluctuations. In this program, the number of units in the system was assessed every twenty four hours, and this number was added into a histogram count. The output from SOMB was kept to a minimum. The total elapsed time of the simulation was printed, the total number of units serviced by each maintenance bay was printed, and finally a histogram of 'queue sizes' was printed. In the context of the program, queue size means the total number of units in the workshops. An example of the type of results obtained from SOMB are shown in figure 7.11.

From the results illustrated it can be seen that the maximum number of units that occur in the workshops is six, thus a total stockholding of six in excess of the numbers required to be in service on aircraft will in this case suffice. If these units are expensive units, say aircraft engines then it would be worth while to extend the simulation to examine the relationship between maximum stockholding and number of service bays. When there are only two service bays, then for the arrival pattern and service pattern used in this program, it was found that the workshops cannot cope and an infinite queue will form, thus two maintenance bays are an impractical proposition. If the simulation is carried out for three loading bays, then the maximum queue size is something like eight units. The economic problem then is whether it is worth increasing the number of maintenance bays from three to four in order

161

to reduce the stockholding from eight units down to six. A further factor that may be considered is reducing the stock still further and incurring a shortage for a short duration. This is where the histogram produced at the end of the simulation run is likely to be the most useful as it enables the proportion of

```
SIMULATION OF ENGINE MAINTENANCE

ELAPSED TIME = 4000 HOURS

NO SERVICED

BAY 1 142

BAY 2 119

BAY 3  96

BAY 4  98



QUEUESIZE (ASSESSED AT 24 HRLY INTERVALS)
COUNT              RANGE
 139                TO     0
  12              1 TO     1
   8              2 TO     2
   3              3 TO     3
   3              4 TO     4
   1              5 TO     5
   0              6 TO     6
   0              7 TO     7
   0              8 TO     8
   0              9 TO
NORMAL EXIT
```

Figure 7.11   Typical output from SOMB

units in excess of a given number to be calculated and costed out at the appropriate shortage rate. If required, the program SOMB could easily be extended to include the economic calculations as described.

Description of Program

The program SOMB is written in CSL to simulate four maintenance bays although it could be easily changed to have the number of bays read in as a variable. The arrays, sets and time-cells are defined in lines 17 and 23 of the program listing given in appendix 12. Inter-arrival times and service times are read in and immediately printed out in lines 24 to 27, and in line 31 the main heading of the output page is printed. The general initialisation stage of the program commences in line 39 where the distributions read in are cumulated, following this two stream variables are initialised in lines 40 and 41. The histogram of queue size to be outputted at the end of the simulation is defined as comprising ten cells with class intervals of one unit. In line 43 the time of arrival of the next unit is pre-set to 2 hours (the choice of this interval is arbitrary but should be typical of the data to be sampled). In lines 44 to 48 the bays are loaded into a FREEBAYS set, the total number repaired by each bay is set to zero, the time each bay finished its last repair is set to −1, and the total number of units serviced is set to zero. Finally, in line 49 a time-cell called T.INTERVAL is set to 24. This time-cell is reduced gradually as the simulation proceeds until it reaches zero; at this stage the number of units in the system is added to the queue size histogram and the time cell reset to twenty four hours. By this means the number of units in the system is noted every twenty four hours. In the context of a stock situation, this is similar to taking the stock levels as recorded at the end of every day, say, and regarding this as a true picture of the stock fluctuations. The problem here is that the stock fluctuations take place on a continuous time scale, but if a histogram is to be compiled then it should be based upon uniform increments of time.

The start of the simulation begins at line 50, and the first BEGIN section checks whether twenty four hours have elapsed, and, if so, adds the number of units to the histogram queue size. Line 62 is the beginning of the section concerning a unit arriving. When a unit has arrived i.e. its time-cell is equal to 0, the time to the next unit arriving is sampled in line 67, and in line 68 the number of units is increased by one. The next section down to line 77 updates the FREEBAYS set. Each bay having a time-cell equal to zero is added to the FREEBAYS set, and the number repaired by that bay is increased by one. Line 82 tests whether any units are in the system; if there are no units in the system the program jumps to line 102 where the total length of simulation is tested. If there are units to be serviced, then line 86 finds the bay with min index in FREEBAYS and the number of units is reduced by one. Line 92 removes the free bay from the FREEBAYS set and line 93 samples a service time for the unit to be repaired in that bay. This service time becomes the time-cell for the appropriate bay. The next line causes the program to recycle to meet any further changes as necessary. When no further action can be taken, the program moves to line 95. If the simulation has reached the end, then lines 103 to 112 output the various details as previously shown in figure 7.11.

A similar problem to SOMB is described in chapter 9 where the emphasis is on the throughput time of the units being repaired. This type of problem is associated with production control applications, and the program LOAD described in chapter 9 is concerned with simulating the lateness of units being processed through a refurbishing facility.

Chapter 8

Forecasting and Inventory Control

INTRODUCTION

This chapter considers the main factors in developing forecasting systems and illustrates various forms of exponential smoothing by reference to a FORTRAN program, FORE. The chapter then considers the factors that should be taken into account in developing an inventory control system. A typical re-ordering system is then described by reference to a CSL program, STAN.

Forecasting techniques are applied in a wide variety of situations ranging from the short term forecast required for stock control purposes to the forecasts that need to be developed in conjunction with long range planning up to twenty years or more ahead. In recent years, the term 'technological forecasting' has come to be used with reference to examination of the company's position and the market requirements up to as far as fifty years ahead. In this chapter, forecasting is taken to mean short term forecasting that is required in conjunction with day-to-day operating systems. Inventory control systems are typical of such an application that relies on routine day-to-day, or more likely, week-to-week forecasting.

FORECASTING

The one certain thing about forecasts is that they are never right. This is often overlooked by people developing or testing alternative systems, as they search for the elusive method that will give them correct forecasts. Once it is recognised that no forecasting system will yield perfect results, then it becomes important to examine other aspects of the forecasting system in order to select the most suitable. A good forecasting system is one that has the following three qualities;

(1) *A small size error* The average size of the error is critical in determining how suitable a forecasting system is for a particular application. In general, given two alternative forecasting systems, the one chosen would be

the one having the smallest average errors. This is however a generalisation and as such may not always be true. In some applications the average error may not be so important as the maximum error that is likely to occur. For this reason, it is usual to monitor the performance of alternative forecasting systems and develop measures that reflect the frequency distribution of the errors and their associated standard deviation. In practice, the standard deviation is an awkward measure to calculate in forecasting systems. This is because the total number of readings in the data is constantly being extended by the addition of the latest figure, and data that are very old are probably no longer relevant to the latest situation. For these reasons, it is common to calculate instead a mean absolute deviation (m.a.d.). This is simply the average of the deviations, i.e. errors between forecasted and actual results, taken without regard to their sign. The precise method of calculating the m.a.d. and the method of updating will be described later in the chapter when the forecasting program FORE is being described.

(2) *The ability to adapt*   The development of a suitable forecasting system may require much effort, and this degree of effort cannot be maintained once the forecasting system is implemented. Because of this, the forecasting system should be able ideally to adapt itself to any subsequent changes in the underlying pattern of data being encountered. Prior to the development of self-adaptive systems, a forecasting system would have to be reviewed and assessed every so often. However, nowadays it is possible to design a forecasting system that not only signals when it has failed to track the actual data effectively, but in the meantime, changes its parameters accordingly. The basis of this approach is due to D. W. Trigg and A. G. Leach[29]. The essential features of their approach will be described and illustrated by reference to one of the runs in the forecasting program FORE.

(3) *Easiest to implement and run*   Given that the above two features are present in alternative forecasting systems, then ultimately the choice should be with the simplest system, that is the one that would be easiest to implement and control from a management point of view. Although management may not know the details of all the calculations involved, they should be capable of appreciating the principles upon which it is based so that they can decide when to ignore the forecasts if necessary and revert to using their own judgement.

The Statistical Approach
The ability to interpret and use figures or data intelligently has become a basic requirement of the modern manager. An appreciation of the statistical approach can help ensure that decisions are soundly based instead of being hunches.

Statistical methods of forecasting can range from the simple job of tabulation and presentation of data, such as the Board of Trade type statistics giving house starts, brick production etc. to the more complex analysis of graphs, trends, probability etc. that is involved in planning company policy.

The straightforward presentation of past data is usually by means of an index whereby each years or month's figure is related to a particular base period. From the point of view of management the index may be used as an indicator.

Quantifiable data can be examined for correlation with leading indicators. In addition, past data can be used to determine any trends, cycles and seasonal patterns. Before data are examined in this way however, the necessity for adjustments should be considered.

Variations in data can be due to the fact that the time periods are not uniform. The number of days in a month vary. Due to odd holidays, the number of working days per week varies during the year. It may therefore be necessary to adjust the initial data to obtain a true comparison of a day's or month's figures. In addition, increases in population or prices may necessitate further adjustments.

Leading Indicators and Correlation

Economic indicators can be the basis of future estimates, particularly if they lead the sales they are related to by a period of several months.

There are various correlation techniques concerned with trying to establish the relationship between variables. The simplest form of correlation is between two variables, when the relationship is linear. Although it is possible to establish nonlinear relationships, (providing they exist), it is usually more convenient to transform the readings into a different form, such as logarithms which may then yield a linear relationship. An example of no correlation and close correlation is illustrated in figure 8.1.

When the variable depends upon several independent variables, a more laborious procedure is necessary to establish the relationship. This procedure is known as multiple correlation and enables the relative importance of the different independent variables to be established.

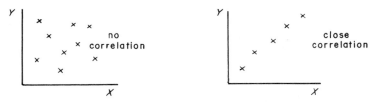

Figure 8.1   The meaning of correlation

The principle of the use of leading indicators is best illustrated by the following hypothetical situation.

A retailer of childrens clothing has compiled a table showing his sales and the corresponding indices of number of marriages (A), number of childrens shoes sold (B) and the sale of nursery wallpaper (C). Which index should be taken as a guide to next year's sales?

Year	Sales	Index A	Index B	Index C
1	20 000	106	112	120
2	70 000	106	116	130
3	90 000	115	104	135
4	50 000	109	101	126
5	40 000	110	107	124

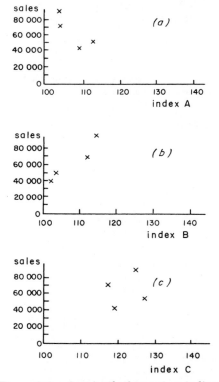

Figure 8.2   Graph of sales against indices

For the sake of simplicity the problem has been devised so that the indicator, index A, B or C leads the sales by exactly a year. In practice of course this period would have to be found. Thus in this example, the value of an index in one year is plotted against the sales in the next year, e.g. taking index A, 106 is plotted against 70 000, then 106 against 90 000, 107 against 50 000 and so on. Plots of the three indices are shown in figure 8.2.

From the graphs it can be seen that only index B shows any correlation with sales. Knowing this, the value of the index in year 5, namely 107, can be interpreted from the graph to indicate sales of 60 000 in year 6.

Coefficient of correlation   It is possible to assess the degree of correlation between sets of data analytically. The preceding example will be used to illustrate how the figures for sales and index B can be analysed to asses (*a*) the degree of correlation, and (*b*) the significance of this value of correlation. The measure of correlation termed the product moment coefficient of correlation, usually designated by the letter *r*, assumes a linear relationship between the pairs of data. When there is perfect correlation between the pairs of data the value of *r* will either be 1 or −1, when there is no correlation at all the value of *r* will be zero. *r* is calculated from the following relationships:

$$r = \frac{S_{xy}}{\sqrt{S_{xx}} \sqrt{S_{yy}}}$$

where

$$S_{xy} = \Sigma xy - \frac{\Sigma x \Sigma y}{n}$$

$$S_{xx} = \Sigma x^2 - \frac{(\Sigma x)^2}{n}$$

$$S_{yy} = \Sigma y^2 - \frac{(\Sigma y)^2}{n}$$

n = number of pair of values, x, y.

Even with unrelated data, a certain degree of correlation may arise by chance. The significant value of *r* therefore needs to be considered. Tables are available that give the critical value of *r* at the 0.05 significance level. The hypothesis is that *r* equals zero; if the value of *r* is found to be greater than the values in the tables then the result is significant and can be interpreted as indicating that a high degree of correlation exists between the pairs of values. Extracts from tables giving the critical value of *r* are given in Appendix 22. It is possible also to assess the significance of *r* by reference to Student's *t* tables.[8]

The calculations involved for finding the correlation coefficient between

A Practical Approach to Computer Simulation

the sales and index B are shown in figure 8.3. It will be seen from the calculations that the value of r is 0.989. From the tables in Appendix 22 the value of r that should be exceeded (for 0.05 level of significance, when d.f. = $n-2 = 2$) should be 0.950. As this data has a higher correlation coefficient, it can be concluded that there is a significant degree of correlation between the pairs of readings.

x	y	x^2	y^2	xy
112	70	12 544	4 900	78 400
116	90	13 456	8 100	10 440
104	50	10 816	2 500	5 200
101	40	10 201	1 600	4 040

$\Sigma x = 433 \quad \Sigma y = 250 \quad \Sigma x^2 = 47\ 017 \quad \Sigma y^2 = 17\ 100 \quad \Sigma xy = 27\ 520$

$$S_{xy} = \Sigma xy - \frac{\Sigma x \Sigma y}{n} = 27\ 520 - \frac{(433)(250)}{4} = 457.5$$

$$S_{xx} = \Sigma x^2 - \frac{(\Sigma x)^2}{n} = 47\ 017 - \frac{(433)^2}{4} = 145$$

$$S_{yy} = \Sigma y^2 - \frac{(\Sigma y)^2}{n} = 17\ 100 - \frac{(250)^2}{4} = 1\ 475$$

$$r = \frac{S_{xy}}{\sqrt{S_{xx}}\ \sqrt{S_{yy}}} = \frac{457.5}{\sqrt{145}\ \sqrt{1\ 475}} = 0.989$$

Figure 8.3   The calculation of r

In this example, the period of lead between the index and the sales was exactly one year. In practice, the lead period may not be so convenient and it is necessary to test for correlation over a range of leading periods. When a series of figures is examined for correlation between successive values of the same series, the value of r is termed the serial correlation coefficient. If the serial correlation coefficient is calculated for the pairs of terms 1, 2, 3 etc. places apart, then the resulting graph of these successive values is termed a correlogram. A correlogram is a useful indication of the potential usefulness in a time series for forecasting purposes. If there is some degree of serial correlation, the correlogram tends to be a smooth curve that oscillates slowly and usually gradually dies away. If however the data being examined are statistically random then the correlogram obtained is an erratic graph showing no sign of damped oscillations. For a further discussion of correlograms and their use, the reader is referred to reference 7, by J. N. Craddock.

Time Series Analysis
The correlation of sales with various indicators is usually disguised by the existence of trends, seasonal patterns etc. These patterns are identified by the application of time series analysis techniques.

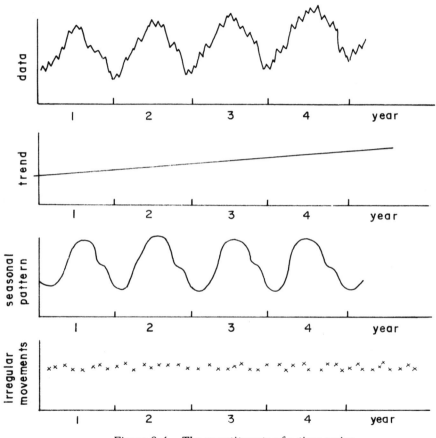

Figure 8.4   The constituents of a time series

Time series analysis is the term used for the analysis of chronological data. Movements in the data can be classified as being due to trend, periodic, cyclical and irregular movements. Usually all four of these movements are present and coexistent.

The trend is usually established by either calculating a twelve-monthly moving average, (which effectively de-seasonalises the data), or more recently

171

by use of a technique termed 'exponential smoothing'. On some occasions the 'method of least squares' is used to fit the best straight line.

The periodic movements, normally seasonal variations, are analysed and expressed as an index of seasonal variation. A common method is to average corresponding data from the previous three years and take these averages as representing the seasonal pattern. The basic data when adjusted for the trend and seasonal pattern will then only show the cyclical and irregular movements. The irregular movements can be further smoothed with exponential smoothing to bring the cyclical movements into prominence. The remaining cyclical movements can then be examined for correlation with other series.

Figure 8.4 illustrates the breaking down of a time series into its constituent parts.

Econometric Models

In some instances it is possible to set up a mathematical model to represent a general economic situation. Econometrics involves the specification of a set of equations to represent the situation, a simple example might be,

$$GNP_t = G_t + I_t + C_t \qquad (8.1)$$
$$C_t = a + bGNP_t \qquad (8.2)$$
$$I_t = m + c(GNP_{t-1} - GNP_{t-2}) \qquad (8.3)$$

where, GNP_t is gross national product in time t, C_t is consumption, I_t is investment and G_t is government spending.

The above equations do not purport to be economically correct, they are meant just to illustrate the principle.

The second step is to estimate the values of the parameters, a, b, m and c above. This may be done using the statistical techniques previously described.

The third step is to verify the model by measuring the errors it gives when applied to past data. Once again, statistical tests can be used to indicate the degree of confidence that may be placed in the results.

Assuming the model is found to be 'correct', the fourth stage is to use it to predict the future. In this example, at time t, the values of GNP_{t-1} and GNP_{t-2} would be known. Therefore, by substituting in equation 8.3 the value of I_t can be calculated. If G_t has been announced then the only remaining unknowns are GNP_t and C_t. As there are two equations and two unknowns, the values of GNP_t and C_t can be solved.

Once the complete set of equations has been solved, the whole procedure can be repeated for the next time interval $t + 1$. However, owing to the complexity of this approach, econometric models have not been widely applied in industry.

EXPONENTIAL SMOOTHING

In the past, traditional statistical methods were applied to the forecasting problem. This meant that the technique of regression was widely used to fit a line to a series of points. The disadvantage of this method is that all the figures have equal importance, whereas the latest figures are probably more relevant to what is to happen next than the earlier ones. To overcome this rather static approach to forecasting, 'dynamic' methods of forecasting have been developed.

The 'dynamic' methods place more weight on the latest figures. An extreme example of this approach is when the latest figure is taken as the forecast for the next period. In general this method is too erratic, but at least it has the advantage of extreme simplicity. A more usual method is to use a twelve monthly moving average. As the latest figure is incorporated into the average the oldest figure (corresponding to the same month last year) is dropped. This method is useful for showing up trends, but relative to modern techniques it is slow to respond to changes and it requires a lot of data to be carried forward.

An extension of the moving average technique, called exponential smoothing, is widely used today. Exponential smoothing places most emphasis on the latest figure and a gradual decreasing emphasis on older figures. The calculations are relatively simple and can be elaborated to take account of any trend and seasonal pattern.

A further development in the last few years is adaptive forecasting. This technique is based upon exponential smoothing but the degree of smoothing used is revised after each observation according to the forecast error. The method thereby adapts itself to the demand pattern.

The type of calculations and method of allowing for trends and errors will be dealt with in the following sections.

Allowing for Trend
In order to identify the trend in a series of data, it is necessary to smooth out the violent fluctuations by calculating some average figure. The calculation of a twelve-monthly moving average results in a forecast that follows the trend slowly. If the recent figures are of more importance, a three-monthly moving average can be tried, this will respond to the recent changes more rapidly, but it will also respond to the random fluctuations.

Exponential smoothing is a particular type of moving average. The usual moving average places equal emphasis on each figure in the period being averaged. Thus in an annual moving average as much weight is given to the figures almost a year old as is given to the most recent data. With exponential smoothing the more recent figures are given increasing importance, the weighting factor following an exponential distribution.

A 'weight' is chosen, between 0 and 1 to give to the latest figure. This weight is termed the smoothing constant, a.

From this, a weight of $(1 - a)$ is calculated and given to the old forecast. Then,

$$\text{The new forecast} = a(\text{latest figure}) + (1 - a)\,(\text{old forecast}) \qquad (8.4)$$

Example:

Let the smoothing constant be: 0.4

then, $(1 - a) = (1 - 0.4)$ $= 0.6$

If the old forecast was 35 and the actual value was 30, then,

New forecast = 0.4 x 30 + 0.6 x 35

=   12   +   21

= 33

One advantage with this technique is that it is necessary only to carry forward one figure to the next period, namely the old forecast. With conventional moving average methods all the data in the averaging period have to be carried forward.

The choice of the 'best' smoothing constant is a matter of experience and judgement. Some works[22] suggest that if the problem warrants detailed analysis, two or three alternative values can be used on past data and the results compared. On the other hand others, (e.g. reference 1) say that with the development of adaptive forecasting this is unnecessary.

It does not follow that the smoothing constant that gave the best results in the past will continue to give the best results in the future. The nature of the demand might change. Therefore unless the system is adaptive, regular checks as to the best constant should be made. A broad guide as to the value of the smoothing constant to be used is:

if there is no trend, let $a = 0.1$

if there is a slight trend, let $a = 0.5$

if there is a marked trend, let $a = 0.9$

In general to suppress random variations, one should reduce the smoothing constant. To respond to changes in the trend quicker, one should increase the smoothing constant. The effect of the choice of the smoothing constant is shown in the following example.

174

Month	Demand	Forecast, $a = 0.1$ Last forecast = 10	Forecast, $a = 0.9$ Last forecast = 10
1	10	10	10
2	14	10.4	13.6
3	15	10.9	14.8
4	11	10.9	12.4
5	8	10.6	8.4
6	10	10.5	9.8
7	6	10.1	6.6
8	8	9.9	7.9
9	10	9.9	9.8
10	9	9.8	9.1
11	11	9.9	10.8
12	10	9.9	10.1

These results are shown for comparison in figure 8.5. The data in this example do not have any substantial trend; the effect of a set of data having a marked trend is shown in figure 8.6.

It can be seen that the use of a small smoothing constant in this case causes the forecast to lag behind the actual figures. Provided an estimate of the trend can be obtained however, a correction can be made to the forecast to eliminate this lag.

One estimate of the current trend could be the difference between the

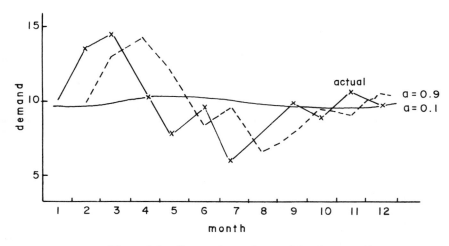

Figure 8.5   Comparison of smoothing (no trend)

175

newly calculated forecast and the old forecast. If this approach is used then the basic exponential smoothing formulae are elaborated into:

current trend = new smoothed average − old smoothed average

new trend = b(current trend) + $(1 − b)$ (old trend)

$$\text{expected demand} = \text{new average} + \frac{(1 − a)}{a} \text{ (new trend)}$$

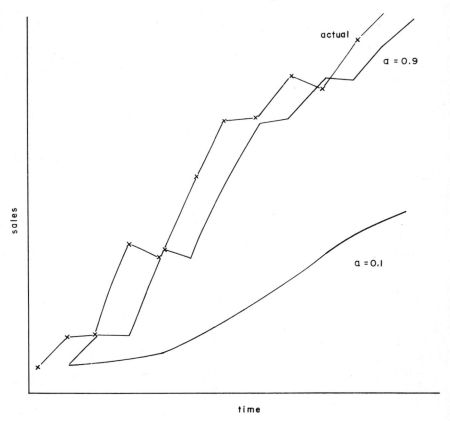

Figure 8.6   Comparison of smoothing with trend present

where b is a further smoothing constant for the trend equation, and is not necessarily the same as a. Note that the correction to the new average, $(1 − a)/a$, does still use a. With this method it is necessary to carry forward to the next period the previously calculated value of the average *and* the trend.

Other methods based upon similar lines have been developed to correct for the trend in a series[1].

Despite the development of adaptive method, the best method to use cannot be found automatically, it is largely a question of trying different approaches with actual data to find the method that appears to work best. This aspect of trying alternative systems falls within the realms of simulation. However before a simple program (FORE) is described, some mention should be made of methods of tracking and how the errors are used in adaptive systems.

Calculating Forecast Errors

If a forecasting system is working correctly, taking into account trend and seasonal patterns, any errors should be sometimes above the forecast and

Table 8.1   Calculation of cumulative error

Month	Actual demand	Forecast	Error	Cumulative error
Jan.	820	840	+20	+20
Feb.	900	889	−11	+ 9
Mar.	870	843	−27	−18
Apr.	1 050	1 068	+18	0
May	1 350	1 360	+10	+10
Jun.	1 800	1 782	−18	− 8
Jul.	1 890	1 939	+49	+31
Aug.	1 740	1 681	−59	−10
Sep.	1 680	1 679	− 1	−11
Oct.	1 500	1 519	+19	+18
Nov.	1 470	1 462	− 8	+10
Dec.	1 130	1 110	−20	−10

sometimes below the forecast. There are therefore two aspects to consider, firstly, how well the system is tracking, and secondly, how large the errors are that must be accepted.

The tracking of the system can be monitored by keeping a record of the cumulative sum of the errors. The cumulative sum of the errors should oscillate above and below zero. If the cumulative sum of the errors drifts in one direction then changes are occurring which are not being forecast. An example of the necessary calculations are given in table 8.1, and a graph of the cumulative errors, showing how the errors calculated above oscillate about zero, is shown in figure 8.7.

The second aspect of the errors is their size in order that the maximum demand to be expected can be estimated. It is usually assumed that in the absence of data to the contrary, the forecast errors in a system that is tracking correctly are normally distributed. Statistically this means that the frequency distribution of errors follows the familiar 'bell-shape' for which the standard distribution can be calculated. Calculation of the standard deviation is tedious and for convenience the mean absolute deviation (m.a.d.) is used as an approximation. The (m.a.d.) is the average of the forecast errors without regard to their sign and represents approximately 0.8 times the standard distribution.

Figure 8.7   Graph of the cumulative error

In exponential smoothing systems to keep the m.a.d. up to date it is smoothed by use of the following formulae:

$$\text{new m.a.d.} = c\ (\text{absolute current deviation})$$
$$+ (1 - c)\ (\text{old m.a.d.})$$

once again the smoothing constant here may not be the same as a or b.

In a normal distribution, the range of values falls approximately within plus or minus three standard deviations. This can be equated to plus or minus four m.a.d.s, (i.e. 4 x 0.8 = 3.2). The range of the actual demand can be taken to lay within four m.a.d.s of the forecast.

Trigg's Trackings
Referring back to the idea of calculating the cumulative errors to assess whether the forecast is tracking or not, it has been suggested by Trigg[29], that an alternative measure would be to smooth the errors exponentially. An exponentially smoothed error will reflect the cumulative effect of past errors and will fit in more readily with an exponential smoothing system. At this stage then we will be smoothing the errors with regard to their sign to give a new exponentially smoothed error, and we will be smoothing the latest error without regard to its sign to revise the exponentially smoothed m.a.d. If the

178

smoothed errors are then divided by the latest m.a.d., we have the basis of Trigg's tracking signal; this tracking signal must lie between minus 1.0 and plus 1.0. Furthermore, if the tracking signal has its sign disregarded, we have a number lying between nought and one; a tracking signal close to zero indicates effective tracking, a tracking signal close to one indicates loss of tracking. An adaptive method of forecasting now becomes possible by simply making the value of a, the smoothing constant, equal to the latest value of the tracking signal (or the penultimate value to prevent instability). Advocates of the use of Trigg's tracking signal for establishing the value of a maintain that this procedure obviates the necessity to find the best value of a from an analysis of past history. However, it would be a wise precaution for those about to set up a forecasting system for the first time to examine other exponential smoothing methods in addition to the adaptive system based on Trigg's tracking signal, before automatically assuming that this adaptive system is the most effective. An example of the sort of program that could be used to assess the effectiveness of various exponential smoothing methods is given by the program FORE (see also appendix 4).

A SIMPLE FORECASTING PROGRAM (FORE)

This program is one that grew up over a period of time as it was found necessary to try alternative forecasting systems. Basically, the program is capable of reading in up to thirty six values that would normally represent past data. The number of past readings read in is counted within the program and the average value calculated, the past data being stored in an array so that they can be referred to on successive runs as different methods of forecasting are tried out. An incremental count, K, is used within the program to determine which method of forecasting is to be undertaken. When K is initialised at 1 the first run carries out simple exponential smoothing. Initially, the value of a is set to 0.1 and then successive runs are made increasing the value of a by 0.1 until 1.0 is reached.

In order to assess the effectiveness of each of these runs and similar runs with the other forecasting methods, an assessment of the effectiveness of the forecasting system is indicated by printing out with each forecast the error, the cumulative error, the smoothed m.a.d. and finally the tracking signal. Provision is made for the system to quickly adapt itself to the nature of the figures. The first forecast is taken as the first data figure thus the initial error will be zero, for this and the next three runs the value of a used, regardless of the method of forecasting, is 0.7. By the fourth forecast the system should have adapted itself from cold, and from then on the appropriate value of a is used as determined by the run being made.

179

At the end of a run with a particular value of a, a summary of the largest error, the largest cumulative error, the largest m.a.d. and the largest tracking signal is printed. In doing this, the first four results are obviously ignored as they were not relevant to the run.

To summarise the simple forecasting system used in FORE, ten runs are made with a starting at 0.1, increasing by 0.1 up to 1.0. The first four results of each run are not typical as initially a is set to 0.7 in every case. Finally, at the end of each of the ten runs the largest value of the errors, the cumulative errors, the m.a.d. and the tracking is printed.

The next series of runs, when $K = 2$ is based upon a simple exponential smoothing system with trend correction. Apart from the inclusion of a trend correction factor the nature of the output is identical. During all the runs involving trend correction, the smoothing constant used for the trend equation is kept constant at 0.1.

At one stage in the development of the program it was felt that a very simple approach to forecasting should not be overlooked, namely, the idea of just setting up a forecast based upon the average of the past demand. Therefore, when K is incremented to 3, what is termed a constant forecasting system is examined. The forecast is pre-set to a constant level and held at this level throughout the run of data. The obvious constant forecast to use is the average value of the past result. However, this may not be the best constant to pick if the past results are skewed. For this reason five runs are made at 60, 80, 100, 120 and 140 per cent of the calculated mean. As before, the errors, cumulative errors, m.a.d., and tracking signal are printed with each forecast. At the end of each of the five runs the maximum values of the error, cumulative error, m.a.d. and tracking signal are once again printed.

The final series of runs, when $K = 4$, are designed to test the effectiveness of an adaptive system based upon the use of Trigg's tracking signal. These runs are in essence a repeat of the calculations made in the first simple exponential smoothing system, but the value of a is determined and set by the penultimate value of the tracking signal.

Output from FORE
Altogether then the program FORE carries out twenty six runs over an initial set of past figures. Ten runs using a simple exponential smoothing system, ten runs incorporating trend correction, five runs with the forecast being held constant and finally one run with the value of a varying according to the tracking signal. During each run the largest value of the various parameters calculated are printed. At the end of all twenty six runs a summary of the best of these is printed together with the associated forecasting method. Thus the run having the smallest largest error is printed together with the

forecasting method being used, as indicated by the value of the increment K, and the associated value of a (or the constant forecast) being used is also printed. A summary of output from the program is shown in figure 8.8.

These results, which came from an analysis of real data, indicate that the best method leading to the smallest errors, cumulative errors, and m.a.d. is method (3), i.e. a method based upon a constant forecast. Although method (3) is indicated as being best for these three parameters, there is a different constant indicated against each parameter, thus the user has to decide which parameter is most important, in his particular application. Cumulative errors may be more important than individual errors if one is interested only in the

THE SMALLEST VALUES OF THE LARGEST ABSOLUTES

PARAMETER	VALUE	METHOD	CONSTANT
ERROR	1998.59	3	1465.4
CUM ERROR	1905.67	3	1343.3
MAD	780.54	3	1099.1
TRACKING	0.36	2	1.00

Figure 8.8   Final output phase from FORE

net consequence over a long run. Alternatively, it might be felt that the value of m.a.d. is of critical importance in so far as this reflects the standard deviation of the errors and thereby indicates the necessity for buffer stocks, contingency plans, etc. The best method for tracking results is indicated as being an exponential smoothing with trend correction but one that is using an a of 1.0. As it turns out, this is not really exponential smoothing, for, if $a = 1.0$, the last result is being taken as the forecast for the next period, furthermore the trend correction disappears in the calculations as $(1 - a)/a$ becomes zero. Overall then this summary of results presents a picture of data that is extremely erratic and having no trend and therefore management at best should determine a fixed forecast and adhere to it. In the light of this conclusion, it would obviously be prudent to keep a close watch on future developments in the demand pattern.

INVENTORY CONTROL

If a stock control system is to be developed, the simulation of alternative forecasting techniques is only the beginning of the analysis required. Having found what appears to be the most appropriate forecasting method, it is then necessary to analyse the various parameters that govern the performance of a stock control system. Before discussing an example of a simulation in this area, a résumé of basic inventory control theory will be given in order to indicate the factors that need considering. Although in the main these factors feature in all stock control systems, the relative importance of certain factors varies enormously across the range of applications within differing industries. Thus one person may be interested in developing a system that is virtually self-running and will be willing to sacrifice a certain degree of efficiency, or optimality, for the sake of having an automatic system, whereas another person is prepared to devote a lot of thought to the size of an order because it is in the nature of a 'one-off' decision and the question of automatic running from day-to-day is irrelevant. For instance, a buyer of fashionable goods needs a system, or more appropriately a method of analysis, that will enable him to buy correctly at the beginning of the season. Halfway through the season is too late to change any earlier decisions and if all the stocks have already been sold then a 'loss' of profit is incurred, whereas if the season finishes with stocks still on the shelves then these may have to be sold at a loss.

At the other end of the scale is the person involved in multi-batch production where the stock control system is controlled, tens of thousands of items and it is impossible to devote much attention to any in particular. Here the system must be based upon management by exception, that is, the system signals when a particular stock item needs individual investigation. Until that happens management take no interest in the ensuing stock fluctuations. A further type of stock problem is one that is effectively a closed-loop system. This type of system is encountered in maintenance work where items are withdrawn from store to replace items that have failed or broken down in some way, the failed items are eventually repaired and put into stock. Here the problem is usually one of deciding what is the total number of items in the system. An example of this has already been covered by the program SOMB in chapter 7.

Basic Inventory Control Principles
Although there are many specific reasons for holding stocks they can be classified into two types, namely,

(1) to enable production or orders to be made in *economic* quantities,
(2) to protect against variations in *demand.*

In control terms stocks can be regarded as a decoupling device giving preceding and succeeding operations a measure of independence. The main variables to be taken into account in developing a policy are shown in figure 8.9.

In addition to the variables shown in the figure there are the economic aspects. The most widely adopted approach is to consider three elements of cost,

(a) administrative costs, i.e. the cost of obtaining a quantity,
(b) holding costs, i.e. the cost of maintaining a stock,
(c) shortage costs, i.e. loss of profit, goodwill, opportunity etc.

The importance of these costs will vary according to the application. Thus administrative costs may be negligible if material is supplied by the customer

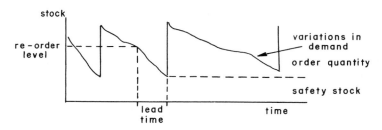

Figure 8.9   Main variables in stock control

as sometimes happens in sub-contracting. Holding cost may be small if extended credit facilities are used, i.e. settlement within three months, etc. Shortage costs may be non-existent or extremely high. In some spares stockholdings, the shortage of one low price item may have serious consequencies.

Whatever type of stock system is used, two questions need answering: (1) *when* should stock orders be placed, and (2) *how much* should be ordered.

When the demand rate is constant the answer to these questions lead to the same policy. However, in practice, due to variations in demand, emphasis is placed on one or the other. This leads to two basic types of system.

When the quantity ordered is fixed, control is obtained by varying the time at which an order is placed. Orders are placed when the stock level reaches a re-order point. This is called the re-order level system and is identical to the two bin system wherein one bin represents the re-order level.

An alternative approach is to fix the time at which an order is to be placed, say once a month and then order a varying amount depending upon the stock level at the time of the review. This is called the periodic review system.

The two systems are compared diagrammatically in figure 8.10.

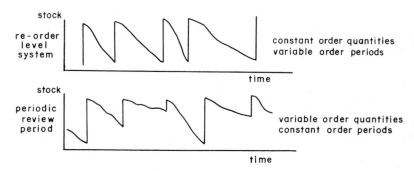

Figure 8.10   Comparison of the two basic systems

Whichever type of system is followed, the calculations leading to the order quantity or the review period would be based upon the *mean* demand. When it is required to meet higher levels of demand whenever they arise, some form of safety stock must be carried.

This characteristic stock graph can be regarded as comprising two components allowing the separate analysis of order quantity and safety stock as mentioned above, (see figure 8.11).

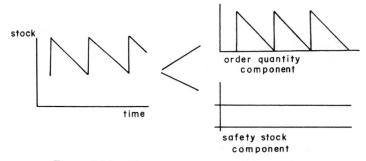

Figure 8.11   The two components of a stock graph

The treatment of the safety stock component as a separate issue simplifies the analysis of the order quantity or review period. As these will be based upon the mean demand, they are simply related by the expression,

$$\text{order quantity} = \frac{\text{annual demand}}{\text{number of review period per year}} \tag{8.5}$$

Although it is mathematically incorrect, for practical purposes it is common to establish the safety stock as a separate issue to calculating the order quantity.

It is worth bearing in mind that in practice the annual demand is a *forecast* of demand. It is assumed that when demand figures are referred to or used they have been obtained by appropriate forecasting techniques.

Summary of Order Quantity Formulae

Many formulae have been developed for specific inventory applications[18]. A brief survey of the main types together with examples is given here.

The simplest inventory formulae is the classical 'economic order quantity', or EOQ relationship. This formula assumes, as do most others, a uniform rate of demand, also that all the order quantity is taken into stock at the same time.

$$Q = \sqrt{\left(\frac{2cd}{ip} \right)} \qquad\qquad (8.6)$$

where,

Q = economic order quantity
c = administrative cost per order
d = annual demand
i = interest on capital (per cent)
p = cost or value per item

For example, a central supply depot issues 10 000 replacement belts in a year. Each belt costs 15p. The cost of placing and order is 75p and the interest on capital invested in stock is 10 per cent. What is the economic order quantity?

Here, $c = 75$, $d = 10\ 000$, $i = 10/100$, $p = 15$

Therefore,

$$Q = \sqrt{\left(\frac{2 \times 75 \times 10\ 000}{0.1 \times 15} \right)}$$

$$= \sqrt{(1\ 000\ 000)}$$

$$= 1\ 000$$

Equation 8.6 is often used in deciding the purchase quantities of raw materials, etc. When it is required to calculate an economic batch quantity, EBQ, a further factor has to be considered—the rate of production.

$$Q = \sqrt{\left\{ \frac{2cd}{ip \left(1 - \frac{d}{r} \right)} \right\}} \qquad\qquad (8.7)$$

where,

r = rate of production, (in same units as d)

This formula might be applied to the following situation. Finished armatures can be produced at the rate of sixty per week. The final assembly programme requires an average output of twenty per week. Each armature is valued at £30. To set up production of finished armatures costs £10. If the interest on capital is ½ per cent per week, what is the economic batch quantity?

In this case,

$$c = 10 \quad d = 20 \quad i = 0.005 \quad p = 30 \quad r = 60$$

Therefore,

$$Q = \sqrt{\left\{\frac{2 \times 10 \times 20}{0.005 \times 30\left(1 - \frac{20}{60}\right)}\right\}}$$

$$= \sqrt{\frac{2 \times 10 \times 20}{0.005 \times 30 \times 2/3}}$$

$$= \sqrt{(4\,000)}$$

$$= 63 \text{ approximately}$$

A convenient batch quantity, near this figure, might be 60.

This formula is likely to cause problems if there are many batches of different products requiring the same facilities. It is necessary to ensure that a batch will last while all the other batches of different products are produced. This is unlikely if each batch quantity is calculated independently. In addition the cost of setting up (part of c) may depend upon the nature of the previous set-up. For these reasons it is best to consider making one batch of each product form a basic production cycle. The problem then is one of calculating the economic production cycle. The formula for this is,

$$n = \sqrt{\left\{\frac{i\Sigma p_j d_j\left(1 - \frac{d_j}{r_j}\right)}{2\Sigma c_j}\right\}} \tag{8.8}$$

where, n = number of production cycles per unit period, and suffix j means the jth product in the cycle.

The above formula assumes each product will be made each cycle. The analysis required when a product is sometimes left out of a cycle is beyond the scope of this résumé but is covered in reference 3.

If the armature production problem involved, say, three types of armatures, then eqn. 8.8 would be applicable. Suppose a summary of the details for types A, B and C armatures is as given here:

Type	A	B	C
set-up cost	£10	£8	£9
demand per week	20	20	40
interest per week	½ per cent	½ per cent	½ per cent
unit cost	£30	£20	£45
rate of production per week	60	40	60

Then

$$n = \sqrt{\left\{ \frac{0.005 \left[30 \times 20\left(1 - \frac{20}{60}\right) + 20 \times 20\left(1 - \frac{20}{40}\right) + 45 \times 40\left(1 - \frac{40}{60}\right)\right]}{2[10 + 8 + 9]} \right\}}$$

$$= \sqrt{\frac{6}{54}}$$

$$= \sqrt{\frac{1}{9}}$$

$$= \frac{1}{3}$$

That is, if the number of production cycles per week is one third, the production cycle is three weeks.

Therefore three weeks supply of A, B and C should be produced, namely batches of 60, 60 and 120 respectively.

In some situations it is necessary to make a decision about the best stock level with no opportunity for re-ordering etc. Such 'once off' stock decisions might occur with highly seasonal goods, fashionable goods, spare stocks holdings, or in the initial stages of a new stock item.

Analysis has shown that an initial stock level can be set by following the principle that if the expected profit exceeds the expected loss then the stock should be increased. It can be shown that following the above principle requires that the stock level should be set so that,

$$\text{the probability of selling the entire stock} = \frac{\text{unit loss}}{\text{unit profit} + \text{unit loss}}$$

(8.9)

For example: a bakery sells cake by the pound (lb). It makes a profit of 35p a pound on every pound sold on the day it is baked. It disposes of all cakes not sold on the date baked at a loss of 5p a pound. If there is an equal chance of selling any quantity between 2 000 to 3 000 lb per day, determine the optimal amount to bake.

$$\text{The probability of selling entire stock should be set} = \frac{5}{35 + 5}$$

$$= 0.125$$

The probability distribution for this situation is shown in figure 8.12. From this distribution it can be established that a stock of 2 875 lb meets the criterion of equation 8.9.

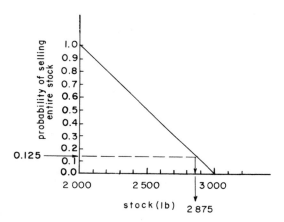

Figure 8.12   Probability of selling entire stock

Safety Stocks

The order quantities used in an inventory system are based upon the average demand. To meet unusually high demand, a buffer or safety stock is carried. The safety stock is therefore based on an analysis of the likely variation in demand. The simplest approach considers the variation of demand within a constant lead time. As in other random variation situations the most likely type of variation is a Poisson distribution, which for convenience is usually assumed to be normal, thus allowing the use of normal distribution tables. It will be assumed in these notes that the demand variations 'fit' a normal curve.

Using standard statistical methods, the standard deviation of the demand can be calculated for the lead time period. The probability of any particular demand can then be read from normal tables such that,

$$z = \frac{u - M}{S} \tag{8.10}$$

188

where,

z = standardised units from mean
u = actual demand
M = mean demand
S = standard deviation

Thus a safety stock giving only a 2 per cent chance of a shortage must cover 98 per cent of the likely demand. Referring to tables (appendix 18), 98 per cent of a standardised normal distribution is covered at 2.05 standard deviations. If the standard deviation of demand is say, 8 tons and the average demand is 20 tons, then from equation 8.10

z = 2.05
M = 20
S = 8

therefore,

$$2.05 = \frac{u - 20}{8}$$

i.e. $u - 20 = 16.4$ tons = safety stock
and $u \quad = 36.4$ tons = re-order point

It is important to realise that the value of M is the mean demand for the period of the lead time. These relationships are illustrated in figure 8.13.

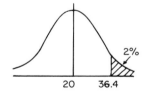
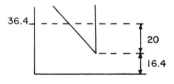

Figure 8.13   Relationship between mean, standard deviation and ROL

Often it is not convenient to calculate the mean demand and standard deviation for the lead time period. It may be more convenient to say analyse the daily variation in demand while the lead time may be, say, ten days. It is therefore necessary to convert the demand parameters to a different time period. This can be done as follows,

$$m \quad = dL \qquad\qquad (8.11)$$
$$S_L^2 = LS_d^2 \qquad\qquad (8.12)$$

189

where,

m = mean demand during lead time,
d = demand per unit time,
L = lead time,
S_L = standard deviation of demand during lead time,
S_d = standard deviation of demand per unit time.

Thus in the previous example if the average demand was 20 tons per week, the safety stock calculated (16.4 tons) and the re-order point (36.4 tons) are based upon a one week lead time. If instead the lead time was four weeks then, from equation 8.11, the average demand over four weeks = 20 x 4 = 80 tons, and from equation 8.12, standard deviation over four weeks = $\sqrt{4}$ (8) = 16 tons. Therefore safety stock for four weeks = 2.05 x 16 = 32.8 tons, and re-order level = 80 + 32.8 = 112.8 tons.

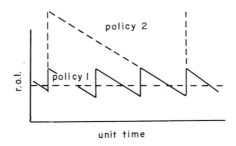

Figure 8.14   Relationship between risk of stockout and order quantity

Although safety stocks are set independently of the order quantity, the risk level used must be based on the number of orders per year. This is because the risk associated for a certain level of safety stock is only incurred when the re-order point is passed. Hence the smaller the order quantity the more frequent this risk is undertaken.

Referring to figure 8.14, a 2 per cent risk of a stockout in policy 1 is taken three times as frequently as in policy 2. Thus the safety stock offering a 2 per cent risk for policy 2 becomes a 3 x 2 = 6 per cent risk for policy 1.

A PROGRAM THAT SIMULATES ALTERNATIVE INVENTORY POLICIES (STAN)

This program (appendix 13) simulates a range of inventory policies for each combination of order levels from five to sixty, in steps of five with order quantities from five to one hundred, in steps of five. For each combination the average stock level and service level is calculated and printed. In this program any shortages encountered are not subsequently made good. The program is not intended to be a general purpose one; in the context of the data used it could be calculated that at any one time there would not be more than three orders outstanding, and therefore in writing the program an array for lead times was fixed at three.

After the initialisation stage of the program, the two main loops are set up with the re-order level loop within the order quantity loop. Within each run of 200 periods there is a certain amount of data to be initialised, namely, the total demand and total service are set to zero, the net stock situation is started at eighty units, and it is assumed no orders are outstanding, thus the provisioned stock level is also set at eighty units and the lead times are set at three ready for a countdown to zero when an order is placed. First test in the simulation is to see whether the lead time is down to zero, if it is, this means a quantity has now been delivered and thus the net stock situation is increased by the order quantity, as determined by the loop. The lead time is then reset to three ready for subsequent use as necessary. The next part of the program samples from a demand pattern that is read in as data. The demand is withdrawn from the net stock if possible, if the demand exceeds the net stock, the net stock is withdrawn bringing the net down to zero, the provisioned stock level is reduced by the net amount withdrawn. The cumulative effect of this sample demand is then reflected in the total demand, the total supplied and the total issued. In the light of the revised stock levels, the provisioned stock level is tested to see whether it is now below the re-order level. If it is below, then a lead time is reduced by 1, and the appropriate order quantity is added to the provisioned stock level. In any case, all the lead times are examined and those that are less that three imply outstanding orders, they therefore have their time reduced by one prior to the next pass through the program. At the end of 200 passes through the program, for a particular combination of order quantity and re-order level, results are printed out. The percentage service is calculated as the proportion of stock issued compared to the total demanded, while the average stock is calculated from the cumulative stock divided by 200.

An example of the output obtained has been shown in figure 4.11. From an analysis of all the output, it was possible to choose the lowest average stock policy for a given level of service (table 8.2). Thus a graph of service level against average stock could be drawn which reflected an amalgam of different combinations of ordering and re-order level quantities. These results are shown in figure 8.15. It is particularly interesting to note from this result that the best policies are not solely based upon the best re-order level, but

Table 8.2   The lowest average stock for a given service level

Service	Average stock	O.Q.	R.O.L.
100	29.2	20	60
99	18.6	20	50
98	15.3	15	55
95	10.7	15	45
93	7.8	15	40
87	6.3	15	35
80	4.9	15	30
70	2.5	10	55
61	2.1	10	20
44	1.7	10	10

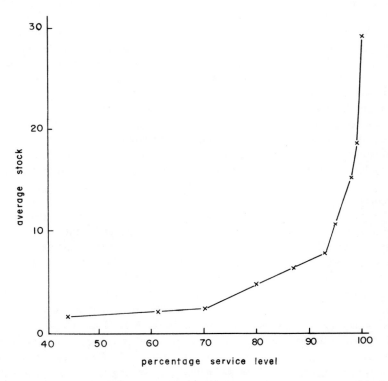

Figure 8.15   Graph of average stock against percentage service level

that the order quantity is a factor in these results. This demonstrates that it is dangerous to establish an order quantity upon the basis of an economic order quantity formula without regard to its effect on the average level of stockholding and the service. For example, the results showed that if an order quantity of forty had to be used (because it was the 'EOQ', say) then, in order to achieve a 98 per cent level of service, a re-order level of forty five would be needed, and under these conditions the average stockholding would be 24.43. This should be compared to the average stock of 15.3 which is capable of giving the desired degree of service, i.e. 98 per cent with the combination of fifteen for order quantity and fifty five for re-order level.

Chapter 9

Simulation of Other Systems

Previous chapters have concentrated on the two most common areas of simulation, that is queueing and inventory control. This chapter will illustrate other possible applications by reference to example programs in the fields of maintenance (ELEM), production scheduling (LOAD), production capacity (CAPF), and profitability analysis (PRAS and PRAC).

THE SIMULATION OF ALTERNATIVE MAINTENANCE POLICIES (ELEM)

The program (appendix 3) developed to illustrate a possible use of simulation in the maintenance function is a development of the combined units situation described earlier in chapter 2. The program (ELEM) has also been used to illustrate the use of subroutines in chapter 5. A brief description of the situation to be simulated is as follows. A company making flow meters uses a baking oven for the hardening of the enamel cases. The oven contains six elements, three down each side, which are subject to failure. The established time to repair one element is three days, to replace three elements down one side four days, and to replace all six elements, six days. An element costs £50 and the cost of having the oven inoperative is £200 per day. Data have been collected on the life of elements and are shown in the form of a frequency distribution in table 9.1. Management wish to ascertain whether it is cheaper to replace a single element as and when it fails (policy A), to replace an element along one side whenever one fails (policy B), or to replace all the elements whenever any one fails (policy C).

This is a simple example of trying to determine the most economic maintenance policy where policy A represents breakdown maintenance, while policies B and C represent a mixture of breakdown and preventive maintenance. Other policies could be suggested for the above situation and, provided they can be expressed in quantitative terms, these other policies could also be simulated and the economic cost ascertained. For instance, one policy which has not been mentioned but which may be used in practice

194

Table 9.1   Frequency distribution of element life

Element life (days)	Frequency
25	7
35	21
45	12
55	20
65	24
75	11
85	3
95	1

would be to replace all elements that are still functioning after they have reached a certain life. Another situation that may present itself is that a superior type element becomes available, at a higher cost. The best policy for the superior type element can then be ascertained by simulation, and it will not necessarily be the same policy as for the cheaper element. For instance, it may be best to replace all the cheap elements whenever any one fails, i.e. policy C, but with a dearer element it may prove more economic to use policy A, that is replace elements as and when they fail individually. Thus there are many possible permutations and situations which could require to be simulated all based upon this basic example. The three policies illustrated here are meant therefore only to be typical policies that may be examined and are not meant to be exhaustive. Because further policies may be needed to be simulated in the future, this program (ELEM) has been written with each maintenance policy as a subroutine.

Policy A does not require simulation at all for replacement theory can be used to calculate the expected costs of this policy given a frequency distribution of element life. By reference to the frequency distribution of element life as given in table 9.1 the mean life can be calculated as follows.

$$\text{mean life} = \frac{\Sigma fx}{n},$$

where
x = element life
f = frequency of that life
n = total frequency

i.e. mean life $= \dfrac{(7 \times 25) + (21 \times 35) + (12 \times 45) + \ldots}{7 + 21 + 12 + \ldots}$

$= \dfrac{5\,295}{99} = 53.4$ days.

Renewal theory tells us that the average time between failures will settle down to be the mean life divided by the total number of units in the system, in this case six, thus the mean time between failures, = 53.4/6 = 8.9 days, the cost of a failure is £650 for policy A, made up of £50 for the element and three days at £200 per day in operative time. Thus the cost of policy A per productive day is

$$\frac{50 + (3 \times 200)}{8.9} = £73 \text{ per day}$$

It should be noted that the cost of the policies should be calculated over the productive time as this is the time during which the costs need to be recovered rather than the total elapsed time. The total elapsed time contains days when the oven is not working and these days in themselves are being costed out at £200 per day. This raises a further aspect of these types of problem, that is, is the objective to find the policy that minimises the cost per day; this might result in a lot of down time. An alternative measure might be the proportion of production time to down time, that is, the policy which gives the most productive time over a given elapsed time period. The correct criteria to use in the valuation of alternative maintenance strategies are only just being examined analytically as operational research techniques are being brought to bear into this area. There are many proposed measures of maintenance efficiency to be found in the literature. For a discussion of this aspect of maintenance see reference 15.

The Output
Program (ELEM) calculates the cost per productive day the implication being that management will choose the policy giving the least cost. The output obtained from ELEM is illustrated in figure 9.1. For each policy the basic cost and overhaul periods are printed out and then as each element fails and a replacement is carried out, the cumulative run time to date, the mean time between failure and the average cost per day is printed out. The program terminates when 200 replacements have been made. Note replacements means 1, 2 or 3 elements according to the policy being simulated. By printing out the cumulative results at the end of each replacement it is possible to see the inherent fluctuations in these figures and to assess to what extent they have settled down by the end of the simulated period. It might be that in the light of the fluctuations that still exist at the end of the simulation that management would require a longer run to be made. The final situation with respect to the three policies simulated are summarised in table 9.2. From this it can be seen that policy A is much dearer than B and C. Due to the cost per day of policies B and C being so close, it may be that a final choice would

SIMULATION OF MAINTENANCE POLICIES FOR STOVING OVEN

POLICY B : REPLACE ALL 3 ELEMENTS DOWN ONE SIDE

TIME REQUIRED = 4 DAYS

COST OF ELEMENTS = £ 50   EACH

COST OF DOWNTIME = £ 200   PER DAY

REPLACEMENT NO.	CUM.RUN.TIME	M.T.B.F.	AV.COST/DAY
1	35	35.00	27.14
2	45	22.50	42.22
3	70	23.33	40.71
4	90	22.50	42.22
5	125	25.00	38.00
6	145	24.17	39.31
7	170	24.29	39.12
8	170	21.25	44.71
....	....	....	....
191	3720	19.48	48.78
192	3740	19.48	48.77
193	3755	19.46	48.83
194	3795	19.56	48.56
195	3830	19.64	48.37
196	3830	19.54	48.62
197	3865	19.62	48.42
198	3865	19.52	48.67
199	3890	19.55	48.60
200	3900	19.50	48.72

Figure 9.1   Typical output from ELEM

197

rest upon other aspects of the simulation. For instance, although the costs are similar the mean time between failure is very different. The mean time

Table 9.2   Summary of results from ELEM

Policy	Mean time between failure (days)	Cost per day £
A	9.18	70.84
B	19.5	48.72
C	33.85	44.31

between failure for policy C is almost double that of policy B. On this score it might be felt that policy C is superior for it would give much longer uninterrupted production runs. In practice therefore the decision that might be made in the light of these results is that policy C should be implemented as being the cheapest policy and the one giving the longest mean time between failure, but because there is little additional cost with policy B this may be resorted to on occasions when it is required to get the oven back into operation as quickly as possible. Only under exceptional circumstances would policy A be followed.

PRODUCTION CONTROL

Production control is an area that in the past has been mainly approached from a commercial programming point of view. Recently this area is being subjected to examination by the developing analytical techniques of management science. The basic problem in this area is that a production control system exists to control the day-to-day running of a factory and as such is largely a commercial application involving purchasing orders, works orders, job tickets, material requisitions etc. A production control system however is concerned with figures, dates, times, durations, deliveries, etc. and as such is amenable to analytical techniques. Thus within the function of production control can be found many applications for the operational research techniques such as queueing theory, linear programming, inventory control, routeing, and of course simulation. The problem in using these techniques in a meaningful way is how to incorporate the application of the techniques into a routine type commercial program. This is necessary as the basic data in a production control system can often change quite rapidly, necessitating a resolving of the problem weekly or even daily. Because of these difficulties, in practice, many firms ignore the scope to apply operational research techniques in this area and treat production control as a purely commercial system. However, operational research techniques can be usefully applied first of all in the general planning aspects of a production control system, that is in assessing the ideal capacity necessary to match a given load or order book economically. Having solved this type of problem and implemented the solution, the situation is lived with for, say, a year until changes in plant facilities are about to be made again. Another aspect that can be examined in general is to ascertain bench marks or guide lines that can be used in the day-to-day running of a production control system, their use day-to-day will not result in optimal solutions but on the other hand they will not be far off optimum. Probably the most basic issue to be resolved in production control is the effective matching of load against capacity. If the load exactly matches the capacity then the slightest trouble will cause delays and throw the whole carefully matched programme out. If the capacity exceeds the load then plant utilisation is likely to be low but on the other hand there is less likelihood of delays to work in process and therefore work in progress is likely to be lower thereby giving a quicker turnover of working capital. Any mismatch between load and capacity may be resolved by the firm holding finished good stock, if this is feasible, or by quoting varying delivery dates. Two problems are examined here with reference to the programs LOAD and CAPF. The program LOAD simulates work going through some facilities and compiles a histogram of how late they are. Examination of a system in this way enables a realistic throughput time to be attached to work, as opposed to the 'theoretical' throughput time. The other program CAPF examines the effect of changing the capacity given a fixed pattern of orders or load. By simulating various plant capacities it is possible to ascertain the best balance that takes into account the cost of having plant idle and on the other hand delaying work and thereby holding it in stock.

Simulation of Work Load (LOAD)

The program LOAD (appendix 5) has been written to simulate the following situation. It is required to simulate the loading of the assembly section in a factory that refurbishes vending machines. Refurbishing requires a quick turnround so that a minimum number of machines are out of commission. There are four models that come in for refurbishing, the daily intake following a Poisson distribution with the following means:

model A has a mean of 1.0
model B has a mean of 2.0
model C has a mean of 1.25
model D has a mean of 2.25.

Management are interested in establishing the probability of exceeding the schedule, i.e. planned throughput time, due to occasional overloads. The results are required in the form of a 'lateness distribution'.

Work coming in on any particular day is batched. That is, the total number of each model constitutes the batch size. If some of each model comes in there will be a maximum of four batches of work to be processed. The batches of work are given a priority based upon consideration of the customers involved. In the simulation the batches will be put in a random sequence to represent this step. Beyond this the work is processed in the date order received. All work being processed requires two days (i.e. 16 hours) to be stripped, cleaned, resprayed and inspected regardless of the batch size. Thereafter the assembly time per unit is as follows:

Model A 10 man hours, B 8 man hours, C 12 man hours, D 5 man hours.

Owing to limitations of space and accessibility, only one man can work on one unit at a time. There are eight assemblers employed in the factory. The factory works an eight hour day, five days a week.

The Input and Output The inputs to the program LOAD are the length of the required simulation and the number of assemblers constituting the capacity of the assembly department. In this case the generation of a random pattern of arrival of the four models is done within the program by means of a Poisson subroutine having preset means. The output obtained from the program is a histogram giving the frequency and cumulative percentage of work that exceeds the planned throughput time, this is shown in figure 9.2. From the results given in figure 9.2 it can be seen that only 58 per cent of the work will go through without any delay and that work can be delayed up to 14 hours. Furthermore, if one wishes to be 99 per cent certain when quoting the throughput time, then from the table an excess of 10 hours should be added on to the 'theoretical' throughput time.

This type of analysis could be carried out for a series of stages in a production process, thereby allowing a more realistic scheduling of work that takes into account the nature of the queues and delays at each stage. Failing this type of analysis, some firms use an efficiency factor of say 70 per cent and scale up the theoretical throughput times suitably, others quite simply allow one operation per week regardless of the actual duration of the operation on a machine. More sophisticated systems break the delay time down into components such as handling time, queueing time, etc. and have variable factors which can be added together to give the total excess time over the theoretical. With a simulation model such as the one shown here, it is

FREQUENCY DISTRIBUTION OF HRS IN EXCESS
OF BASIC PROCESSING TIMES

EXCESS HRS	FREQ	CUM%
0	932	58.47
1	84	63.74
2	179	74.97
3	36	77.23
4	141	86.07
5	61	86.90
6	42	92.53
7	22	93.91
8	62	97.80
9	14	98.68
10	12	99.44
11	4	99.69
12	3	99.87
13	1	99.94
14	1	100.00
15	0	100.00
16	0	100.00
17	0	100.00
18	0	100.00
19	0	100.00
20	0	100.00

Figure 9.2   Typical results from LOAD

possible to simulate the effect of increasing the capacity, i.e. here the number of assemblers on the throughput time.

General Description of LOAD A general listing of the program LOAD is given in appendix 5. The program down to line 54 is initialising various arrays and variables such that the four means of the Poisson distributions are set and the assembly time for the four models is set, the histogram is 'zeroised', as is also the forward load on the men. In line 54 a variable IOUT is set to equal 55. This variable is compared subsequently in the program to the day count and allows the first 55 days of the simulation to be ignored. The reason for this is to allow the model to build up a realistic backlog of work and delay pattern before a count is made of delays for purposes of output. Although this step has not been carried out in previous programs described, it is important in practice to determine to what extent the early results of the simulation should be ignored while the model is settling in. Lines 59, 60 and 61 write headings for 'diagnostic' output during the simulation run.

'Diagnostic' output has been left in this program to illustrate the type of information that could prove useful in monitoring the course of the simulation run. In this case the day being simulated is printed out followed by the quantities of each model followed by the priority sequence. Further 'diagnostics' are printed out at line 137. They consist of the time 'now' plus 16 hours which is printed as a cumulative time from the start in hours, the earliest time that a man is forward loaded expressed as hours from the start, the number of the man, his new forward load, the number of the model he is servicing, and finally the number of hours late. A sample of this diagnostic is shown in figure 9.3. The first line of the diagnostics in the figure shows that it is day 228 of the simulation. The quantity of models A, B, C, D, that have arrived are 1, 0, 0, 2, respectively and the sequence of priorities is 1, 3, 2, 4, i.e. models A, C, B, D. Thus in day 228 there is 1 model A to be processed and 2 model D to be processed in that order.

The 'diagnostics' printed out at line 137 in the listing go on to show that these units will reach the assembly department by the end of the next day, i.e. 1832 hours from the start of the simulation. The first assembler to be free will be free at 1833 hours; this assembler is assembler number six and in dealing with the first job, namely model A, he will now be forward loaded until 1833 plus 10, i.e. 1843 hours. The model he has been loaded with is then printed as being model 1, i.e. A, and the final column shows that this particular unit was delayed one hour in the system thereby taking eleven hours to go through the assembly section instead of the planned ten hours. The next line goes on to give similar details of the next model to be processed, the first man becomes available at 1834 hours (assembler number eight). In taking the first of model D he will now be forward loaded until 1839 hours, and this particular unit of model D (or 4) will take an extra two hours to pass through the assembly section. Finally, the third unit to be dealt with will be seen by assembler number one who becomes available at 1836 hours; he will take this model and therefore be forward loaded until 1841 hours thereby causing the unit to be four hours in excess of the planned time of five hours for model D. The histogram that is finally outputted is therefore a consolidation of the figures in the final column of this part of the diagnostics, i.e. the three units that came in on day 228 took one, two and four hours in excess of their planned throughput time.

IDAY	IQ(1)	IQ(2)	IQ(3)	IQ(4)	N(1)	N(2)	N(3)	N(4)
228	1	0	0	2	1	3	2	4
	1832	1833	6	1843	1	1		
	1832	1834	8	1839	4	2		
	1832	1836	1	1841	4	4		
IDAY	IQ(1)	IQ(2)	IQ(3)	IQ(4)	N(1)	N(2)	N(3)	N(4)
229	3	3	3	0	2	1	3	4

Figure 9.3   Some lines of diagnostics from LOAD

A further aspect to note in this particular problem is the use of a uniform distribution to generate the priority sequence. This starts at line 75 in the listing where a subroutine that samples from a uniform distribution, in this case over the range 1–4, is called. The first number sampled, after being converted to an integer, represents model A, B, C or D, where 1 represents A, 2 represents B, 3 represents C, and 4 represents D. Another random number is generated from the uniform subroutine and converted to an integer. If this gives an integer that has already been picked, the number is discarded and a further number chosen until a second and different number has been sampled. After sampling three numbers along the above lines, the fourth number or model is known by implication. The sum of the numbers 1, 2, 3, 4, is 10, therefore having successfully found the first three numbers for the priority sequence by taking these numbers away from 10, the remainder gives the value of the fourth and last priority. This is done in line 86 on the listing. For example, if the first integer sampled is 1 and then the next different integer sampled is 3 followed by yet a third different integer as 2, then by taking away the sum of 1 + 3 + 2, i.e. 6, from 10 we obtain the answer 4 as being the number yet to be established. The final sequence 1, 3, 2, 4, being interpreted as models: A, C, B and D as already explained above.

Discussion of Results A further refinement of the output would be to output separate histograms of excess hours for each type of model. It can be

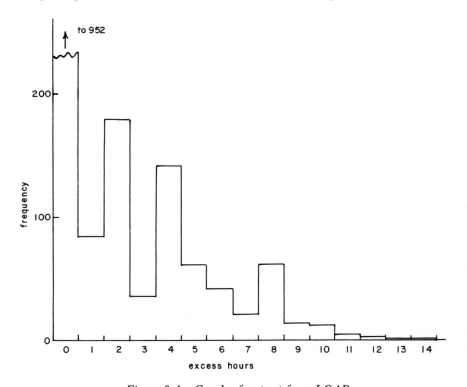

Figure 9.4   Graph of output from LOAD

seen from the results presented in figure 9.4 that the frequency distribution contained peaks at 2 hours, 4 hours, and 8 hours. These peaks may be due to particular models. Only further analysis can determine to what extent it would pay to treat the different models separately. In practice, there are likely to be many more than four models being processed and therefore, although theoretically it would be desirable to analyse these separately and have separate lateness distributions, in practice, it may be justifiable to lump them altogether to speed up the application of this concept. The principle of the 'vital few and the trivial many' should always be borne in mind when investigating production control type situations. This consideration is known as the 80:20 rule or alternatively the Pareto law. It is often quoted with respect to stock control applications and is illustrated in figure 9.5 where 20 per cent of the range of items in stock account for 80 per cent say, of the capital tied up. This shaped curve is often obtained in all sorts of situations. Depending upon the application, the designation of the axis changes but the

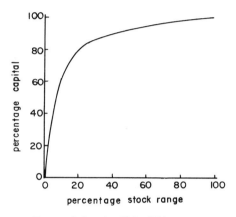

Figure 9.5   An '80 : 20' curve

basic shape remains. For instance, the axis of figure 9.5 may be amended to show that 20 per cent of the parts in a design account for 80 per cent of the cost, or that 20 per cent of the orders loaded on to the factory account for 80 per cent of the imposed load. Thus it may be that in a situation where a large number of products are being processed, a detailed simulation of the few product lines that account for the bulk of the factory load will be quite adequate to bring about a drastic improvement in the situation.

Simulation of Alternative Plant Capacities (CAPF)
A further simulation in the field of production control is illustrated by the program CAPF, appendix 1. This program has been written to simulate work being processed by a factory of known plant capacity where the cost of having a machine idle is £5 per hour and the cost of delaying the work is £1 per machine hour per day. This cost can be taken as a stockholding cost combined with any penalty costs associated with delayed work. There is an equal chance that 1, 2, 3, . . . 10 orders are received per day, and there are

240 working days in a year. A frequency table of the machine hours per order is given in table 9.3. The objective of the simulation is to find the production capacity where the combined cost of machine idle time and the penalty for waiting orders will be at a minimum.

Table 9.3   Frequency distribution of machine hours per order

Machine hours per order	Order frequency
0 – 5	79
5.01 – 10	53
10.01 – 15	132
15.01 – 20	159
20.01 – 25	185
25.01 – 30	185
30.01 – 35	185
35.01 – 40	132
40.01 – 45	79
45.01 – 50	79
50.01 – 55	26
55.01 – 60	26

A plot of the machine hours per order on arithmetic probability paper shows that the frequency distribution given in table 9.3 is normally distributed with a mean of 24 and a standard deviation of 15, see figure 9.6. This means that the machine hours per order can be generated from a standard normal subroutine as described in chapter 4. The number of orders received per day can be generated from a rectangular, or uniform distribution again as described in chapter 4, the parameters being a range of 10 with increments of one.

The program (CAPF) has therefore been written without any input data, the generation of orders and associated machine hours is carried out by means of standard subroutines having prescribed parameters. The length of the simulated run was also set within the program to 240 days. In other circumstances, the parameters for the normal frequency distribution and the uniform distribution may be read in at run time, also the length of the simulation may be read in as required.

Estimating Results   The output from this program is a table of total costs against various plant capacities. From this, a graph can be drawn to determine the precise optimum plant capacity and also to ascertain how sensitive the

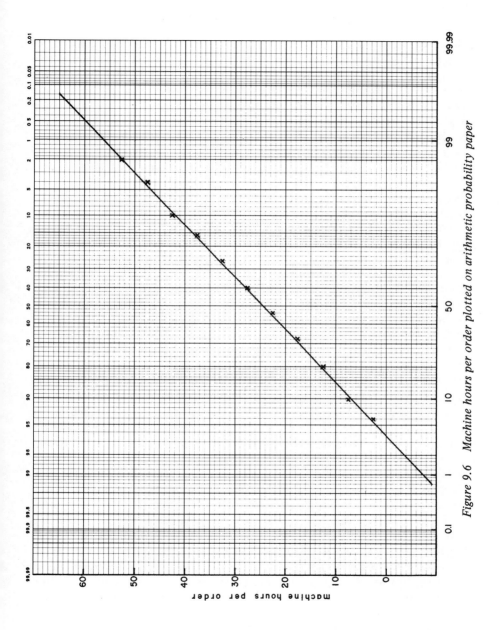

Figure 9.6   Machine hours per order plotted on arithmetic probability paper

costs are to a change in plant capacity. In writing the program, it was necessary to estimate the ideal plant capacity to ensure that the plant capacity simulated was read either side of the optimum. This was approximated by simply taking the mean machine hours per order as twenty four hours and multiplying by the mean number of orders per day, i.e. 5.5. This gives a mean load of 132 machine hours per day. If this is correct, then the ideal plant capacity is 132 machine hours, and therefore plant capacities over the range 120 to 150 machine hours were simulated. It was decided to use this program to demonstrate how a program could be made to change its incremental steps as it approached the optimum thereby giving greater detail on output around the optimum value. The general listing of CAPF is given in appendix 1.

Description of Variable Incrementing At line 82 a test is made to determine whether 240 days have been simulated, if not the program returns to line 38, but if 240 days have been simulated then in line 83 the total cost is divided by the number of days simulated to give the cost per day. Line 84 prints the plant capacity and cost per day for this particular capacity level. The next sequence of statements determine the increment to be made to the existing plant capacity. Line 86 tests the results of taking the exiting total cost away from the previous total cost and dividing by the plant capacity increment being used. While the total cost is falling, the result of this test will always be positive. However, as soon as the optimum point has been reached, or overshot, the latest cost will be higher than the previous cost and therefore this test will give a zero or negative result. Thus at line 86 while the result of the test is positive the simulation can proceed by incrementing the plant capacity by five machine hours; this is done in line 97 onwards providing the maximum capacity of 150 has not been exceeded. If the test in line 86 shows that the minimum has been reached or passed then the program in line 87 checks, by reference to the indicator J, that J has the initialised value of zero, If this is so, the plant capacity is reduced by 10 machine hours, thereby backtracking on the previous calculations, and the increment is changed to 1 machine hour. The indicator J is set then to 1 so that this backtracking will not occur on any subsequent passes through the program.

To summarise so far, the plant capacity is initialised at 120 machine hours and 240 days are simulated. The plant capacity is then increased by five machine hours and another 240 days simulated. Further simulations are made in steps of five machine hours until the program finds that the minimum cost has been reached or passed. At this point, the program reverts to a plant capacity that is ten machine hours smaller than the present capacity and reapproaches the minimum in increments of one machine hour. The next section of the program, starting at line 91, is concerned with testing to terminate the increments of one and revert to increments of five. This is done by testing in line 91 whether the latest cost is greater than the previous cost. This test will give a positive result once the minimum point has been passed, in this case, the program then goes into a count down routine to simulate four more plant capacities in increments of one. This is done by successively reducing the index I by one, once the minimum has been passed (see line 93). As the indicator I was set to 4 in line 20 of the listing, the value of I will become zero after four further runs as required. When this happens, the test in line 92 will transfer the program to line 95 where the incremental value of the plant capacity is reset to five machine hours. Line 96 reduces the value of I by a further one so that on the next pass through the program I will be negative. On this occasion, the test of I in line 92 will cause the program to jump to line 97 without amending the incremental value which will remain therefore at five.

Output from CAPF The results obtained from CAPF are shown in figure 9.7 and clearly illustrate the action of the program in following the statements described above. The first output is for a capacity of 120 and gives a cost of 349. The simulation continues by incrementing the capacity in steps of five machine hours up to a capacity of 140. At this point, the cost associated with a capacity of 140 indicates the minimum cost has been passed, the program therefore reduces the plant capacity by ten units i.e. to 130, and then commences to simulate further capacities in increments of one. The next simulated capacity is therefore 131. Simulation continues in increments of one until the cost figures indicate that the minimum has been passed. This occurs in the results given in figure 9.7 at a capacity of 138. At this stage in the program, the indicator I will be reduced by one thereby allowing the simulation to continue in increments of one for three more runs. Thus when the capacity of 141 is reached the value of I in the program has become zero and the incremental steps revert to five. This means the next simulated capacity is for 146 and the program continues until a capacity of 150 is reached or exceeded. In this case, the program terminates at a capacity of 151. These results are presented graphically in figure 9.8 where it can be seen that greater detail is obtained automatically around the region of the minimum value.

In this case the program was kept simple by having fixed incremental values of five or one. There is no reason why the program could not be elaborated to choose an incremental value that is a function of the slope of the line. It would be equally easy to write a program that outputs only the optimum value and no other, however this is less useful to management. A graph such as the one shown in figure 9.8 indicates not only the optimum but

CAPACITY	TOTAL COST
120	349
125	270
130	200
135	177
140	179
131	187
132	182
133	179
134	177
135	177
136	177
137	177
138	178
139	178
140	179
141	180
146	189
151	205

Figure 9.7   Typical output from CAPF

also how important it is to aim for the optimum. In this case, the minimum is flat over the range 134 to 137 and furthermore the rate of increase is less as excess capacity is permitted. It is not intended to suggest by this example that the capacity, in practice should be known to within one machine hour. This small increment was chosen only to illustrate the technique of variable incrementing.

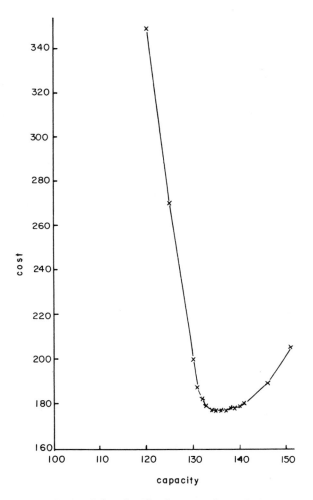

Figure 9.8   Graph of output from CAPF

PROFITABILITY ANALYSIS

Profitability analysis is an area where some packages, e.g. ICL Prop Users Guide[24] make use of simulation techniques. Two programs are presented here to assess the profitability of a proposed project, one PRAS simulates a profitability profile while the other PRAC calculates the profile exactly. It

211

will be seen from the program listings contained in appendices 8 and 9 that there is little to choose between the two methods on the grounds of programming effort. On the grounds of accuracy, the simulation method is obviously not as accurate as the precise method, while on the grounds of run time there is little to choose between either program. Both programs have been written in BASIC for use on a terminal (see chapter 5) and in obtaining the results presented in this book the terminal time for either program was substantially the same. The background to the programs is as follows.

The factors considered in the assessing of the possible profitability of a proposed project have been classified under three cost categories, namely, labour, overheads and income. Owing to the uncertainty and assumptions inherent in forward planning, the discounted cash flows cannot be stated with certainty. For each cost category, a set of cash flows have been calculated together with an associated probability of achievement. A summary of the complete data is given in table 9.4. The net profitability of any combination of outcomes will be given by,

$$\text{Profit} = \text{income} - (\text{labour} + \text{overheads})$$

Table 9.4   Summary of profitability data

Labour		Overheads		Income	
Cash flow	Probability	Cash flow	Probability	Cash flow	Probability
30 000	0.1	14 000	0.05	40 000	0.20
32 000	0.3	16 000	0.15	45 000	0.25
34 000	0.4	18 000	0.50	55 000	0.30
36 000	0.2	20 000	0.20	60 000	0.25
		22 000	0.10		

Assuming that cash flow outcomes for each cost category are equally likely, the total number of combinations and therefore possible profits is 80 (from 4 x 5 x 4). However, the cash flows are not equally likely, and therefore any profitability analysis should take into account the weighting of the probabilities. The results are best presented as a frequency distribution of profitability so that management can assess the implications of its range, mode, skewness, etc.

Simulation of Net Profitability
If a simulated approach is to be adopted, then Monte Carlo methods are used to build up the profitability frequency distribution. The procedure is simply that the three cash flows are sampled *pro rata* to their probabilities to give a

simulated net profitability. The number of simulations required to build up a representative frequency distribution can be estimated by considering the lowest probabilities in each cost category, namely 0.1, 0.05, and 0.20. The associated profit (or in this case loss) is:

$$40\ 000 - (30\ 000 + 14\ 000) = -4\ 000$$

and the probability of experiencing this outcome is:

$$0.1 \times 0.05 \times 0.20 = 0.001$$

Thus, provided a simulation of at least 1 000 runs is carried out, the results should be representative of all possible outcomes.

In this example, the purely combinatorial approach requires, as has been shown, eighty possible profit combinations to be calculated. Associated with each combination, a net profitability figure has also to be calculated. The eighty pairs or results then need sorting to yield a profit probability distribution.

As these programs (PRAC) and (PRAS) were written in BASIC for running over a terminal, they have been written to take advantage of some of the facilities of a terminal. Both programs are essentially the same apart from the stage where the costs are being calculated. For this reason, the method of input and output obtained are similar. the details of PRAS will be described and then the differences in PRAC will be noted; both programs are listed in appendices 8 and 9. The input phase to PRAS has been explained in chapter 5.

The histogram details provided were number of cells required, the value of the lowest cell and the class intervals (see figure 5.12). These three items of information fully describe the proposed histogram and can be determined easily by considering, in turn, the best possible outcome (regardless of its probability), and the worst possible outcome (regardless of probability). In this case, the best outcome is a profit of £16 000 and the worst outcome is a loss of £18 000. In the light of the range of values it seems reasonable to go up in steps of £1 000. The final input request from the program occurs at line 414 where the length of the simulation is required. In the run undertaken, as already described, the length of the simulation was made 1 000 runs. The program goes on to output the data received from the user in a consolidated form to give the user an opportunity to terminate the run if any data seems amiss. A heading is printed out in line 418 and then lines 421 to 460 result in the cash flows associated frequencies, histogram details, and length of run being outputted. Line 485 to line 494 is concerned with cumulating the frequencies so that the random numbers can be allocated to the correct one. A loop is set up for the number of runs in line 520, this loop ends at line 800. Within the loop various cash flows are simulated and the net profitability

PROJECT PROFITABILITY ANALYSIS HISTOGRAM

COUNT	CUM PROBABILITY	RANGE		
0	1		TO	-30000
0	1	-29999	TO	-29000
0	1	-28999	TO	-28000
0	1	-27999	TO	-27000
0	1	-26999	TO	-26000
0	1	-25999	TO	-25000
0	1	-24999	TO	-24000
0	1	-23999	TO	-23000
0	1	-22999	TO	-22000
0	1	-21999	TO	-21000
0	1	-20999	TO	-20000
0	1	-19999	TO	-19000
1	.999	-18999	TO	-18000
0	.999	-17999	TO	-17000
9	.99	-16999	TO	-16000
0	.99	-15999	TO	-15000
33	.957	-14999	TO	-14000
1	.956	-13999	TO	-13000
72	.884	-12999	TO	-12000
11	.873	-11999	TO	-11000
49	.824	-10999	TO	-10000
50	.774	-9999	TO	-9000
36	.738	-8999	TO	-8000
107	.631	-7999	TO	-7000
3	.628	-6999	TO	-6000
117	.511	-5999	TO	-5000
0	.511	-4999	TO	-4000
62	.449	-3999	TO	-3000
0	.449	-2999	TO	-2000
22	.427	-1999	TO	-1000
0	.427	-999	TO	0
49	.378	1	TO	1000
1	.377	1001	TO	2000
115	.262	2001	TO	3000
1	.261	3001	TO	4000
91	.17	4001	TO	5000
24	.146	5001	TO	6000
56	8.99999E-02	6001	TO	7000
36	5.39999E-02	7001	TO	8000
16	.038	8001	TO	9000
22	.016	9001	TO	10000
1	.015	10001	TO	11000
12	2.99995E-03	11001	TO	12000
0	2.99995E-03	12001	TO	13000
3	-4.98258E-08	13001	TO	14000
0	-4.98258E-08	14001	TO	15000
0	-4.98258E-08	15001	TO	16000
0	-4.98258E-08	16001	TO	17000
0	-4.98258E-08	17001	TO	18000
0	-4.98258E-08	18001	TO	

DONE

Figure 9.9   Output from PRAS

assessed. On each occasion the profitability is noted in the appropriate histogram cell. Lines 801 to 910 are concerned with the output phase and a copy of the output obtained is given in figure 9.9. From this, it will be seen that for every interval in the histogram, a count is given and a cumulative probability figure printed. The cumulative probability is set at 1 initially and is reduced progressively according to the count. Thus the cumulative probability figure quoted in the output represents the probability of achieving or exceeding that particular profitability.

For example, figure 9.9 indicates that there is a 0.262 probability of achieving or exceeding a net profit of £2 001. It will be noted that this cumulative probability figure never reaches zero but for practical purposes has reached an extremely small value at the maximum end of the histogram, i.e. there is in practice no chance of reaching or exceeding £13 001. The probability figure does not reach zero but overshoots and becomes negative due to rounding errors on the part of the computer. In the cases when the output is in E format, i.e. 5.39999E-02, this is interpreted as the decimal part, 5.39999 multiplied by 10 raised to the value of the exponent, i.e. -02. This means, 5.39999×10^{-02}, i.e. 0.0539999.

The Calculation of Net Profitability
The program PRAC differs only slightly from PRAS. The input phase is identical apart from omitting the length of the simulation required. The output from PRAC is identical apart from presenting the results of simulating the probabilities as actual probabilities instead of simulated frequencies. An example of the output obtained from PRAC is given in figure 9.10. In this case, it can be seen that the cumulative probability figure does not go negative, as would be expected, but still does not quite reach zero in the last three entries due to computer rounding errors. It is probably better for management to have these results printed graphically, and an example of the output from PRAC when graphed is given in figure 9.11. The histogram shows in a marked way how erratic the probability of profit or loss is likely to be. The net effect of the cash flows is not a normal frequency distribution as might be expected, but looks slightly bimodal with a reasonable chance of making either a fair amount of profit or a fair loss but a smaller chance of breaking even. The cumulative probability curve is probably the more important measure that management would pay attention to, for this smooths out the individual fluctuations on the histogram and gives a clearer picture of the chance of breaking even (in this case 45.7 per cent).

Discussion of Output
These programs could be elaborated so that the number of cash flows became a variable determined by the user at run time, and the graph as presented in

215

```
PROJECT PROFITABILITY ANALYSIS -
PROBABILITY DISTRIBUTION
```

PROBABILITY	CUM PROBABILITY		RANGE	
0	1		TO	-30000
0	1	-29999	TO	-29000
0	1	-28999	TO	-28000
0	1	-27999	TO	-27000
0	1	-26999	TO	-26000
0	1	-25999	TO	-25000
0	1	-24999	TO	-24000
0	1	-23999	TO	-23000
0	1	-22999	TO	-22000
0	1	-21999	TO	-21000
0	1	-20999	TO	-20000
0	1	-19999	TO	-19000
.004	.996	-18999	TO	-18000
0	.996	-17999	TO	-17000
.016	.98	-16999	TO	-16000
0	.98	-15999	TO	-15000
.042	.938	-14999	TO	-14000
.005	.933	-13999	TO	-13000
.06	.873	-12999	TO	-12000
.02	.853	-11999	TO	-11000
.048	.805	-10999	TO	-10000
.0525	.7525	-9999	TO	-9000
.023	.7295	-8999	TO	-8000
.075	.6545	-7999	TO	-7000
.006	.6485	-6999	TO	-6000
.06	.5885	-5999	TO	-5000
.001	.5875	-4999	TO	-4000
.03475	.55275	-3999	TO	-3000
0	.55275	-2999	TO	-2000
.0315	.52125	-1999	TO	-1000
0	.52125	-999	TO	0
.06425	.457	1	TO	1000
.005	.452	1001	TO	2000
.09	.362	2001	TO	3000
.02	.342	3001	TO	4000
.072	.27	4001	TO	5000
.0525	.2175	5001	TO	6000
.0345	.183	6001	TO	7000
.075	.108	7001	TO	8000
.009	.099	8001	TO	9000
.06	.039	9001	TO	10000
.0015	.0375	10001	TO	11000'
.02875	8.75002E-03	11001	TO	12000
0	8.75002E-03	12001	TO	13000
.0075	1.25002E-03	13001	TO	14000
0	1.25002E-03	14001	TO	15000
.00125	1.74623E-08	15001	TO	16000
0	1.74623E-08	16001	TO	17000
0	1.74623E-08	17001	TO	18000
0	1.74623E-08	18001	TO	

```
DONE
```

Figure 9.10   Output from PRAC

figure 9.11 could be produced on the terminal with slightly more programming effort. The analytical aspects of the program should only be elaborated with caution for in this type of application management are being asked to put probability figures against cash flows, and the data by implication is not certain. It would therefore be dangerous to draw very sophisticated conclusions on the basis of original data empirically derived.

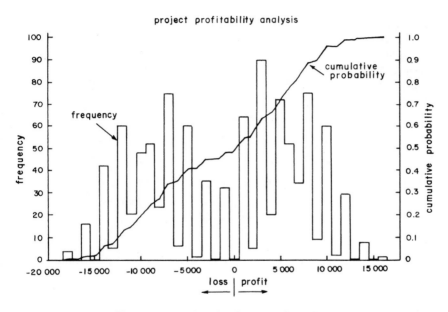

Figure 9.11   Graph of output from PRAC

Nevertheless, although this particular application uses only simple mathematics, it does enable alternative projects to be assessed in an objective manner and also compared on a common basis. Thus, in practice, management are not likely to make a decision on the grounds of a single figure arising from the analysis, but are more likely to be influenced by the shape of the histogram presented. A histogram that is erratic, for instance, will be less desirable from a management point of view than one that is compact. This is because with the former, management would be in a greater state of uncertainty, and from the point of view of control, this is a bad situation to encourage.

Although there is little to choose between the run times of PRAS and

PRAC as presented in the appendices, the run time of PRAS was considerably extended in the first version where diagnostics were included. During the simulation period of the run, approximately 5 min elapses without any response on the part of the terminal. To check that the programming is functioning correctly the first version required the program to print out the random numbers as they were chosen, together with their appropriate cash flows and then after three such pairs of numbers had been printed the net profitability figure. This would have meant something like 4 000 lines of output with the program as written for a run of 1 000 simulations. Because of this, the runs that included 'diagnostic' output were kept as short as practicable. One could ascertain after, say, ten simulations that the program was operating correctly. The first short trial runs also enable the format statements to be checked to ensure a neat layout of output.

Chapter 10

Summary and Conclusion

DEVELOPING AND USING A COMPUTER SIMULATION MODEL

The considerations in developing and using a computer simulation model may be summarised as follows:

(*1*) *Model Building*   A critical examination should be made of the proposed simulation project to provide well-defined terms of reference and to identify relevant factors. The representation of the model in suitable terms should be carried out by means of a schematic diagram, e.g. industrial dynamics (see chapter 4).

(*2*) *Choice of Language*   This will depend upon the nature and complexity of the model and the availability of suitable compilers.

(*3*) *Flow-charting*   A flowchart of the logical steps to be performed by the computer should be drawn in appropriate detail for the language chosen.

(*4*) *Design of Test Data*   Suitable data should be developed to fully test the program logic and validity of the model.

(*5*) *Program Writing*   It may be advantageous to write the program in the form of subroutines to allow easy implementation of subsequent changes in the model. The program should include intermediate print statements to allow 'diagnostic' information to be output at critical stages in the program to assist in the subsequent validation. These 'diagnostic' statements may be removed before the running of the validated program. The format of the final output should be designed for easy interpretation by management.

(*6*) *Validation*   When the simulated system exists in real life, the model should be validated against the actual situation before making experimental changes in the parameters. Where actual data are to be used in a model for a proposed system, the validity of the data may be checked by first building a model of the existing system. In this case, the final results obtained from the proposed model should not be assumed correct, despite their apparent feasibility, until the validity of this model has been confirmed. This may be carried out by using suitable test data and 'diagnostic' output. In many aspects of detailed validation statistical tests can be used, e.g. significance testing (see chapter 3).

(7) Interpretation of the Results

(*a*) Graphical representation of output may give a better understanding of the results as demonstrated by a comparison of figures 9.10 and 9.11 (PRAC).

(*b*) Further changes in the model or policies may be suggested by the results obtained and introduced into the model (see figure 7.11 (SOMB)).

(*c*) Alternative policies may be shown to lead to the same outcome, thereby allowing management to select one according to factors outside the model (see table 9.2 (ELEM)).

(*d*) In some cases, the results point to an 'optimum solution' (see figure 9.8 (CAPF)).

SUGGESTED EXERCISES

As all the programs discussed have been given in the appendices, these should provide a useful basis for exercises for the potential practitioner. Exercises based on material in this book might include:

(1) the drawing of flowcharts for the given programs,

(2) the development of test data to validate the program logic,

(3) the introduction of 'diagnostic' output to trace the running of the programs,

(4) the statistical testing of output,

(5) the introduction of changes in the models, e.g. length of run, alternative input/output, alternative policies.

CONCLUSION

The purpose in writing this book has been to introduce managers, systems analysts, industrial engineers and operational research workers to simulation in a practical manner. It is hoped that the wide range of programs included will help these people to appreciate the potential usefulness of simulation techniques in their own companies.

References and Bibliography

1. BARRETT, D. A., *Automatic Inventory Control Techniques*, Business Books, London, 1969.
2. *BASIC FORTRAN*, Technical Publication 4023, I.C.T. Ltd., April 1967.
3. BATTERSBY, A. *A Guide to Stock Control*, Pitman, London, 1962.
4. BUXTON, J. N. and LASKI, J. G., 'Control and Simulation Language', *The Computer Journal*, vol. 5, 1962, p. 194.
5. CORKE, D. K., *Production Control is Management*, Arnold, London, 1969.
6. COX, D. R. and SMITH, W. L., *Queues*, Methuen, London, 1961.
7. CRADDOCK, J. M., *Statistics in the Computer Age*, E.U.P., London, 1968.
8. CROFT, D., *Applied Statistics for Management Studies*, Macdonald and Evans, London, 1969.
9. *CSL Reference Manual*, IBM United Kingdom Ltd. and Esso Petroleum Co. Ltd., 1962.
10. *CSL Reference Manual*, IBM United Kingdom Ltd., 1965.
11. *Control and Simulation Language Manual*, Honeywell Electronic Data Processing, 1967.
12. FORRESTER, J., *Industrial Dynamics*, M.I.T. Press, 1961.
13. *Hocus*, P-E Consulting Group, London.
14. HOULDEN, B. T., *Some Techniques of Operational Research*, E.U.P., London, 1962.
15. JARDINE, A. K. S., *Operational Research in Maintenance*, Manchester University Press, Manchester, 1970.
16. KRASNOW, H. S. and MERKALLIO, R. A., 'The Past, Present, and Future of General Simulation Languages', *Management Science*, vol. 11, No. 2, Nov. 1964, p. 236.
17. LANGLEY, R., *Practical Statistics*, Pan, London, 1968.
18. LEWIS, C. D., *Scientific Inventory Control*, Butterworths, London, 1970.
19. MOORE, P. G., *Basic Operational Research*, Pitman, London, 1968.
20. NAYLOR, T. H., BALINTFY, J. L., BURDICK, D. S. and CHU, K., *Computer Simulation Techniques*, John Wiley, New York, 1968.
21. NEWELL, G. F., *Applications of Queueing Theory*, Chapman and Hall, London, 1971.
22. NILAND, P., *Production Planning, Scheduling and Inventory Control*. Macmillan, London, 1970.
23. *Programming Language FORTRAN*, ISO Draft Recommendation No. 1539.

24. *Prop Users Guide*, Technical Publication 3389, I.C.T. Ltd., 1967.
25. *Scientific Subroutines*, Technical Publication 4096, ICT Ltd., 1969.
26. *Standard FORTRAN Programming Manual*, National Computing Centre Ltd., 1970.
27. THOMAS, A. B., *Stock Control in Manufacturing Industries*, Gower Press, London, 1970.
28. TOCHER, K. D., 'Review of Simulation Languages', *O.R. Quarterly*, vol. 16, No. 2, June 1965, p. 189.
29. TRIGG, D. W. and LEACH, A. G., 'Exponential Smoothing with an adaptive response rate', *O.R. Quarterly*, vol. 18, No. 1, p. 53.
30. *USA Standard FORTRAN*, USASI X3.9–1966.
31. *1900 C.S.L.*, Technical Publication 3386, ICL September, 1968.

Appendix 1

FORTRAN Programs: CAPF

```
1              LIST(LP)
2              SEND TO(MT)
3              PROGRAM(CAPF)
4              OUTPUT 6=LPO
5              END
6              MASTER PLANT
7       C
8       C   THIS PROGRAM SIMULATES THE LOADING OF A MACHINE SHOP
9       C   AND IS USED TO FIND THE PLANT CAPACITY GIVING A
10      C   MINIMUM COST, TAKING INTO ACCOUNT THE COST OF HAVING
11      C   PLANT IDLE AND PENALTIES ASSOCIATED WITH DELAYED
12      C   WORK.
13      C
14             WRITE(6,1)
15           1 FORMAT(29H1     CAPACITY     TOTAL COST)
16      C
17      C   SET INITIAL PLANT CAPACITY AS IPC.
18      C
19             J=0
20             I=4
21             IPC=120
22             INC=5
23             IOC=100000
24      C
25      C   SET UP INITIAL CONDITIONS FOR 240 DAYS AT GIVEN
26      C   PLANT CAPACITY I.E. NO EXCESS LOAD, ZERO TOTAL COST
27      C   AT DAY 0.
28      C
29      70     IEX=0
30             ITC=0
31             IDAY=0
32             STREAMU=0.1
33             STREAMN=0.2
34      C
35      C   SET DAY'S TOTAL LOAD TO ZERO AND SAMPLE NO OF ORDERS
36      C   RECEIVED (RECTANGULAR DISTRIBUTION).
37      C
38      10     ITDAY=0
39             CALL UNIFM(1.0,10.0,ORDS,STREAMU)
40             IORDS=ORDS
41      C
42      C   SIMULATE LOAD FOR EACH ORDER BY SAMPLING FROM A NORMAL
```

223

```
43      C    DISTRIBUTION, AND IF NEGATIVE SET TO ZERO.
44      C
45      20   CALL NORM(24.0,15.0,TIME,STREAMN)
46           MTIME=TIME
47           IF(MTIME)21,22,22
48      21   MTIME=0
49      22   ITDAY=ITDAY+MTIME
50           IORDS=IORDS-1
51           IF(IORDS)20,23,20
52      C
53      C    UPDATE TOTAL LOAD FOR DAY AND REPEAT UNTIL PLANT HAS
54      C    BEEN LOADED WITH ALL THE ORDERS. TOTAL LOAD MUST
55      C    INCLUDE ORDERS NOT DEALT WITH ON PREVIOUS DAY (EXCESS),
56      C    AND ANY EXCESS LOAD MUST BE CARRIED FORWARD TO NEXT
57      C    DAY.
58      C
59      23   ITDAY=ITDAY+IEX
60           IDIFF=IPC-ITDAY
61           IF(IDIFF)11,12,12
62      C
63      C    CALCULATE COST FOR EACH DAY AS £5/HOUR IF A MACHINE
64      C    IS IDLE, AND £1/MACHINE HOUR PER DAY FOR DELAYING
65      C    AN ORDER.
66      C
67      12   ICOST=5 * IDIFF
68           IEX=0
69           GO TO 30
70      11   ICOST=-1 * IDIFF
71           IEX=-1 * IDIFF
72      30   ITC=ITC + ICOST
73           IDAY=IDAY+1
74      C
75      C    CONTINUE THE SIMULATION FOR 240 DAYS FOR EACH PLANT
76      C    CAPACITY, FROM INITIAL CAPACITY AND GOING UP IN
77      C    STEPS OF 5 UNTIL SLOPE CHANGES SIGN. BACKSTEP PLANT
78      C    CAPACITY BY 10 UNITS AND CONTINUE IN STEPS OF 1 UNTIL
79      C    COST INCREASES. CALCULATE 4 FURTHER VALUES WITH INCREMENT
80      C    OF 1, THEN IN STEPS OF 5 UNTIL FINAL VALUE IS REACHED.
81      C
82           IF(IDAY-240)10,9,10
83      9    ITC=ITC/IDAY
84           WRITE(6,2)IPC,ITC
85      2    FORMAT(1H0,I12,I14)
86           IF(IOC-ITC)/INC)300,300,200
87      300  IF(J)302,301,302
88      301  IPC=IPC-10
89           INC=1
90           J=1
91      302  IF(ITC-IOC)200,200,303
92      303  IF(I)200,304,305
93      305  I=I-1
94           GO TO 200
95      304  INC=5
96           I=I-1
97      200  IF(IPC-150)400,60,60
98      400  IOC=ITC
```

224

```
 99            IPC=IPC+INC
100            GO TO 70
101      60    STOP
102            END
103            SUBROUTINE UNIFM(A,B,X,STREAM)
104            R=FPMCRV(STREAM)
105            X=A+(B-A)*R
106            RETURN
107            END
108            SUBROUTINE NORM(EX,STDX,X,STREAM)
109            SUM=0.0
110            DO 5 I=1,12
111            R=FPMCRV(STREAM)
112       5    SUM=SUM+R
113            X=STDX*(SUM-6.0)+EX
114            RETURN
115            END
116            LIBRARY
117            READ FROM(MT,-.FSCE)
118            FINISH
```

Appendix 2

FORTRAN Programs: COMF

```
 1              LIST(LP)
 2              SEND TO(MT)
 3              PROGRAM(COMF)
 4              INPUT 1=CRO
 5              OUTPUT 2,(MONITOR)=LPO
 6              TRACE
 7              END
 8              MASTER CUNIT
 9       C
10       C THIS PROGRAM SIMULATES THE FAILURE PATTERN OF A COMBINED
11       C UNIT, WHICH CONSISTS OF TWO BASIC UNITS (MOTOR+GEAR) OF
12       C KNOWN FAILURE PATTERNS.
13       C
14              DIMENSION MUNIT(6),IGUNIT(5),IHIST(6)
15       C
16       C READ IN CUMULATIVE FREQUENCIES FOR UNITS AND HISTOGRAM
17       C DETAILS.
18       C
19              READ(1,1) (MUNIT(I),I=1,6),(IGUNIT(J),J=1,5),N,IR,IW
20       1      FORMAT(14I3)
21              WRITE(2,45)(MUNIT(I),I=1,6),(IGUNIT(J),J=1,5),N,IR,IW
22       45     FORMAT(1H0,14I6)
23       C
24       C ZEROISE HISTOGRAM CELLS.
25       C
26              DO 7 I=1,N
27       7      IHIST(I)=0
28       C
29       C SET UP LOOP FOR 100 FAILURES.
30       C
31              STREAM=0.7
32              DO 8 K=1,100
33       C
34       C SELECT TWO RANDOM NUMBERS.
35       C
36       42     CALL FPMCRV(STREAM)
37              IRN1=100.*STREAM
38              IF(IRN1-100)41,42,42
39       41     CALL FPMCRV(STREAM)
40              IRN2=100.*STREAM
41              IF(IRN2-100)43,41,41
42       C
```

```
43      C USE THE RANDOM NUMBERS TO FIND NO OF WEEKS UNITS RUN
44      C BEFORE FAILING.
45      C
46              DO 10 I=1,6
47              IF(MUNIT(I)-IRN1+1)10,20,20
48      10      CONTINUE
49      20      DO 11 J=1,5
50              IF(IGUNIT(J)-IRN2+1)11,22,22
51      11      CONTINUE
52      C
53      C TEST WHICH UNIT FAILS FIRST AND ADD 1 TO APPROPRIATE
54      C HISTOGRAM CELL.
55      C
56      22      IF(I-J)24,24,25
57      24      IHIST(I)=IHIST(I)+1
58              GO TO 8
59      25      IHIST(J)=IHIST(J)+1
60      8       CONTINUE
61      C
62      C PRINT HEADINGS AND HISTOGRAM.
63      C
64              WRITE(2,2)
65          2 FORMAT(24H1HISTOGRAM COMBINED UNIT)
66              WRITE(2,5)
67          5 FORMAT(19HOCOUNT         RANGE)
68              WRITE(2,6)IHIST(1),IR
69          6 FORMAT(1H ,I4,10X,2HTO,I4)
70              NO=N-1
71              DO 30 I=2,NO
72              L=IW*(I-1)+1
73              M=IW*I
74      30      WRITE(2,3)IHIST(I),L,M
75      3       FORMAT(1H ,I4,I8,2HTO,I4)
76              L=IW*(N-1)+1
77              WRITE(2,4)IHIST(I),L
78      4       FORMAT(1H ,I4,I8,2HTO)
79              STOP
80              END
81              LIBRARY
82              READ FROM(MT,-.FSCE)
83              FINISH
```

FORTRAN Programs: ELEM

```
 1              LIST(LP)
 2              PROGRAM(ELEM)
 3              INPUT 1=CRO
 4              OUTPUT (MONITOR),2=LPO
 5              TRACE
 6              END
 7              MASTER MAIN
 8      C
 9      C   THIS PROGRAM SIMULATES THE MAINTENANCE OF A BAKING
10      C   OVEN USED FOR THE HARDENING OF ENAMEL CASES OF FLOW
11      C   METERS. THE OVEN CONTAINS SIX ELEMENTS, THREE DOWN
12      C   EACH SIDE, WHICH ARE SUBJECT TO FAILURE.
13      C   THE ESTABLISHED TIME TO REPAIR ONE ELEMENT IS THREE
14      C   DAYS, TO REPLACE THREE ELEMENTS DOWN ONE SIDE, FOUR
15      C   DAYS, AND TO REPLACE ALL SIX ELEMENTS, SIX DAYS.
16      C   AN ELEMENT COSTS £50 AND THE COST OF HAVING THE
17      C   OVEN INOPERATIVE IS £200 PER DAY.
18      C   THREE POLICIES A,B AND C WILL BE SIMULATED TO
19      C   DETERMINE WHICH IS THE CHEAPEST.
20      C
21              DIMENSION L(8),LF(8)
22              READ(1,1)L,LF
23      1       FORMAT(16I2)
24              WRITE(2,2)L,LF
25      2       FORMAT(5H1DATA,16I4)
26              CALL POLICYA(L,LF)
27              CALL POLICYB(L,LF)
28              CALL POLICYC(L,LF)
29              STOP
30              END
31              SUBROUTINE POLICYA(L,LF)
32      C
33      C   POLICY A : REPLACE AN ELEMENT WHEN IT FAILS.
34      C
35              DIMENSION L(8),LF(8),LIFE(6)
36              STREAM=0.1
37              IREP=0
38              IRT=0
39      C
40      C   SAMPLE LIFE OF SIX ELEMENTS FROM DISTRIBUTION.
41      C
42              DO 20 J=1,6
```

```
43    20     CALL SLIFE(L,LF,STREAM,LIFE(J))
44    C
45    C    PRINT HEADINGS.
46    C
47           WRITE(2,100)
48    100 FORMAT(35H1SIMULATION OF MAINTENANCE POLICIES,
49        117H FOR STOVING OVEN//
50        241H POLICY A : REPLACE ELEMENTS INDIVIDUALLY)
51           WRITE(2,101)
52    101 FORMAT(23HOTIME REQUIRED = 3 DAYS//
53        130H COST OF ELEMENTS = £ 50  EACH//
54        234H COST OF DOWNTIME = £ 200  PER DAY/)
55           WRITE(2,102)
56    102 FORMAT(31HOREPLACEMENT NO.   CUM.RUN.TIME,
57        125H    M.T.B.F.  AV.COST/DAY)
58    C
59    C    FIND SHORTEST LIFE AND DEDUCT THIS VALUE FROM
60    C    ALL THE 6 LIVES. SAMPLE NEW LIFE FOR FAILED ELEMENT.
61    C
62    40     CALL MLIFE(LIFE,I,MIN)
63           DO 30 J=1,6
64    30     LIFE(J)=LIFE(J)-MIN
65           CALL SLIFE(L,LF,STREAM,LIFE(I))
66    C
67    C    UPDATE TOTAL RUNNING TIME AND INCREASE REPLACEMENTS
68    C    BY 1.
69    C
70           IRT=IRT+MIN
71           IREP=IREP+1
72           ATBF=FLOAT(IRT)/IREP
73           COST=650.0/ATBF
74           WRITE(2,103)IREP,IRT,ATBF,COST
75    103 FORMAT(1H0,I8,I17,F14.2,F12.2)
76           IF(IREP-200)40,41,41
77    41     RETURN
78           END
79           SUBROUTINE POLICYB(L,LF)
80    C
81    C POLICY B : REPLACE THE ELEMENTS ALONG ONE SIDE
82    C WHENEVER ONE FAILS.
83    C
84           DIMENSION L(8),LF(8),LIFE(6)
85           STREAM=0.1
86           IREP=0
87           IRT=0
88    C
89    C    SAMPLE LIVES FOR 6 ELEMENTS AND FIND SHORTEST LIFE.
90    C
91           DO 20 J=1,6
92    20     CALL SLIFE(L,LF,STREAM,LIFE(J))
93    C
94    C    PRINT HEADINGS.
95    C
96           WRITE(2,100)
97    100 FORMAT(35H1SIMULATION OF MAINTENANCE POLICIES,
98        117H FOR STOVING OVEN//
```

```
 99              248H POLICY B : REPLACE ALL 3 ELEMENTS DOWN ONE SIDE)
100              WRITE(2,101)
101       101 FORMAT(23HOTIME REQUIRED = 4 DAYS//
102              130H COST OF ELEMENTS = £ 50  EACH//
103              234H COST OF DOWNTIME = £ 200  PER DAY/)
104              WRITE(2,102)
105       102 FORMAT(31HOREPLACEMENT NO.   CUM.RUN.TIME,
106              125H    M.T.B.F.  AV.COST/DAY)
107       25    CALL MLIFE(LIFE,I,MIN)
108       C
109       C     TEST ON WHICH SIDE ELEMENT FAILED AND REPLACE ALL
110       C     ELEMENTS ON THAT SIDE. DEDUCT SHORTEST LIFE FROM
111       C     ELEMENTS ON OTHER SIDE.
112       C
113              IF(I-3)30,30,31
114       30    DO 40 J=4,6
115       40    LIFE(J)=LIFE(J)-MIN
116              DO 41 J=1,3
117       41    CALL SLIFE(L,LF,STREAM,LIFE(J))
118              GO TO 60
119       31    DO 50 J=1,3
120       50    LIFE(J)=LIFE(J)-MIN
121              DO 51 J=4,6
122       51    CALL SLIFE(L,LF,STREAM,LIFE(J))
123       60    IRT=IRT+MIN
124              IREP=IREP+1
125              ATBF=FLOAT(IRT)/IREP
126              COST=950.0/ATBF
127              WRITE(2,113)IREP,IRT,ATBF,COST
128       113   FORMAT(1HO,I8,I17,F14.2,F12.2)
129              IF(IREP-200)25,70,70
130       70    RETURN
131              END
132              SUBROUTINE POLICYC(L,LF)
133       C
134       C   POLICY C : REPLACE ALL THE ELEMENTS WHENEVER
135       C   ONE FAILS.
136       C
137              DIMENSION L(8),LF(8),LIFE(6)
138              STREAM=0.1
139              IREP=0
140              IRT=0
141       C
142       C   PRINT HEADINGS.
143       C
144              WRITE(2,100)
145       100 FORMAT(35H1SIMULATION OF MAINTENANCE POLICIES,
146              117H FOR STOVING OVEN//
147              234H POLICY C : REPLACE ALL 6 ELEMENTS)
148              WRITE(2,101)
149       101 FORMAT(23HOTIME REQUIRED = 6 DAYS//
150              130H COST OF ELEMENTS = £ 50  EACH//
151              234H COST OF DOWNTIME = £ 200  PER DAY/)
152              WRITE(2,102)
153       102 FORMAT(31HOREPLACEMENT NO.   CUM.RUN.TIME,
154              125H    M.T.B.F.  AV.COST/DAY)
```

230

```
155    C
156    C        SAMPLE LIVES FOR 6 ELEMENTS AND FIND SHORTEST LIFE.
157    C
158    10       DO 20 J=1,6
159    20       CALL SLIFE(L,LF,STREAM,LIFE(J))
160             CALL MLIFE(LIFE,I,MIN)
161             IRT=IRT+MIN
162             IREP=IREP+1
163             ATBF=FLOAT(IRT)/IREP
164             CCST=1500.0/ATBF
165             WRITE(2,113)IREP,IRT,ATBF,COST
166    113      FORMAT(1H0,I8,I17,F14.2,F12.2)
167             IF(IREP-200)10,50,50
168    50       RETURN
169             END
170             SUBROUTINE SLIFE(L,LF,STREAM,LIFE)
171    C
172    C        THIS SUBROUTINE SAMPLES THE LIFE OF AN ELEMENT
173    C        FROM A FREQUENCY DISTRIBUTION OBTAINED FROM THE
174    C        MAIN PROGRAM.
175    C
176             DIMENSION L(8),LF(8)
177             CALL FPMCRV(STREAM)
178             IRAND=100.0*STREAM
179             LIFE=L(1)
180             DO 11 I=2,8
181             IF(IRAND-LF(I-1))12,12,11
182    11       LIFE=L(I)
183    12       RETURN
184             END
185             SUBROUTINE MLIFE(LIFE,I,MIN)
186    C
187    C        THIS SUBROUTINE FINDS THE ELEMENT HAVING
188    C        THE SHORTEST REMAINING LIFE.
189    C
190             DIMENSION LIFE(6)
191             MIN=LIFE(1)
192             I=1
193             DO 22 J=2,6
194             IF(LIFE(J)-MIN)21,22,22
195    21       MIN=LIFE(J)
196             I=J
197    22       CONTINUE
198             RETURN
199             END
200             LIBRARY
201             READ FROM(MT,-.FSCE)
202             FINISH
```

Appendix 4

FORTRAN Programs: FORE

```
 1              LIST(LP)
 2              PROGRAM(FORE)
 3              INPUT 1=CRO
 4              OUTPUT 2,(MONITOR)=LPO
 5              TRACE
 6              END
 7              MASTER(FORE)
 8      C   THIS PROGRAM USES FOUR FORECASTING METHODS ON UP TO 36
 9      C   PAST READINGS. THE METHOD USED IS DETERMINED BY THE
10      C   VALUE OF K, WHICH IS INITIALISED AT 1 AND THEN INCREASED
11      C   IN STEPS OF 1 UP TO 4 WITHIN THE PROGRAM.
12      C
13      C   WHEN K = 1, A SIMPLE EXPONENTIAL SMOOTHING ROUTINE IS
14      C   USED FOR 10 RUNS AS ALPHA IS INCREASED FROM 0.1 TO 1.0
15      C   IN INCREMENTS OF 0.1.
16      C   WHEN K = 2, A TREND CORRECTION IS INCORPORATED INTO THE
17      C   SMOOTHING ROUTINES. THE ALPHA USED FOR TREND SMOOTHING
18      C   IS KEPT CONSTANT AT 0.1.
19      C
20      C   WHEN K = 3, THE PROGRAM USES THE MEAN DEMAND AS A BASIS
21      C   OF 5 CONSTANT FORECAST RUNS AT 60, 80, 100, 120, AND
22      C   140% OF THE CALCULATED MEAN.
23      C   WHEN K = 4, THE PROGRAM USES THE METHOD OF K = 1 BUT
24      C   SETS ALPHA TO THE PENULTIMATE VALUE OF THE TRACKING
25      C   SIGNAL.
26      C
27      C   DURING EACH RUN THE LARGEST ABSOLUTE VALUES ARE FOUND
28      C   FOR VARIOUS PARAMETERS. AT THE END OF THE 25 RUNS A
29      C   SUMMARY OF THE BEST OF THESE IS PRINTED TOGETHER WITH
30      C   THE ASSOCIATED FORECASTING METHOD.
31      C
32      C   READ IN INPUT DATA AND PRINT
33      C
34              DIMENSION DF(36)
35              READ(1,10) DF
36      10      FORMAT(20F4.0)
37              WRITE(2,100)DF
38      100     FORMAT(5H1DATA,(/1H0,12F7.0))
39      C
40      C   INITIALISE VALUES.
41      C   B BECOMES THE VALUE OF ALPHA DURING ANY PARTICULAR RUN BUT -
42      C   C IS THE VALUE OF ALPHA FOR THE FIRST 3 CALCULATIONS OF EACH RUN.
```

232

```
43    C
44          B=0.1
45          C=0.7
46          K=1
47          SEMAX=9999
48          SADMX=9999
49          STMAX=9999
50          SCMAX=9999
51          TOT=0
52          I=1
53          TL=0.7
54    16    IF(DF(I)-0)14,14,13
55    C
56    C     THE AVERAGE OF THE DATA IS CALCULATED AND CALLED AVE.
57    C
58    13    TOT=TOT+DF(I)
59          N=I
60          I=I+1
61          IF(I-36)16,16,14
62    14    AVE=TOT/N
63          CON=(0.8)*AVE
64          ADD=(0.1)*AVE
65          J=1
66    C
67    C     THIS IS THE STARTING POINT OF EACH PAGE OF OUTPUT.
68    C     OUTPUT APPROPRIATE HEADING.
69    C
70    80    A=B
71    25    IF(K-2)17,15,18
72    17    WRITE(2,19)A
73    19    FORMAT(35H1    EXPONENTIAL SMOOTHING NO TREND,10X,
74          16HALPHA=,F4.1
75          GO TO 27
76    18    WRITE(2,26)AVE
77    26    FORMAT(22H1    CONSTANT FORECAST,15X,12HMEAN DEMAND= ,F6.1)
78          GO TO 27
79    67    WRITE(2,64)
80    64    FORMAT(35H1    ADAPTIVE EXPONENTIAL SMOOTHING)
81          GO TO 27
82    15    WRITE(2,11)A
83    11    FORMAT(37H1    EXPONENTIAL SMOOTHING WITH TREND,10X,
84          16HALPHA=,F4.1)
85    27    WRITE(2,12)
86    12    FORMAT(44H0    DEMAND   FORECAST     ERROR   CUM ERROR,
87          119H   MAD    TRACKING)
88    C
89    C     INITIALISED BEGINNING OF EACH RUN.
90    C
91          ADM=0.8*((DF(1))**0.5)
92          OE=0
93          OF=DF(1)
94          OT=0
95          EMAX=0
96          ADMX=0
97          TMAX=0
98          CMAX=0
```

```
 99            I=1
100            OA=DF(I)
101            CE=0
102            TL=0.7
103     20     D=DF(I)
104     C
105     C    READ NEXT FIGURE.
106     C    THE FIRST 3 CALCULATIONS ARE DONE WITH SMOOTHING CONSTANTS
107     C    SET TO 0.7 TO ALLOW RAPID SETTLING IN.
108     C
109            IF(I-3)31,31,39
110     31     A=C
111            Y=C
112            GOTO 32
113     39     IF(J-5)65,65,66
114     66     A=ABS(TOLD)
115            Y=0.1
116            GO TO 32
117     65     A=B
118            Y=0.1
119     32     SA=A*D+(1-A)*OA
120     C
121     C    TEST VALUE OF K TO DECIDE METHOD OF FORECASTING.
122     C
123            IF(K-4)68,22,68
124     68     IF(K-2)22,21,23
125     21     CT=SA-OA
126            NT=Y*CT+(1-Y)*OT
127            F=SA+((1.-A)/A)*NT
128            GO TO 24
129     22     F=SA
130            GO TO 24
131     23     F=CON
132            A=CON
133     C
134     C    CALCULATE CONSEQUENCES OF FORECAST IN TERMS OF ERRORS ETC.
135     C
136     24     E=OF-D
137            SE=Y*E+(1-Y)*OE
138            CE=CE+E
139            AD=ABS(OF-D)
140            ADM=Y*AD+(1-Y)*ADM
141            IF(ADM-0)60,60,70
142     60     ADM=1
143     70     T=SE/ADM
144            IF(T)73,72,73
145     72     T=0.01
146     C
147     C    TEST TO FIND LARGEST ABSOLUTE VALUES ,AFTER 1ST FOUR RESULTS
148     C
149     73     IF(I-4)33,33,71
150     71     AE=ABS(E)
151            IF(AE-EMAX)35,35,34
152     34     EMAX=AE
153     35     IF(ADM-ADMX)37,37,36
154     36     ADMX=ADM
```

234

```
155    37     ATX=ABS(T)
156           IF(ATX-TMAX)48,48,38
157    38     TMAX=ATX
158    48     ACE=ABS(CE)
159           IF(ACE-CMAX)33,33,90
160    90     CMAX=ACE
161    C
162    C      OUTPUT LINE OF RESULTS.
163    C
164    33     WRITE(2,30)D,F,E,CE,ADM,T
165    30     FORMAT(1H ,5F10.1,F10.2)
166    C
167    C      INDEX VALUES UP READY FOR NEXT PASS
168    C
169           TOLD=TL
170           TL=T
171           OF=F
172           OA=SA
173           OT=NT
174           OE=SE
175           I=I+1
176           IF(I-N)20,20,40
177    C
178    C      FIND MIN OF MAXIMUMS ,AND OUTPUT MAXS OF THIS RUN
179    C
180    40     IF(EMAX-SEMAX)42,43,43
181    42     SEMAX=EMAX
182           SEE=A
183           M1=K
184    43     IF(ADMX-SADMX)44,45,45
185    44     SADMX=ADMX
186           SAA=A
187           M3=K
188    45     IF(TMAX-STMAX)46,47,47
189    46     STMAX=TMAX
190           STA=A
191           M4=K
192    47     IF(CMAX-SCMAX)91,92,92
193    91     SCMAX=CMAX
194           SCE=A
195           M2=K
196    92     WRITE(2,41)EMAX,CMAX,ADMX,TMAX
197    41     FORMAT(21H0    ABSOLUTE MAXIMUM,3F10.1,F10.2)
198    C
199    C
200    C      TEST FOR END OF RUN AND METHOD.
201    C
202           IF(K-3)54,62,51
203    54     B=B+0.1
204           IF(B-1.00)80,80,50
205    50     IF(K-3)61,62,62
206    61     K=K+1
207           B=0.1
208           GO TO 80
209    62     CON=CON+ADD
210           J=J+1
```

235

```
211          IF(J-5)25,25,63
212   63     K=4
213          TOLD=0.7
214          GO TO 67
215   C
216   C    AFTER LAST RUN OF FOURTH METHOD OUTPUT FINAL SUMMARY
217   C
218   51     WRITE(2,52)
219   52     FORMAT(46H1 THE SMALLEST VALUES OF THE LARGEST ABSOLUTES)
220          WRITE(2,57)
221   57     FORMAT(45HOPARAMETER       VALUE       METHOD     CONSTANT)
222          WRITE(2,53)SEMAX,M1,SEE
223   53     FORMAT(6HOERROR,F16.2,7X,I1,F14.1)
224          WRITE(2,55)SCMAX,M2,SCE
225   55     FORMAT(10HOCUM ERROR,F12.2,7X,I1,F14.1)
226          WRITE(2,56)SADMX,M3,SAA
227   56     FORMAT(4HOMAD,F18.2,7X,I1,F14.1)
228          WRITE(2,58)STMAX,M4,STA
229   58     FORMAT(9HOTRACKING,F13.2,7X,I1,F15.2)
230          STOP
231          END
232          FINISH
```

FORTRAN Programs: LOAD

```
  1            LIST(LP)
  2            SEND TO(MT)
  3            PROGRAM(LOAD)
  4            INPUT 1=CRO
  5            OUTPUT 2,(MONITOR)=LPO
  6            TRACE
  7            END
  8            MASTER LOAD
  9     C
 10     C      THIS PROGRAM SIMULATES THE LOADING OF THE ASSEMBLY
 11     C      SECTION IN A FACTORY THAT REFURBISHES VENDING
 12     C      MACHINES.
 13     C
 14     C
 15     C      ALLOCATE STORAGE FOR MAXIMUM SIZE OF ARRAYS AND
 16     C      SET INITIAL VALUE OF STREAM VARIABLE.
 17     C
 18            DIMENSION A(4),IAT(4),IQ(4),N(4),MAN(9),LATE(4),IHIST(21)
 19            STREAM=0.3
 20     C
 21     C      READ IN NO OF DAYS FOR SIMULATION (IEND) AND
 22     C      NO OF ASSEMBLERS.  PRINT DATA.
 23     C
 24            READ(1,2)IEND,NO
 25     2      FORMAT(I4,I2)
 26            WRITE(2,3)IEND,NO
 27     3      FORMAT(5H1DATA,I5,I4)
 28     C
 29     C      SET UP INITIAL CONDITIONS : A(1) - (4) ARE THE FOUR
 30     C      POISSON MEANS AND IAT(1) - (4) ARE THE ASSEMBLY TIMES
 31     C      FOR THE FOUR MODELS.
 32     C
 33            A(1)=1.0
 34            A(2)=2.0
 35            A(3)=1.25
 36            A(4)=2.25
 37            IAT(1)=10
 38            IAT(2)=8
 39            IAT(3)=12
 40            IAT(4)=5
 41     C
 42     C      ZEORISE 21 CELLS OF HISTOGRAM (IHIST) FOR
```

237

```
43    C      EXCESS HOURS.
44    C
45           DO 300 I=1,21
46    300    IHIST(I)=0
47    C
48    C      ALL MEN ARE FREE AT DAY 1 AND THE FIRST 55 DAYS
49    C      ARE TO BE IGNORED.
50    C
51           DO 50 I=1,NO
52    50     MAN(I)=0
53           IDAY=1
54           IOUT=55
55    C
56    C      PRINT HEADINGS FOR DIAGNOSTIC INFORMATION : DAY,
57    C      QUANTITIES FOR EACH MODEL AND PRIORITY.
58    C
59    1      WRITE(2,4)
60    4      FORMAT(39H0    IDAY IQ(1) IQ(2) IQ(3) IQ(4)  N(1),
61           118H  N(2)  N(3)  N(4))
62    C
63    C      DETERMINE QUANTITIES FOR EACH MODEL USING A
64    C      POISSON DISTRIBUTION (SUBROUTINE POISN).
65    C
66           DO 10 I=1,4
67           CALL POISN((A(I)),X,STREAM)
68    10     IQ(I)=X
69           DO 9 I=1,4
70    9      N(I)=0
71    C
72    C      DETERMINE PRIORITY OF MODELS USING A RECTANGULAR
73    C      DISTRIBUTION (SUBROUTINE UNIFM).
74    C
75           CALL UNIFM(1.0,4.0,X,STREAM)
76           N(1)=X
77    13     CALL UNIFM(1.0,4.0,X,STREAM)
78           IX=X
79           IF(N(1)-IX)15,13,15
80    15     N(2)=IX
81    11     CALL UNIFM(1.0,4.0,X,STREAM)
82           IX=X
83           IF(N(1)-IX)14,11,14
84    14     IF(N(2)-IX)12,11,12
85    12     N(3)=IX
86           N(4)=10-(N(1)+N(2)+N(3))
87    C
88    C      PRINT QUANTITIES AND PRIORITY OF MODELS.
89    C
90           WRITE(2,200)IDAY,(IQ(I1),I1=1,4),(N(I2),I2=1,4)
91    200    FORMAT(1H0,9I6)
92    C
93    C      TO FIND FIRST PRIORITY MODEL.
94    C
95           J=1
96    C
97    C      TO FIND JTH. PRIORITY MODEL AND SET SUFFIX TO L.
98    C
```

```
 99     25     L=N(J)
100     C
101     C      TO ESTABLISH WHETHER ANY MODEL 'L' HAVE ARRIVED.
102     C
103     20     IF(IQ(L)-1)26,28,28
104     26     IF(J-4)27,30,30
105     27     J=J+1
106            GO TO 25
107     C
108     C      IF SO SET NA TO NUMBER TO BE PROCESSED.
109     C
110     28     NA=IQ(L)
111     C
112     C      NOW LOAD MEN WITH MODEL 'L', NA TIMES.
113     C      FIRST FIND EARLIEST MAN AVAILABLE AND SET TO MAN(K).
114     C
115     24     K=1
116            MIN=MAN(1)
117            DO 6 I=2,NO
118            IF(MIN-MAN(I))6,6,7
119     7      MIN=MAN(I)
120            K=I
121     6      CONTINUE
122     C
123     C      TEST IF MAN(K) IS FORWARD LOADED,
124     C      IF NOT BRING UP TO 'NOW' + 16 HRS.
125     C
126            ITIME=IDAY*8+8
127            IF(MAN(K)-ITIME)36,32,32
128     36     MAN(K)=ITIME
129     C
130     C      NOW FORWARD LOAD MAN(K) WITH MODEL 'L'.
131     C
132     32     MAN(K)=MAN(K)+IAT(L)
133     C
134     C      CALCULATE LATENESS BEYOND BASIC TIME AND OUTPUT.
135     C
136            LATE(L)=MAN(K)-8-IAT(L)-(IDAY*8)
137            WRITE(2,206)ITIME,MIN,K,MAN(K),L,LATE(L)
138     206    FORMAT(1H0,6I9)
139            IF(IDAY-5)400,400,401
140     C
141     C      UPDATE APPROPRIATE CELL OF HISTOGRAM (EXCESS HOURS).
142     C
143     401    DO 301 I=1,21
144            IC=I-1
145            IF(IC-LATE(L))301,302,301
146     302    IH=I
147            GO TO 303
148     301    CONTINUE
149     303    IHIST(IH)=IHIST(IH)+1
150     C
151     C      REVISE NUMBER OF MODEL 'L' TO BE PROCESSED AND
152     C      TEST IF ZERO.
153     C
154     400    NA=NA-1
```

```
155          IF(NA-1)29,24,24
156    C
157    C     IF NONE LEFT, SET UP FOR J+1 PRIORITY AND
158    C     TEST IF OVER 4.
159    C
160    29    J=J+1
161          IF(J-5)25,30,30
162    C
163    C     AS NO MODELS LEFT ADVANCE TO NEXT DAY AND
164    C     TEST FOR END OF RUN,IEND.
165    C
166    30    IDAY=IDAY+1
167          IF(IDAY-IOUT)1,1,100
168    100   WRITE(2,310)
169    310   FORMAT(40H1FREQUENCY DISTRIBUTION OF HRS IN EXCESS/
170          126H OF BASIC PROCESSING TIMES//
171          128HOEXCESS HRS     FREQ    CUM%/)
172          IOUT=IOUT+50
173          IFREQT=0
174          CUM=0
175          DO 320 I=1,21
176    320   IFREQT=IFREQT+IHIST(I)
177          DO 340 I=1,21
178          CUM=CUM+IHIST(I)*100.0/IFREQT
179          IEX=I-1
180    340   WRITE(2,330)IEX,IHIST(I),CUM
181    330   FORMAT(1HO,I5,I13,F9.2)
182          IF(IDAY-IEND)1,1,402
183    402   STOP
184          END
185          SUBROUTINE UNIFM(A,B,X,STREAM)
186          R=FPMCRV(STREAM)
187          X=A+(B-A)*R
188          RETURN
189          END
190          SUBROUTINE POISN(P,X,STREAM)
191          X=0.0
192          B=EXP(-P)
193          TR=1.0
194    5     R=FPMCRV(STREAM)
195          TR=TR * R
196          IF(TR-B)10,8,8
197    8     X=X+1.0
198          GO TO 5
199    10    RETURN
200          END
201          LIBRARY
202          READ FROM(MT,-.FSCE)
203          FINISH
```

Appendix 6

FORTRAN Programs: SIMQ

```
 1              LIST(LP)
 2              PROGRAM(SIMQ)
 3              INPUT 1=CR0
 4              OUTPUT 2,(MONITOR)=LP0
 5              END
 6              MASTER SIMQ
 7      C
 8      C   THIS PROGRAM SIMULATES A GENERAL QUEUEING SITUATION.
 9      C
10      C
11      C   ALLOCATE STORAGE FOR ARRAYS : FREQUENCY DISTRIBUTIONS
12      C   OF INTERARRIVAL TIMES (A,AF) AND SERVICE TIMES (S,SF);
13      C   CHANNEL ELAPSED TIMES (AMINT).
14      C
15              DIMENSION A(10),AF(10),S(10),SF(10),AMINT(10)
16      C
17      C   READ AND PRINT FREQUENCY DISTRIBUTIONS.
18      C
19              READ(1,2)A,AF,S,SF
20      2       FORMAT(10F3.0)
21              WRITE(2,7)A,AF,S,SF
22      7       FORMAT(5H1DATA,20F4.1/1H0,20F4.1)
23      C
24      C   SET UP INITIAL CONDITIONS (ALL PARAMETERS TO ZERO).
25      C   CALCULATE MEAN ARRIVAL AND SERVICE RATES FOR
26      C   INPUT DATA (AMEAN,SMEAN) AND GENERATED VALUES
27      C   (AAT,AST).
28      C
29              AMAF=0
30              AMFA=0
31              AMSF=0
32              AMFS=0
33              DO 5 M=1,10
34              AMAF=AMAF+AF(M)
35              AMFA=AMFA+(AF(M)*A(M) )
36              AMSF=AMSF+SF(M)
37      5       AMFS=AMFS+(SF(M)*S(M))
38              AMEAN=AMAF/AMFA
39              SMEAN=AMSF/AMFS
40              STREAM=0.1
41              L=50
42              T=0
```

```
43              TST=0
44              CAT=0
45              WT=0
46              AMWT=0
47              ISEEN=0
48      C
49      C   CONVERT FREQUENCY DISTRIBUTIONS TO CUMULATIVE FORM.
50      C
51              DO 9 I=2,10
52              AF(I)=AF(I)+AF(I-1)
53      9       SF(I)=SF(I)+SF(I-1)
54      C
55      C   READ NUMBER OF CHANNELS AND LENGTH OF FIRST SIMULATION.
56      C
57              READ(1,3)N,IEND
58      3       FORMAT(2I4)
59              DO 10 I=1,N
60      10      AMINT(I)=0
61      C
62      C   SAMPLE INTERARRIVAL TIME AND CALCULATE
63      C   CUMULATIVE ARRIVAL TIME (CAT).
64      C
65      11      CALL FPMCRV(STREAM)
66              RAND=100.*STREAM
67              AT=A(1)
68              DO 22 I=2,10
69              IF(RAND-AF(I-1))30,30,22
70      22      AT=A(I)
71      30      CAT=CAT+AT
72      C
73      C   FIND CHANNEL WITH MINIMUM ELAPSED TIME (AMINT(J)).
74      C
75              AMET=AMINT(1)
76              J=1
77              DO 40 I=1,N
78              IF(AMINT(I)-AMET)41,40,40
79      41      AMET=AMINT(I)
80              J=I
81      40      CONTINUE
82      C
83      C   IF CUMULATIVE ARRIVAL TIME IS GREATER THAN AMINT(J),
84      C   ADD DIFFERENCE TO CHANNEL IDLE TIME (T), AND SET
85      C   CHANNEL ELAPSED TIME TO CUMULATIVE ARRIVAL TIME.
86      C   OTHERWISE ADD DIFFERENCE TO ARRIVAL WAITING TIME (WT)
87      C   AND SET MAXIMUM WAITING TIME (AMWT).
88      C
89              IF(CAT-AMINT(J))45,45,46
90      46      DIFF=CAT-AMINT(J)
91              T=T+DIFF
92              AMINT(J)=CAT
93              GO TO 60
94      45      DIFF=AMINT(J)-CAT
95              WT=WT+DIFF
96              IF(AMWT-DIFF)47,47,60
97      47      AMWT=DIFF
98      C
```

```
 99    C    INCREASE TOTAL SERVED BY 1.
100    C
101    60     ISEEN=ISEEN+1
102    C
103    C    SAMPLE SERVICE TIME AND ADD TO CHANNEL ELAPSED TIME.
104    C
105           CALL FPMCRV(STREAM)
106           RAND=100.*STREAM
107           ST=S(1)
108           DO 65 I=2,10
109           IF(RAND-SF(I-1))67,67,65
110    65     ST=S(I)
111    67     AMINT(J)=AMINT(J)+ST
112           TST=TST+ST
113           IF(CAT-FLOAT(L))11,68,68
114    C
115    C    END OF PRESENT SIMULATION. PRINT RESULTS.
116    C
117    68     AWT=WT/FLOAT(ISEEN)
118           AAT=FLOAT(ISEEN)/CAT
119           AST=FLOAT(ISEEN)/TST
120           PCUT=100.*(FLOAT(N)*CAT-T)/(FLOAT(N)*CAT)
121           WRITE(2,8)N,L
122    8      FORMAT(23H1SIMULATION OF QUEUEING,5X,
123           13HN =,I2,3X,3HL =,I5/)
124           WRITE(2,4)AMEAN,SMEAN,AAT,AST
125    4      FORMAT(27HOMEAN ARRIVAL RATE (DATA) =,F7.3//
126           127HOMEAN SERVICE RATE (DATA) =,F7.3//
127           232HOMEAN ARRIVAL RATE (GENERATED) =,F7.3//
128           332HOMEAN SERVICE RATE (GENERATED) =,F7.3/)
129           WRITE(2,6)N,CAT,ISEEN,WT,AWT,AMWT,T,PCUT
130    6      FORMAT(16HONO OF CHANNELS=,I3//14HOELAPSED TIME=,F7.2//
131           116HOTOTAL SERVICED=,I5//20HOTOTAL WAITING TIME=,F7.2//
132           222HOAVERAGE WAITING TIME=,F7.2//
133           322HOMAXIMUM WAITING TIME=,F7.2//
134           425HOTOTAL CHANNEL IDLE TIME=,F7.2//
135           522HO%CHANNEL UTILISATION=,F7.2)
136    C
137    C    INCREASE LENGTH OF SIMULATION UNTIL IEND DAYS HAVE
138    C    BEEN SIMULATED.
139    C
140           IF(L-IEND)70,100,100
141    70     L=L+50
142           GO TO 11
143    100    STOP
144           END
145           LIBRARY
146           READ FROM(MT,-.FSCE)
147           FINISH
```

Appendix 7

FORTRAN Programs: SUBF

```
 1              LIST(LP)
 2              SEND TO (MT)
 3              PROGRAM(SUBF)
 4              OUTPUT 2,(MONITOR) =LPO
 5              CREATE 6=MTO/UNFORMATTED(NUMBERS)
 6              TRACE
 7              END
 8              MASTER SUBF
 9              DIMENSION X(5),Y(5),Z(5),V(5),IV(5)
10              STREAM=0.3
11              WRITE(2,100)
12      100     FORMAT(44H1100 GENERATED RANDOM VALUES FROM SUBROUTINE)
13              WRITE(2,110)
14      110     FORMAT(1H+,44X,7HUNIFORM)
15              WRITE(2,111)
16      111     FORMAT(15HORANGE = 1 TO 4)
17      200     FORMAT(1H0/19H SIMULATED : MEAN =,F6.2,5X,
18             120HSTANDARD DEVIATION =,F6.2)
19              DO 20 J=1,4
20              WRITE(2,103)
21      103     FORMAT(1H0//)
22              DO 20 K=1,5
23              DO 30 L=1,5
24              CALL UNIFM(1.0,4.0,X(L),STREAM)
25      30      WRITE(6)X(L)
26      20      WRITE(2,104)(X(I),I=1,5)
27      104     FORMAT(1H ,5F10.2)
28              REWIND 6
29              CALL SDEV(2.5,100,SD,CMEAN)
30              WRITE(2,200)CMEAN,SD
31              REWIND 6
32              WRITE(2,100)
33              WRITE(2,112)
34      112     FORMAT(1H+,44X,6HNORMAL)
35              WRITE(2,113)
36      113     FORMAT(29HOMEAN = 10.0  DEVIATION = 2.0)
37              DO 40 J=1,4
38              WRITE(2,103)
39              DO 40 K=1,5
40              DO 50 L=1,5
41              CALL NORM(10.0,2.0,Y(L),STREAM)
42      50      WRITE(6)Y(L)
```

```
43    40      WRITE(2,104)(Y(I),I=1,5)
44            REWIND 6
45            CALL SDEV(10.0,100,SD,CMEAN)
46            WRITE(2,200)CMEAN,SD
47            REWIND 6
48            WRITE(2,100)
49            WRITE(2,114)
50    114     FORMAT(1H+,44X,20HNEGATIVE EXPONENTIAL)
51            WRITE(2,115)
52    115     FORMAT(10HOMEAN = 50)
53            DO 60 J=1,4
54            WRITE(2,103)
55            DO 60 K=1,5
56            DO 70 L=1,5
57            CALL EXPON(50.0,Z(L),STREAM)
58    70      WRITE(6)Z(L)
59    60      WRITE(2,104)(Z(I),I=1,5)
60            REWIND 6
61            CALL SDEV(50.0,100,SD,CMEAN)
62            WRITE(2,200)CMEAN,SD
63            REWIND 6
64            WRITE(2,100)
65            WRITE(2,116)
66    116     FORMAT(1H+,44X,7HPOISSON)
67            WRITE(2,117)
68    117     FORMAT(11HOMEAN = 2.0)
69            DO 80 J=1,4
70            WRITE(2,103)
71            DO 80 K=1,5
72            DO 90 L=1,5
73            CALL POISN(2.0,V(L),STREAM)
74            WRITE(6)V(L)
75    90      IV(L)=V(L)
76    80      WRITE(2,120)(IV(I),I=1,5)
77    120     FORMAT(1H ,5I10)
78            REWIND 6
79            CALL SDEV(2.0,100,SD,CMEAN)
80            WRITE(2,200)CMEAN,SD
81            STOP
82            END
83            SUBROUTINE UNIFM(A,B,X,STREAM)
84            R=FPMCRV(STREAM)
85            X=A+(B-A)*R
86            RETURN
87            END
88            SUBROUTINE NORM(EX,STDX,X,STREAM)
89            SUM=0.0
90            DO 5 I=1,12
91            R=FPMCRV(STREAM)
92    5       SUM=SUM+R
93            X=STDX * (SUM-6.0)+EX
94            RETURN
95            END
96            SUBROUTINE EXPON(EX,X,STREAM)
97            R=FPMCRV(STREAM)
98            X=-EX * ALOG(R)
```

```
 99           RETURN
100           END
101           SUBROUTINE POISN(P,X,STREAM)
102           X=0.0
103           B=EXP(-P)
104           TR=1.0
105    5      R=FPMCRV(STREAM)
106           TR=TR * R
107           IF(TR-B)10,8,8
108    8      X=X+1.0
109           GO TO 5
110    10     RETURN
111           END
112           SUBROUTINE SDEV(AMEAN,NO,SD,CMEAN)
113           SUMX=0
114           SUMXM=0
115           SUMXMSQ=0
116           DO 10 I=1,NO
117           READ(6)X
118           SUMX=SUMX + X
119           XM=X - AMEAN
120           SUMXM=SUMXM + XM
121    10     SUMXMSQ=SUMXMSQ + XM * XM
122           ANO=NO
123           SD=SQRT(SUMXMSQ/ANO - (SUMXM/ANO)**2)
124           CMEAN=SUMX/ANO
125           RETURN
126           END
127           LIBRARY
128           READ FROM(MT,-.FSCE)
129           FINISH
```

100 GENERATED RANDOM VALUES FROM SUBROUTINE UNIFORM

RANGE = 1 TO 4

1.90	1.30	3.70	2.50	3.70
3.69	1.86	2.98	2.09	1.75
1.64	1.10	1.86	2.24	3.67
2.88	3.27	3.66	2.58	1.53
1.95	1.89	3.84	1.00	2.48

3.86	1.86	1.40	1.68	1.48
3.72	1.03	3.69	1.85	2.87
1.54	2.41	1.65	1.14	2.04
2.96	3.39	3.76	2.01	3.21
2.24	3.51	1.89	1.77	3.64

3.86	3.43	1.84	2.15	3.38
1.90	2.95	1.61	2.15	2.34
1.75	2.39	2.64	1.31	3.10
1.80	1.92	2.28	3.44	1.07
3.52	3.47	2.13	3.53	3.03

2.44	3.36	2.17	1.81	1.37
1.88	2.96	1.86	3.57	2.63
2.69	2.42	3.34	2.25	2.42
1.29	1.91	3.88	1.08	2.57
3.69	3.01	3.84	2.91	1.91

SIMULATED : MEAN = 2.48   STANDARD DEVIATION = 0.84

100 GENERATED RANDOM VALUES FROM SUBROUTINE NORMAL

MEAN = 10.0 DEVIATION = 2.0

```
 8.78    12.59    10.56     8.83    11.72
10.86    14.49    12.52     9.84    12.62
11.04    10.22     7.74    10.58     6.79
15.78     9.58     7.86    10.09     8.68
 9.48     8.37     7.42    10.38     9.88


11.19    11.76    12.66     9.92    10.93
11.00    12.06     9.80    10.14    12.27
 8.21    11.17    11.63    10.34    10.22
 9.53    10.91     9.98    11.07     8.53
 6.49    12.37    11.94     8.43     6.34


 9.42     6.63    12.42    10.19    12.19
 9.91     7.02     9.94    11.26     9.93
 8.45    10.05     7.08    12.53     8.98
11.87    12.35    11.67     9.36    10.06
10.43     5.80    11.13    10.95    11.67


 8.21    13.06     6.88     9.83    11.42
 7.46    10.65    12.39    11.56     8.61
 9.80     8.99     8.73     9.11    11.09
 7.79    11.39     8.24    10.79    11.81
14.72     8.37    11.08     7.34    13.02
```

SIMULATED : MEAN = 10.19   STANDARD DEVIATION = 1.92

100 GENERATED RANDOM VALUES FROM SUBROUTINE NEGATIVE EXPONENTIAL

MEAN = 50

79.66	271.58	81.31	98.09	130.43
86.75	46.37	12.03	92.64	7.26
12.58	6.27	61.02	9.26	55.52
34.79	180.48	19.68	10.88	14.06
62.13	3.18	171.53	14.45	79.85

37.30	188.17	6.92	206.32	67.47
44.44	101.14	118.59	49.81	48.94
3.55	78.93	7.83	64.78	2.70
75.44	11.18	10.72	21.86	24.55
7.58	21.73	94.33	124.96	102.59

172.53	169.47	4.34	81.11	3.46
9.80	31.44	11.03	216.97	7.58
162.24	34.73	21.93	48.89	39.66
55.60	5.18	39.94	26.86	39.08
36.03	11.16	43.19	55.44	84.15

96.52	80.97	6.25	33.43	101.03
84.70	4.75	10.99	23.00	28.67
17.84	103.32	38.77	23.64	25.97
2.03	44.92	11.03	95.76	20.35
20.14	198.23	115.93	43.41	22.91

SIMULATED : MEAN = 58.30   STANDARD DEVIATION = 56.95

100 GENERATED RANDOM VALUES FROM SUBROUTINE POISSON

MEAN = 2.0

0	1	1	2	2
0	1	2	4	1
2	3	0	2	0
3	4	1	3	7
3	1	1	4	2
3	2	4	0	2
3	1	1	2	0
5	0	3	4	5
5	1	3	4	1
0	2	4	0	2
1	1	1	2	1
3	3	0	3	3
1	3	4	4	1
2	0	6	3	4
0	3	2	1	1
1	2	2	1	5
1	3	0	1	2
2	4	2	4	2
3	2	2	1	5
2	2	3	1	2

SIMULATED : MEAN = 2.15   STANDARD DEVIATION = 1.51

BASIC Programs: PRAC

```
10    REM:
20    REM:   THIS PROGRAM IS AN EXAMPLE OF PROJECT PROFITABILITY ANALYSIS.
30    REM:
40    REM:   A SET OF CASH FLOWS HAVE BEEN CALCULATED TOGETHER WITH AN
50    REM:   ASSOCIATED PROBABILITY OF ACHIEVEMENT FOR EACH OF THREE
60    REM:   COST CATEGORIES : LABOUR, OVERHEADS AND INCOME.
70    REM:   NET PROFITABILITY(P) = INCOME(M) - (LABOUR(R) + O'HEADS(D)).
80    REM:
90    REM:   A PROBABILITY DISTRIBUTION OF PROFITABILITY WILL BE
100   REM:   CALCULATED BY MULTIPLYING THE PROBABILITIES OF ALL
110   REM:   COMBINATIONS OF INCOME, LABOUR AND O'HEADS. THIS
120   REM:   ENABLES MANAGMENT TO ASSESS THE IMPLICATIONS WITH
130   REM:   RESPECT TO THE RANGE, MODE AND SKEWNESS OF THE
131   REM:   RESULTING HISTOGRAM.
132   REM:
140   REM:
150   REM:   ALLOCATE STORAGE FOR FREQUENCY DISTRIBUTION AND
160   REM:   HISTOGRAM ARRAYS.
170   REM:
180   DIM L[4],A[4],O[5],B[5],I[4],C[4],H[50]
190   REM:
200   REM:   ZEROISE HISTOGRAM CELLS; READ AND PRINT DATA.
210   REM:
220   MAT H=ZER
221   PRINT
222   PRINT "TYPE 1 TO OBTAIN NOTES ON INPUTTING DATA,"
223   PRINT "OR 2 IF THESE INSTRUCTIONS ARE NOT REQUIRED."
224   PRINT
225   INPUT Q
226   IF Q=2 THEN 381
230   PRINT "TYPE DATA OR READ IN DATA TAPE FOR THE FOLLOWING:-"
240   PRINT "LABOUR CASH FLOW(L) : 4 VALUES; FREQUENCY(A) : 4 VALUES;"
250   PRINT "O'HEADS CASH FLOW(O) : 5 VALUES; FREQUENCY(B) : 5 VALUES;"
260   PRINT "INCOME CASH FLOW(I) : 4 VALUES; FREQUENCY(C) : 4 VALUES;"
270   PRINT "NO OF HISTOGRAM CELLS(N),RANGE OF FIRST CELL(F)"
280   PRINT "AND WIDTH OF CELLS(W)."
300   PRINT
310   PRINT "NOTE : LETTERS IN BRACKETS ARE VARIABLE NAMES USED"
320   PRINT "IN PROGRAM. THE COMPUTER WILL PRINT A QUESTION MARK"
330   PRINT "TO INDICATE THAT INPUT IS EXPECTED. YOU SHOULD RESPOND"
340   PRINT "BY TYPING IN THE DATA AS LISTED ABOVE (SEPARATED BY"
350   PRINT "COMMAS AND FOLLOWED BY A RETURN AT THE END OF EACH LINE)."
```

```
370   PRINT "TO INPUT FROM PAPER TAPE TYPE IN TAPE."
371   PRINT
380   PRINT
381   PRINT "LABOUR CASH FLOW(L), 4 VALUES PLEASE"
382   MAT   INPUT L[4]
383   PRINT "ASSOCIATED FREQUENCIES PLEASE"
384   MAT   INPUT A[4]
385   T=A[1]+A[2]+A[3]+A[4]
386   IF T=100 THEN 389
387   PRINT "YOUR FREQUENCIES DO NOT ADD UP TO 100, TRY AGAIN"
388   GOTO 383
389   PRINT
390   PRINT "O'HEAD CASH FLOWS(O), 5 VALUES PLEASE"
391   MAT   INPUT O[5]
392   PRINT "ASSOCIATED FREQUENCIES PLEASE"
393   MAT   INPUT B[5]
394   T=B[1]+B[2]+B[3]+B[4]+B[5]
395   IF T=100 THEN 398
396   PRINT "YOUR FREQUENCIES DO NO ADD UP TO 100, TRY AGAIN"
397   GOTO 392
398   PRINT
399   PRINT "INCOME CASH FLOW(I), 4 VALUES PLEASE"
400   MAT   INPUT I[4]
401   PRINT "ASSOCIATED FREQUENCIES PLEASE"
402   MAT   INPUT C[4]
403   T=C[1]+C[2]+C[3]+C[4]
404   IF T=100 THEN 407
405   PRINT "YOUR FREQUENCIES DO NO ADD UP TO 100, TRY AGAIN"
406   GOTO 401
407   PRINT
408   PRINT "NO OF HISTOGRAM CELLS REQUIRED"
409   INPUT N
410   PRINT "VALUE OF LOWEST CELL"
411   INPUT F
412   PRINT "CLASS INTERVALS"
413   INPUT W
416   PRINT
417   PRINT
418   PRINT "PROJECT PROFITABILITY ANALYSIS DATA"
419   PRINT
420   PRINT
421   PRINT "LABOUR CASH FLOW";TAB(20);L[1];TAB(28);L[2];TAB(36);L[3];
422   PRINT TAB(44);L[4]
423   PRINT "FREQUENCIES";TAB(20);A[1];TAB(28);A[2];
424   PRINT TAB(36);A[3];TAB(44);A[4]
425   PRINT
430   PRINT "O'HEAD CASH FLOW";TAB(20);O[1];TAB(28);O[2];TAB(36);
431   PRINT O[3];TAB(44);O[4];TAB(52);O[5]
432   PRINT "FREQUENCIES";TAB(20);B[1];TAB(28);B[2];TAB(36);
433   PRINT B[3];TAB(44);B[4];TAB(52);B[5]
434   PRINT
440   PRINT "INCOME CASH FLOW";TAB(20);I[1];TAB(28);I[2];TAB(36);
441   PRINT I[3];TAB(44);I[4]
442   PRINT "FREQUENCIES";TAB(20);C[1];TAB(28);C[2];TAB(36);C[3];
443   PRINT TAB(44);C[4]
444   PRINT
```

```
450    PRINT "NO OF CELLS, LOWEST, INTERVALS";N,F,W
451    PRINT
470    PRINT
480    PRINT
490    PRINT
660    FOR X=1 TO 4
670    FOR G=1 TO 4
680    FOR Z=1 TO 5
690    P=I[X]-L[G]-O[Z]
700    P1=C[X]*A[G]*B[Z]/1.E+06
710    Y=1
720    FOR J=F TO (F+W*(N-1)) STEP W
730    IF P< = J THEN 760
740    Y=Y+1
750    NEXT J
760    H[Y]=H[Y]+P1
770    NEXT Z
780    NEXT G
790    NEXT X
801    C1=1-H[1]
802    PRINT
803    PRINT
804    PRINT
810    REM:
820    REM:PRINT HISTOGRAM.
830    REM:
840    PRINT "PROJECT PROFITABILITY ANALYSIS - PROBABILITY DISTRIBUTION"
850    PRINT
860    PRINT "PROBABILITY    CUM PROBABILITY              RANGE"
870    PRINT TAB(4);H[1];TAB(18);C1;TAB(40)"TO   ";TAB(45);F
880    FOR J=2 TO N-1
881    C1=C1-H[J]
890    PRINT TAB(4);H[J];TAB(18);C1;TAB(32);
891    PRINT F+(W*(J-2))+1;TAB(40)"TO   ";F+(W*(J-1))
900    NEXT J
901    C1=C1-H[N]
910    PRINT TAB(4);H[N];TAB(18);C1;TAB(32);
911    PRINT F+(W*(N-2))+1;TAB(40)"TO"
920    END
```

Appendix 9

BASIC Programs: PRAS

```
10    REM:
20    REM:   THIS PROGRAM IS AN EXAMPLE OF PROJECT PRÔFITABILITY ANALYSIS.
30    REM:
40    REM:   A SET OF CASH FLOWS HAVE BEEN CALCULATED TOGETHER WITH AN
50    REM:·  ASSOCIATED PROBABILITY OF ACHIEVEMENT FOR EACH OF THREE
60    REM:   COST CATEGORIES : LABOUR, OVERHEADS AND INCOME.
70    REM:   NET PROFITABILITY(P) = INCOME(M) - (LABOUR(R) + O'HEADS(D)).
80    REM:
90    REM:   A FREQUENCY DISTRIBUTION (HISTOGRAM) OF PROFITABILITY
100   REM:   WILL BE BUILT UP USING MONTE CARLO METHODS TO ENABLE
110   REM:   MANAGEMENT TO ASSESS THE IMPLICATIONS OF ITS RANGE,
120   REM:   MODE,SKEWNESS ETC.
130   REM:
140   REM:
150   REM:   ALLOCATE STORAGE FOR FREQUENCY DISTRIBUTION AND
160   REM:   HISTOGRAM ARRAYS.
170   REM:
180   DIM L[4],A[4],O[5],B[5],I[4],C[4],H[50]
190   REM:
200   REM:   ZEROISE HISTOGRAM CELLS; READ AND PRINT DATA.
210   REM:
220   MAT H=ZER
221   PRINT
222   PRINT "TYPE 1 TO OBTAIN NOTES ON INPUTTING DATA,"
223   PRINT "OR 2 IF THESE INSTRUCTIONS ARE NOT REQUIRED."
224   PRINT
225   INPUT Q
226   IF Q=2 THEN 381
230   PRINT "TYPE DATA OR READ IN DATA TAPE FOR THE FOLLOWING:-"
240   PRINT "LABOUR CASH FLOW(L) : 4 VALUES; FREQUENCY(A) : 4 VALUES;"
250   PRINT "O'HEADS CASH FLOW(O)) : 5 VALUES; FREQUENCY(B) : 5 VALUES;"
260   PRINT "INCOME CASH FLOW(I) : 4 VALUES; FREQUENCY(C) : 4 VALUES;"
270   PRINT "NO OF HISTOGRAM CELLS(N),RANGE OF FIRST CELL(F)"
280   PRINT "AND WIDTH OF CELLS(W)."
290   PRINT "NO OF RUNS REQUIRED(N1)."
300   PRINT
310   PRINT "NOTE : LETTERS IN BRACKETS ARE VARIABLE NAMES USED"
320   PRINT "IN PROGRAM. THE COMPUTER WILL PRINT A QUESTION MARK"
330   PRINT "TO INDICATE THAT INPUT IS EXPECTED. YOU SHOULD RESPOND"
340   PRINT "BY TYPING IN THE DATA AS LISTED ABOVE (SEPARATED BY"
350   PRINT "COMMAS AND FOLLOWED BY A RETURN AT THE END OF EACH LINE)."
370   PRINT "TO INPUT FROM PAPER TAPE TYPE IN TAPE."
```

```
371   PRINT
380   PRINT
381   PRINT "LABOUR CASH FLOW(L), 4 VALUES PLEASE"
382   MAT INPUT L(4)
383   PRINT "ASSOCIATED FREQUENCIES PLEASE"
384   MAT INPUT A(4)
385   T = A(1)+A(2)+A(3)+A(4)
386   IF T = 100 THEN 389
387   PRINT "YOUR FREQUENCIES DO NOT ADD UP TO 100, TRY AGAIN"
388   GOTO 383
389   PRINT
390   PRINT "O'HEAD CASH FLOWS(O), 5 VALUES PLEASE"
391   MAT INPUT O(5)
392   PRINT "ASSOCIATED FREQUENCIES PLEASE"
393   MAT INPUT B(5)
394   T = B(1)+B(2)+B(3)+B(4)+B(5)
395   IF T = 100 THEN 398
396   PRINT "YOUR FREQUENCIES DO NO ADD UP TO 100, TRY AGAIN"
397   GOTO 392
398   PRINT
399   PRINT "INCOME CASH FLOW(I), 4 VALUES PLEASE"
400   MAT INPUT I(4)
401   PRINT "ASSOCIATED FREQUENCIES PLEASE"
402   MAT INPUT C(4)
403   T = C(1)+C(2)+C(3)+C(4)
404   IF T = 100 THEN 407
405   PRINT "YOUR FREQUENCIES DO NO ADD UP TO 100, TRY AGAIN"
406   GOTO 401
407   PRINT
408   PRINT "NO OF HISTOGRAM CELLS REQUIRED"
409   INPUT N
410   PRINT "VALUE OF LOWEST CELL"
411   INPUT F
412   PRINT "CLASS INTERVALS"
413   INPUT W
414   PRINT "NO OF SIMULATED RUNS REQUIRED"
415   INPUT N1
416   PRINT
417   PRINT
418   PRINT "PROJECT PROFITABILITY ANALYSIS DATA"
419   PRINT
420   PRINT
421   PRINT "LABOUR CASH FLOW";TAB(20);L(1);TAB(28);L(2);TAB(36);L(3);
422   PRINT TAB(44);L(4)
423   PRINT "FREQUENCIES";TAB(20);A(1);TAB(28);A(2);
424   PRINT TAB(36);A(3);TAB(44);A(4)
425   PRINT
430   PRINT "O'HEAD CASH FLOW";TAB(20);O(1);TAB(28);O(2);TAB(36);
431   PRINT O(3);TAB(44);O(4);TAB(52);O(5)
432   PRINT "FREQUENCIES";TAB(20);B(1);TAB(28);B(2);TAB(36);
433   PRINT B(3);TAB(44);B(4);TAB(52);B(5)
434   PRINT
440   PRINT "INCOME CASH FLOW";TAB(20);I(1);TAB(28);I(2);TAB(36);
441   PRINT I(3);TAB(44);I(4)
442   PRINT "FREQUENCIES";TAB(20);C(1);TAB(28);C(2);TAB(36);C(3);
443   PRINT TAB(44);C(4)
```

```
444   PRINT
450   PRINT "NO OF CELLS, LOWEST, INTERVALS";N,F,W
451   PRINT
460   PRINT "LENGTH OF RUN";N1
470   PRINT
471   PRINT
472   PRINT
480   REM:
481   REM:  CUMULATE FREQUENCIES
482   REM:
485   A(2)=A(1)+A(2)
486   A(3)=A(3)+A(2)
487   A(4)=A(4)+A(3)
488   B(2)=B(1)+B(2)
489   B(3)=B(3)+B(2)
490   B(4)=B(4)+B(3)
491   B(5)=B(5)+B(4)
492   C(2)=C(1)+C(2)
493   C(3)=C(3)+C(2)
494   C(4)=C(4)+C(3)
499   REM:
500   REM:  SET UP LOOP FOR NO OF RUNS.
510   REM:
520   FOR X=1 TO N1
530   REM:
540   REM:  SAMPLE FROM EACH OF THE FREQUENCY DISTRIBUTIONS
550   REM:  AND CALCULATE NET PROFITABILITY.
560   REM:
570   R=L[1]
580   FOR S1=2 TO 4
590   IF (RND(0)*100)< = A[S1-1] THEN 620
600   R=L[S1]
610   NEXT S1
620   D=O[1]
630   FOR S2=2 TO 5
640   IF (RND(0)*100)< = B[S2-1] THEN 670
650   D=O[S2]
660   NEXT S2
670   M=I[1]
680   FOR S3=2 TO 4
690   IF (RND(0)*100)< = C[S3-1] THEN 720
700   M=I[S3]
710   NEXT S3
720   P=M-R-D
730   REM:
740   REM:  ADD 1 TO APPROPRIATE HISTOGRAM CELL.
750   REM:
759   Y=1
760   FOR J=F TO (F+W*(N-1)) STEP W
770   IF P< = J THEN 790
775   Y=Y+1
780   NEXT J
790   H[Y]=H[Y]+1
800   NEXT X

801   C1=1-H[1]/N1
```

```
810   REM:
820   REM:PRINT HISTOGRAM.
830   REM:
840   PRINT "PROJECT PROFITABILITY ANALYSIS HISTOGRAM"
850   PRINT
860   PRINT "COUNT    CUM PROBABILITY              RANGE"
870   PRINT TAB(1);H(1);TAB(12);C1;TAB(36)"TO   ";TAB(40);F
880   FOR J=2 TO N-1
881   C1=C1-H(J)/N1
890   PRINT TAB(1);H(J);TAB(12);C1;TAB(28);
891   PRINT F+(W*(J-2))+1;TAB(36)"TO   ";F+(W*(J-1))
900   NEXT J
901   C1=C1-H(N)/N1
910   PRINT TAB(1);H(N);TAB(12);C1;TAB(28);F+(W*(N-2))+1;TAB(36)"TO"
920   END
```

Appendix 10

CSL Programs: BOWS

```
 1              LISTING(3)
 2              SOURCE(CR,S1)
 3              LABEL(,BOWSERS,999)
 4              OBJECT(MT,BOWSERS.EH1)
 5      *       PROGRAM(BOWS)
 6      *       COMPRESS INTEGER AND LOGICAL
 7      *       INPUT 1=CRO
 8      *       OUTPUT 2=LPO
 9      *       END
10              MASTER REFUELLING
11      C
12      C   THIS PROGRAM SIMULATES REFUELLING OF AIRCRAFT BY
13      C   FOUR BOWSERS (REFUELLING LORRIES).
14      C
15      C   TWO CLASSES OF ENTITIES ARE DEFINED : 1000 AIRCRAFT AND
16      C   4 BOWSERS.  THE AIRCRAFT ENTITIES EACH HAVE 2
17      C   ATTRIBUTES : (1) = FUEL REQUIRED AND (2) = TIME
18      C   AIRCRAFT JOINS THE QUEUE (SET AIRQUEUE).
19      C   THE BOWSER ENTITIES ARE ADDED TO A SET FREEBOW WHEN
20      C   THEY BECOME AVAILABLE FOR REFUELLING I.E. WHEN THE
21      C   ASSOCIATED TIME VALUES BECOME ZERO.
22      C
23              CLASS TIME AIRCRAFT.1000(2) SET AIRQUEUE
24      C       CLASS TIME BOWSER.4(1) SET FREEBOWS
25              CLASS PARTFILLED.4(1) SET EXT,AV
26      C   MAXIMUM DIMENSIONS OF ARRAYS ARE DEFINED AND
27      C   DISTRIBUTIONS FOR AIRCRAFT INTERARRIVAL TIMES AND
28      C   FUEL REQUIRED FOR AIRCRAFT ARE READ IN AND PRINTED
29      C
30              ARRAY ARRIVETIME(2,10),FUELREQ(2,8),ACFILLTIME(4),
31             1REFUELTIME(4),FUELPC(4),REFILLPC(4),WAITPC(4),
32             2TACTIME(4),TRTIME(4)
33              READ(1,500)L
34          500 FORMAT(I3)
35              READ(1,2)ARRIVETIME, FUELREQ
36            2 FORMAT(20I4/16I4)
37              WRITE(2,4)ARRIVETIME,FUELREQ
38            4 FORMAT(5H1DATA//1H0,20I5//1H0,16I5)
39      C
40      C   THE DISTRIBUTIONS ARE CONVERTED TO CUMULATIVE FORM AND
41      C   A HISTOGRAM IS DEFINED FOR THE WAITING TIMES (6 CELLS
42      C   OF WIDTH 5).  THE INITIAL CONDITIONS ARE SET UP WITH THE
```

258

```
43   C    BOWSERS CONTAINING 10000 GALLONS OF FUEL, AND THE NEXT
44   C    AIRCRAFT DUE IN 10 MINS.
45   C
46        DIST ARRIVETIME,FUELREQ
47        STREAMA=5
48        STREAMB=9
49        HIST WAITING(14,0,20)
50        T.NEXT=10
51        BOWSER LOAD FREEBOWS
52        ZERO AIRQUEUE
53        ZERO EXT
54        PARTFILLED LOAD AV
55        MAXWAIT=0
56        CRAFT=0
57        FILLED=0
58        J=0
59        MAXQ=0
60        FOR I=1,4
61          BOWSER.I(1)=10000
62          T.BOWSER.I=-1
63          ACFILLTIME(I)=0
64          REFUELTIME(I)=0
65          TACTIME(I)=0
66          TRTIME(I)=0
67   C
68   C    START OF SIMULATION.
69   C
70        ACTIVITIES
71        BEGIN AIRCRAFT ARRIVAL
72        T.NEXT EQ 0
73   C
74   C    AN AIRCRAFT HAS ARRIVED AND JOINS THE QUEUE (AIRQUEUE).
75   C    ITS ARRIVAL TIME AND THE AMOUNT OF FUEL REQUIRED ARE
76   C    RECORDED.  THE TIME OF ARRIVAL OF THE NEXT AIRCRAFT
77   C    IS SAMPLED.
78   C
79        J+1
80        AIRCRAFT.J TAIL AIRQUEUE
81        AIRCRAFT.J(2) = CLOCK
82        AIRCRAFT.J(1) = SAMPLE(1,FUELREQ,STREAMB)
83        T.NEXT = SAMPLE(1,ARRIVETIME,STREAMA)
84        CRAFT+1
85        CRAFT GT MAXQ @ 5
86        MAXQ = CRAFT
87      5 WRITE(2,100)J,AIRCRAFT.J(1),AIRCRAFT.J(2),CRAFT,T.NEXT
88    100 FORMAT(38HOA/C : FUEL : ARRIVE : QUEUE : NEXT : ,5I7)
89        BEGIN UPDATE FREEBOWS
90   C
91   C    BOWSERS WHICH HAVE BECOME AVAILABLE ARE ADDED TO END
92   C    OF SET FREEBOWS.
93   C
94        FOR IX=1,4
95          T.BOWSER.IX EQ 0 @ 9
96          ACFILLTIME(IX)=0
97          REFUELTIME(IX)=0
98          WRITE(2,200)IX,CLOCK
```

```
 99                 BOWSER.IX TAIL FREEBOWS @ 9
100          9  DUMMY
101     200 FORMAT(14H0IX : CLOCK : ,2I7)
102             BEGIN REFUEL
103     C
104     C   THE FIRST AVAILABLE BOWSER (IF ANY) STARTS REFUELLING
105     C   THE FIRST AIRCRAFT IN THE QUEUE.
106     C
107             FOR MX=1,4
108                FIND K EXT FIRST @ 11
109                N=PARTFILLED.K(1)
110                T.AIRCRAFT.N EQ 0 @ 600
111                AIRCRAFT.N HEAD AIRQUEUE
112                PARTFILLED.K FROM EXT
113                PARTFILLED.K TO AV
114                GO TO 11
115        600     DUMMY
116      11 FIND M AIRQUEUE FIRST
117             FINE I FREEBOWS FIRST
118             BOWSER.I FROM FREEBOWS
119             AIRCRAFT.M FROM AIRQUEUE
120     C
121     C   THE REFUELLING TIME AND THE AMOUNT OF FUEL USED BY THE
122     C   BOWSER IS CALCULATED.
123     C
124             ACFILLTIME(I) = AIRCRAFT.M(1)/50 + 10
125             TACTIME(I) = TACTIME(I) + ACFILLTIME(I)
126             BOWSER.I(1) = BOWSER.I(1) - AIRCRAFT.M(1)
127             WRITE(2,201)M,I,BOWSER.I(1),ACFILLTIME(I),CLOCK
128     201 FORMAT(45H0A/C : BNO : BFUEL : A/C FILL-TIME : CLOCK : ,
129         15I7)
130             BOWSER.I(1) LE 0 @ 12
131     C
132     C   THE BOWSER IS EMPTY AND GOES TO BE RE-FILLED (TO 14).
133     C   THE FUEL STILL REQUIRED BY THE AIRCRAFT IS RECORDED,
134     C   AND IT IS RETURNED TO THE BEGINNING OF THE QUEUE.
135     C
136             AIRCRAFT.M(1) = - BOWSER.I(1)
137             ACFILLTIME(I) = ACFILLTIME(I) - AIRCRAFT.M(1)/50
138             TACTIME(I) = TACTIME(I) - AIRCRAFT.M(1)/50
139             T.AIRCRAFT.M = ACFILLTIME(I)
140             FIND K AV FIRST
141             PARTFILLED.K FROM AV
142             PARTFILLED.K(1) = M
143             PARTFILLED.K TAIL EXT
144             WRITE(2,560)(PARTFILLED.K(1),K=1,4)
145     560 FORMAT(28H0PARTFILLED 1 : 2 : 3 : 4 : ,4I7)
146             WRITE(2,202)M,AIRCRAFT.M(1),T.AIRCRAFT.M
147     202 FORMAT(22H0A/C : FUEL : EXTRA : ,3I7)
148             BOWSER.I(1) = 0
149             GO TO 14
150     C
151     C   WHEN THE AIRCRAFT HAS BEEN REFUELLED, THE WAITING TIME
152     C   IS RECORDED AND THE MAXIMUM WAITING TIME TO DATE IS
153     C   FOUND. 1 IS ADDED TO THE NUMBER REFUELLED.
154     C
```

```
155        12 WAIT = CLOCK - AIRCRAFT.M(2)
156           WRITE(2,203)M,WAIT
157       203 FORMAT(14HOA/C : WAIT : ,2I7)
158           WAIT GT MAXWAIT @ 13
159           MAXWAIT = WAIT
160        13 ADD WAIT,WAITING
161           WRITE(2,101)WAIT,MAXWAIT
162       101 FORMAT(18HOWAIT : MAXWAIT : ,2I7)
163           FILLED+1
164           CRAFT-1
165           WRITE(2,204)(BOWSER.IY(1),IY=1,4)
166       204 FORMAT(29HOBOWSER FUEL 1 : 2 : 3 : 4 : ,4I7)
167           BOWSER.I(1) LT 1500 @ 15
168    C
169    C   THE BOWSER CONTAINS LESS THAN 1500 GALLONS OF FUEL
170    C   AND IS SENT FOR RE-FILLING. THE FILLING TIME IS
171    C   CALCULATED.
172    C
173        14 REFUELTIME(I) = 210 + (10000 - BOWSER.I(1))/100
174           TRTIME(I) = TRTIME(I) + REFUELTIME(I)
175           WRITE(2,205)I,REFUELTIME(I)
176       205 FORMAT(21HOBNO : REFUEL TIME : ,2I7)
177           BOWSER.I(1)=10000
178        15 T.BOWSER.I = ACFILLTIME(I) + REFUELTIME(I)
179           RECYCLE
180           BEGIN FINISH
181    C
182    C   IF MORE THAN L AIRCRAFT HAVE BEEN REFUELED , THE
183    C   MAXIMUM WAITING TIME AND HISTOGRAM ARE PRINTED,
184    C   OTHERWISE TIME IS ADVANCED AND THE SIMULATION IS
185    C   CONTINUED
186    C
187           FILLED GT L @ 17
188           FOR I=1,4
189             FUELPC(I) = 100*TACTIME(I)/(CLOCK+T.BOWSER.I)
190             REFILLPC(I) = 100*TRTIME(I)/(CLOCK+T.BOWSER.I)
191             WAITPC(I) = 100 -FUELPC(I) - REFILLPC(I)
192           WRITE(2,1)
193         1 FORMAT(34H1SIMULATION OF AIRCRAFT TURN ROUND//)
194           WRITE(2,300) (FUELPC(I),I=1,4),(WAITPC(J),J=1,4),
195         1(REFILLPC(K),K=1,4)
196       300 FORMAT(38HOBOWSERS          1      2      3      4/
197           114HO%FUELLING A/C,4I6/9HO%WAITING,I11,3I6/
198           211HO%REFILLING,I9,3I6//)
199           WRITE(2,301)MAXQ ,MAXWAIT
200       301 FORMAT(23HOMAXIMUM QUEUE LENGTH =,I4//
201           123HOMAXIMUM WAITING TIME =,I4//
202           241HOHISTOGRAM WAITING TIME (SCALED UP BY 10)/)
203           OUTPUT WAITING
204           EXIT
205        17 DUMMY
206           END
207           ENDSUBFILE
208           READ FROM(MT,BOWSERS.EH1)
209           LIBRARY
210           READ FROM(MT,-.SRC2)
211           FINISH
```

Appendix 11

CSL Programs: PSIM

```
 1              LISTING(3)
 2              SOURCE(CR,S1)
 3              LABEL(,FORTFILE,7)
 4              OBJECT(MT,FORTFILE.EHSUBFILE1)
 5      *       PROGRAM(PSIM)
 6      *       COMPRESS INTEGER AND LOGICAL
 7      *       INPUT 1=CRO
 8      *       OUTPUT 6=LPO
 9      *       END
10              MASTER PATROLSIM
11      C
12      C THIS PROGRAM SIMULATES TWO MOBILE SERVICING UNITS WHO
13      C SERVICE CUSTOMERS AS CALLED UPON.  WHEN BOTH PATROLS ARE
14      C FREE THE ONE HAVING THE SHORTEST DRIVE TIME ATTENDS TO
15      C THE CALL.  THE PATROLS START AT 08.00 HRS. THEY WILL
16      C COMPLETE ANY JOB ONCE THEY HAVE SET OUT, HOWEVER THEY
17      C WILL SET OUT TO A NEW JOB AFTER 19.29 HRS. ONLY IF THE
18      C CALL WAS RECEIVED BEFORE 18.59 HRS.
19      C
20      C CALLS MAY BE RECEIVED UP TO 22.00 HRS.; IF THEY CANNOT
21      C BE ATTENDED TO BY THE PATROLS THEY ARE REFERRED TO A
22      C 'GARAGE'.
23      C
24      C THE DAILY COST OF THE PATROLS IS CALCULATED AND FROM
25      C THIS AN AVERAGE COST PER JOB IS DERIVED.
26      C
27      C VARIOUS ASPECTS OF THE SITUATION ARE PRINTED OUT AFTER
28      C A SIMULATION OF 350 DAYS.
29      C
30              CLASS MEMBER.200(1) SET MEMWAITING
31              CLASS TIME PATROL.2 SET PATROLFREE
32              FLOAT AVCOSTPERJOB,CDAYCOST,DCOST,CJOBCOUNT,
33             1JOBCOUNT,AMTIME,PATUT
34              ARRAY CALLTIME(2,25),DRIVETIME(2,12),JOBTIME(2,7),
35             1JTIME(2),DTIME(2)
36      C
37      C READ IN AND PRINT FREQUENCY DISTRIBUTIONS FOR
38      C CALL INTERVAL,JOB AND DRIVING TIMES.
39      C
40              READ(1,1) CALLTIME,DRIVETIME,JOBTIME
41            1 FORMAT(26I3)
42              WRITE(6,98)CALLTIME,DRIVETIME,JOBTIME
```

```
43     98 FORMAT(5H1DATA/(1H0,26I4))
44        WRITE(6,500)
45    500 FORMAT(38H0  DAY  JOBS  GJOBS  LMT    TMT   ,
46       123H  TPT    EXT   CJOBS )
47  C
48  C SET UP INITIAL CONDITIONS FOR SIMULATION.
49  C
50        HIST WTIME(25,0,5),GJOBS(20,0,1),JPERDAY(26,0,1),
51       1AVJOBCOST(30,0,25)
52        DIST CALLTIME,DRIVETIME,JOBTIME
53        STREAMA=1
54        STREAMB=2
55        STREAMC=3
56        DCOUNT=0
57        CJOBCOUNT=0
58        CDAYCOST=0
59        TMEMTIME=0
60        LMEMTIME=0
61        TPTIME=0
62  C
63  C SET UP INITIAL CONDITIONS FOR DAY AND START
64  C DAY AT 08.00 (CLOCK=0) WITH BOTH PATROLS FREE.
65  C
66    100 CALLS=0
67        M=0
68        ZERO MEMWAITING
69        T.CALLS=5
70        GCOUNT=0
71        IJOBCOUNT=0
72        CLOCK=0
73        T.PATROL.1=-1
74        T.PATROL.2=-1
75        PATROL LOAD PATROLFREE
76        JTIME(1)=0
77        JTIME(2)=0
78        DTIME(1)=0
79        DTIME(2)=0
80        EXTRATIME=0
81        EXTIME =0
82        ACTIVITIES
83        BEGIN CALLS
84        T.CALLS EQ 0
85        CLOCK LE 840 @ 70
86  C
87  C SAMPLE CALL-TIME INTERVAL AND ADD 1 TO NO OF CALLS(M).
88  C NOTE TIME CALL WAS RECEIVED.
89  C
90        T.CALLS = SAMPLE(1,CALLTIME,STREAMA)
91        M+1
92        MEMBER.M TAIL MEMWAITING
93        MEMBER.M(1)=CLOCK
94        BEGIN FREE PATROLS
95        FOR I=1,2
96          T.PATROL.I EQ 0 @ 6
97          PATROL.I TAIL PATROLFREE
98      6   DUMMY
```

```
 99          BEGIN ANYMORE
100   C
101   C IF ANY MEMBERS ARE WAITING, FIND THE PATROL WHICH WILL
102   C GET THERE FIRST.  PATROL WILL ONLY SET OUT IF CALL
103   C RECEIVED BEFORE 18.59 HRS.,OTHERWISE CALL IS PASSED TO
104   C GARAGE.
105   C
106      70 FIND MI MEMWAITING FIRST @ 55
107         MEMBER.MI(1) LE 659 @ 50
108         FIND I PATROLFREE FIRST @ 56
109         DTIME(I)=SAMPLE(1,DRIVETIME,STREAMB)
110         PATROL.I FROM PATROLFREE
111         FIND J PATROLFREE FIRST @ 10
112         DTIME(J)=SAMPLE(1,DRIVETIME,STREAMB)
113         DTIME(I) LT DTIME(J) @ 20
114      10 K=I
115         DTIME(J)=0
116         GO TO 30
117      20 K=J
118         PATROL.J FROM PATROLFREE
119         PATROL.I TO PATROLFREE
120         DTIME(I)=0
121   C
122   C CALCULATE MEMBER'S WAITING TIME.
123   C
124      30 MEMTIME = DTIME(K) + CLOCK - MEMBER.MI(1)
125   C
126   C CALL WILL BE SERVICED ONLY IF PATROL ARRIVES
127   C BEFORE 19.30 HRS.
128   C
129         ARTIME = CLOCK + DTIME(K)
130         ARTIME LT 690 @ 50
131         TMEMTIME = TMEMTIME + MEMTIME
132         LMEMTIME LT MEMTIME @ 60
133         LMEMTIME=MEMTIME
134      60 ADD MEMTIME,WTIME
135   C
136   C DETERMINE TIME WHEN PATROL BECOMES FREE, ADD 1 TO NO
137   C OF JOBS AND CALCULATE TIME WORKED AFTER 19.00. HRS.
138   C
139         JTIME(K) = SAMPLE(1,JOBTIME,STREAMC)
140         T.PATROL.K = DTIME(K) + JTIME(K)
141         TPTIME = TPTIME + T.PATROL.K
142         IJOBCOUNT+1
143         EXTIME = ARTIME + JTIME(K)
144         EXTIME GT 660 @ 49
145         EXTRATIME=EXTRATIME+EXTIME-660
146      49 GO TO 51
147   C
148   C ADD 1 TO NO OF CALLS PASSED TO GARAGES.
149   C
150      50 GCOUNT+1
151      51 MEMBER.MI FROM MEMWAITING
152         RECYCLE
153         BEGIN END OF DAY
154   C
```

```
155   C IF TIME IS GREATER THAN 19.00 HRS., UPDATE HISTOGRAMS AND
156   C CALCULATE COST PER DAY @ £1/HR., COST PER JOB AND
157   C CUMULATIVE COST. IF LESS THAN 18.59 HRS., ADVANCE TIME
158   C AND CONTINUE SIMULATION.
159   C
160      55 CLOCK GT 840 @ 56
161      57 ADD GCOUNT,GJOBS
162         ADD IJOBCOUNT,JPERDAY
163         DCOST=(1320 + EXTRATIME)/60
164         JOBCOUNT=IJOBCOUNT
165         CPJOB=DCOST*100/JOBCOUNT
166         ADD CPJOB,AVJOBCOST
167         DCOUNT+1
168         CDAYCOST=CDAYCOST + DCOST
169         CJOBCOUNT = CJOBCOUNT + JOBCOUNT
170         ICJOBCOUNT=CJOBCOUNT
171         WRITE(6,7)DCOUNT,IJOBCOUNT,GCOUNT,LMEMTIME,
172        1TMEMTIME,TPTIME,EXTRATIME,ICJOBCOUNT
173       7 FORMAT(1H ,I5,I6,2I7,2I9,2I7)
174         DCOUNT EQ 350 @ 100
175         BEGIN FINISH
176   C
177   C PRINT SUMMARY OF SIMULATED RESULTS.
178   C
179         AVCOSTPERJOB=CDAYCOST/CJOBCOUNT
180         WRITE(6,2)
181       2 FORMAT(39H1SIMULATION OF MOBILE SERVICING PATROLS)
182         WRITE(6,4)DCOUNT
183       4 FORMAT(18HONO OF PATROLS = 2//
184        131H TOTAL SIMULATED PERIOD(DAYS) =,I4)
185         IJCOUNT=CJOBCOUNT
186         AVSERDAY=CJOBCOUNT/DCOUNT
187         AVWTIME=TMEMTIME/CJOBCOUNT
188         WRITE(6,5)IJCOUNT,AVSERDAY
189       5 FORMAT(17HOTOTAL SERVICED =,I7//
190        127H AVERAGE SERVICED PER DAY =,I4//
191        219HOHISTOGRAM JOBS/DAY)
192         OUTPUT JPERDAY
193         WRITE(6,200)
194     200 FORMAT(22H1HISTOGRAM GARAGE JOBS)
195         OUTPUT GJOBS
196         WRITE(6,201)TMEMTIME,AVWTIME,LMEMTIME
197         FORMAT(21H1TOTAL WAITING TIME =,I7//
198        123H AVERAGE WAITING TIME =,I4//
199        223H MAXIMUM WAITING TIME =,I4)
200         TPITIME=1320*350-TPTIME
201         AMTIME=TPTIME
202         PATUT=AMTIME/(1320*350)*100
203         WRITE(6,203)TPITIME,PATUT
204     203 FORMAT(25HOTOTAL PATROL IDLE TIME =,I8//
205        129H PATROL UTILISATION PERCENT =,F6.2//)
206         WRITE(6,205)
207     205 FORMAT(23HOHISTOGRAM WAITING TIME)
208         OUTPUT WTIME
209         WRITE(6,202)CDAYCOST ,AVCOSTPERJOB
210     202 FORMAT(25H1TOTAL COST OF JOBS (£) =,F8.2//
```

265

```
211          127H AVERAGE COST PER JOB (£) =,F5.2//
212          238HOHISTOGRAM AVERAGE JOBCOST (NEW PENCE))
213           OUTPUT AVJOBCOST
214           EXIT
215       56 DUMMY
216           END
217           ENDSUBFILE
218           READ FROM (MT,FORTFILE.EHSUBFILE1)
219           LIBRARY
220           READ FROM (MT,-.SRC2)
221           FINISH
```

Appendix 12

CSL Programs: SOMB

```
 1              LISTING(3)
 2              SOURCE(CR,S1)
 3              LABEL(,SOMB,999)
 4              OBJECT(MT,SOMB.EH)
 5      *       PROGRAM(SOMB)
 6      *       COMPRESS INTEGER AND LOGICAL
 7      *       INPUT 1=CRO
 8      *       OUTPUT 6=LPO
 9      *       END
10              MASTER MAINTENANCE
11      C
12      C THIS PROGRAM SIMULATES A MAINTENANCE PROBLEM
13      C DEFINE CLASS OF ENTITIES(BAY) AND ASSOCIATED ORDERED SET
14      C (FREEBAYS).  TIME VALUES ARE TO BE ASSOCIATED WITH THE
15      C ENTITIES.
16      C
17              CLASS TIME BAY.4 SET FREEBAYS
18      C
19      C DEFINE MAXIMUM DIMENSION OF ARRAYS FOR BAYSERVICE TIME AND
20      C READ IN FREQUENCY DISTRIBUTIONS: SERVICING TIMES(BAYTIME)
21      C AND INTERARRIVAL TIMES. THEN PRINT DATA.
22      C
23              ARRAY REPAIRED(4),BAYTIME(2,8),ARRIVETIME(2,10)
24              READ(1,100) BAYTIME,ARRIVETIME
25      100 FORMAT(36I2)
26              WRITE(6,101) BAYTIME,ARRIVETIME
27      101 FORMAT( 5H1DATA,36I3)
28      C
29      C PRINT HEADING.
30      C
31              WRITE(6,102)
32      102 FORMAT(33H1SIMULATION OF ENGINE MAINTENANCE)
33      C
34      C CONVERT DISTRIBUTIONS TO CUMULATIVE FORM.
35      C DEFINE QUEUESIZE AS HISTOGRAM (10 CELLS OF WIDTH 1).
36      C SET UP INITIAL CONDITIONS: ALL BAYS FREE AT -1 HRS,
37      C NEXT UNIT DUE IN 2 HRS, NO UNITS IN SYSTEM.
38      C
39              DIST BAYTIME,ARRIVETIME
40              STREAMA=13
41              STREAMB=17
42              HIST QUEUESIZE(10,0,1)
```

```
43              T.UNIT=2
44              BAY LOAD FREEBAYS
45              FOR I=1,4
46                REPAIRED(I)=0
47                T.BAY.I=-1
48              UNITS=0
49              T.INTERVAL=24
50              ACTIVITIES
51      C
52      C START OF SIMULATION
53      C
54              BEGIN SERVICING
55      C
56      C NO OF UNITS IN SYSTEM COUNTED EVERY 24 HRS AND
57      C HISTOGRAM UPDATED.
58      C
59              T.INTERVAL EQ 0
60              T.INTERVAL=24
61              ADD UNITS,QUEUESIZE
62              BEGIN UNIT ARRIVAL
63      C
64      C TIME OF NEXT ARRIVAL SAMPLED WHEN A UNIT ARRIVES.
65      C
66              T.UNIT EQ 0
67              T.UNIT=SAMPLE(1,ARRIVETIME,STREAMB)
68              UNITS+1
69              BEGIN UPDATE FREEBAYS
70      C
71      C FREE BAYS ADDED TO END OF SET AND NO SERVICED NOTED.
72      C
73              FOR I=1,4
74                T.BAY.I EQ 0 @ 108
75                BAY.I TAIL FREEBAYS @ 108
76                REPAIRED(I)+1
77      108     DUMMY
78              BEGIN UNIT ENTERS BAY
79      C
80      C TEST IF ANY UNITS IN SYSTEM (IF NONE GO TO BEGIN FINISH).
81      C
82              UNITS GT 0
83      C
84      C TEST IF A BAY IS FREE (IF NONE GO TO BEGIN FINISH).
85      C
86              FIND I FREEBAYS MIN(I)
87              UNITS-1
88      C
89      C SELECT FREEBAY AND START SERVICE OF A UNIT.
90      C REMOVE BAY FROM FREEBAYS SET.
91      C
92              BAY.I FROM FREEBAYS
93              T.BAY.I=SAMPLE(1,BAYTIME,STREAMA)
94              RECYCLE
95              BEGIN FINISH
96      C
97      C TEST IF ELAPSED TIME IS > OR = 4000 HRS.
98      C IF NO, ADVANCE TIME AND CONTINUE SIMULATION.
```

```
99    C IF YES, PRINT ELAPSED TIME, NO SERVICED BY BAYS AND
100   C QUEUESIZE HISTOGRAM.
101   C
102         CLOCK GE 4000 112 @ 113
103     112 WRITE(6,114)CLOCK
104     114 FORMAT(15HOELAPSED TIME =,I5,6H HOURS)
105         WRITE(6,115)
106     115 FORMAT(12HONO SERVICED)
107         FOR I=1,4
108           WRITE(6,116)I,REPAIRED(I)
109     116   FORMAT(4HOBAY,I2,I4)
110         WRITE(6,117)
111     117 FORMAT(1HO/42HOQUEUESIZE (ASSESSED AT 24 HRLY INVERVALS)/)
112         OUTPUT QUEUESIZE
113         EXIT
114     113 DUMMY
115         END
116         ENDSUBFILE
117         READ FROM(MT,SOMB.EH)
118         LIBRARY
119         READ FROM (MT,-.SRC2)
120         FINISH
```

Appendix 13

CSL Programs: STAN

```
 1          LISTING(3)
 2          SOURCE(CR,S1)
 3          LABEL(,STAN,999)
 4          OBJECT(MT,STAN.EHSUBFILE)
 5   *      PROGRAM(STAN)
 6   *      COMPRESS INTEGER AND LOGICAL
 7   *      INPUT 1=CRO
 8   *      OUTPUT 2=LPO
 9   *      END
10          MASTER STAN
11   C
12   C THIS PROGRAM SIMULATES A RANGE OF INVENTORY POLICIES.
13   C FOR EACH COMBINATION OF ORDER QUANTITY AND ROL THE AVERAGE
14   C STOCK AND SERVICE LEVEL IS CALCULATED. IN THIS PROGRAM
15   C ANY SHORTAGES ENCOUNTERED ARE NOT SUBSEQUENTLY MADE GOOD.
16   C
17   C DEFINE ARRAYS FOR DEMAND DISTRIBUTION AND FOR LEAD TIMES.
18   C READ IN FREQUENCY DISTRIBUTION: DEMAND, PRINT DEMAND DATA.
19   C
20          ARRAY DEMAND(2,6),LI(3)
21          READ(1,1)DEMAND
22        1 FORMAT(12I2)
23          WRITE(2,20)DEMAND
24       20 FORMAT(5H1DATA,12I4)
25          STREAM=5
26          DIST DEMAND
27          FLOAT SERVICE,AVN
28   C
29   C SPECIFY FORMAT OF HEADINGS.
30   C
31        2 FORMAT(19H1INVENTORY POLICIES)
32        3 FORMAT(43H0    ORDER QUANTITY    R.O.L.    SERVICE,
33         114H    AV. STOCK)
34       30 FORMAT(1H0)
35   C
36   C DEFINE ORDER QUANTITIES TO BE SIMULATED IN AN INCREMENTAL
37   C FOR LOOP.
38   C
39   C PRINT PAGE HEADINGS.
40   C
41          FOR OQ=5,100,5
42            WRITE(2,2)
```

```
43              WRITE(2,3)
44              WRITE(2,30)
45    C
46    C DEFINE ROLS  TO BE SIMULATED FOR EACH ORDER QUANTITY LOOP.
47    C INIALISE BEGINNING OF RUN, INITIAL STOCK SET TO 80 UNITS.
48    C THREE LEAD TIMES SET TO 3 READY FOR COUNT DOWN.
49    C
50              FOR ROL=5,60,5
51                TD=0
52                TC=0
53                FOR I=1,3
54                  LI(I)=3
55                N=80
56                P=80
57                AVN=0
58    C
59    C START OF 200 WEEK SIMULATION FOR A PARTICULAR COMBINATION
60    C OF ORDER QUANTITY AND ROL.
61    C
62                FOR WK=1,200
63    C
64    C TEST LEAD TIMES, IF DOWN TO ZERO ADD ORDER QUANTITY TO
65    C STOCK AND RESET APPROPRIATE LEAD TIME.
66    C
67                  FOR I=1,3
68                    LI(I) EQ 0 @ 21
69                    N=N+OQ
70                    LI(I)=3
71        21        DUMMY
72    C
73    C SAMPLE DEMAND, IF IN EXCESS OF NET STOCK ISSUE STOCK
74    C AVAILABLE. ADJUST PROVISIONED STOCK LEVEL ACCORDINGLY.
75    C CUMULATE TOTAL DEMAND (TD), TOTAL ISSUED (TC),.
76    C AND NET (AVN).
77    C
78        4        D=SAMPLE(1,DEMAND,STREAM)
79                 IF(N-D)6,6,7
80        6        TC=TC+N
81                 P=P-N
82                 N=0
83                 GO TO 8
84        7        N=N-D
85                 P=P-D
86                 TC=TC+D
87        8        TD=TD+D
88                 AVN=AVN+N
89    C
90    C TEST IF PROVISIONED STOCK LEVEL IS BELOW ROL.
91    C
92                 P LE ROL @ 9
93    C
94    C FIND FIRST UNALLOCATED LEAD TIME AND REDUCE BY 1.
95    C ADD ORDER QUANTITY TO PROVISIONED STOCK LEVEL.
96    C
97                 FOR I=1,3
98                   LI(I) EQ 3 @ 22
```

```
 99                      P=P+OQ
100                      LI(I)-1
101                      J=I
102                      GO TO 23
103        22           DUMMY
104         9      J=0
105   C
106   C REDUCE LEAD TIMES IN USE BY 1.
107   C
108        23       FOR I=1,3
109                    I  NE J @ 24
110                    LI(I) NE 3 @ 24
111                    LI(I)-1
112        24         DUMMY
113        10     DUMMY
114   C
115   C OUTPUT RESULT AT END OF EACH RUN.
116   C
117                  SERVICE=TC*100/TD
118                  AVN=AVN/200.
119                  WRITE(2,11)OQ,ROL,SERVICE,AVN
120        11 FORMAT(1H ,12X,I3,11X,I2,F13.1,F13.2)
121             DUMMY
122         EXIT
123         END
124         ENDSUBFILE
125         READ FROM(MT,STAN.EHSUBFILE)
126         LIBRARY
127         READ FROM(MT,-.SRC2)
128         FINISH
```

Appendix 14

CSL Programs: SUBC

```
 1              LISTING(3)
 2              SOURCE(CR,S1)
 3              LABEL(,SUBC,999)
 4              OBJECT(MT,SUBC.EH)
 5              MASTER SUBC
 6              FLOAT X,Y,Z,V,SD,CMEAN
 7              ARRAY X(5),Y(5),Z(5),V(5),IV(5)
 8              STREAM=3
 9        300 FORMAT(1H0/19H SIMULATED : MEAN =,F6.2,5X,
10            120HSTANDARD DEVIATION =,F6.2)
11              WRITE(2,100)
12        100 FORMAT(44H1100 GENERATED RANDOM VALUES FROM SUBROUTINE)
13              WRITE(2,200)
14        200 FORMAT(1H+,44X,16HUNIFORM (RANDOM))
15              WRITE(2,210)
16        210 FORMAT(15HORANGE = 1 TO 4)
17        220 FORMAT(1H ,5I10)
18              FOR J=1,4
19                WRITE(2,103)
20                FOR K=1,5
21                  FOR L=1,5
22                    X(L)=RANDOM(STREAM,4)
23                    WRITE(6)X(L)
24                  WRITE(2,104)(X(I),I=1,5)
25                  DUMMY
26              DUMMY
27    F         REWIND 6
28    F         CALL SDEV(2.5,100,A005,A006)
29              WRITE(2,300)CMEAN,SD
30    F         REWIND 6
31              WRITE(2,100)
32              WRITE(2,101)
33        101 FORMAT(1H+,44X,16HNORMAL (DEVIATE))
34              WRITE(2,102)
35        102 FORMAT(29HOMEAN = 10.0  DEVIATION = 2.0)
36        103 FORMAT(1H0//)
37        104 FORMAT(1H ,5F10.2)
38              FOR J=1,4
39                WRITE(2,103)
40                FOR K=1,5
41                  FOR L=1,5
42                    Y(L)=DEVIATE(STREAM,200,1000)
```

```
43                      Y(L)=Y(L)/100.0
44                       WRITE(6)Y(L)
45                      WRITE(2,104)(Y(I),I=1,5)
46                   DUMMY
47                DUMMY
48       F        REWIND 6
49       F        CALL SDEV(10.0,100,A005,A006)
50                WRITE(2,300)CMEAN,SD
51       F        REWIND 6
52                WRITE(2,100)
53                WRITE(2,230)
54          230 FORMAT(1H+,44X,29HNEGATIVE EXPONENTIAL (NEGEXP))
55                WRITE(2,240)
56          240 FORMAT(10HOMEAN = 50)
57                FOR J=1,4
58                  WRITE(2,103)
59                  FOR K=1,5
60                    FOR L=1,5
61                      Z(L)=NEGEXP(STREAM,50)
62                       WRITE(6)Z(L)
63                      WRITE(2,104)(Z(I),I=1,5)
64                   DUMMY
65                DUMMY
66       F        REWIND 6
67       F        CALL SDEV(50.0,100,A005,A006)
68                WRITE(2,300)CMEAN,SD
69       F        REWIND 6
70                WRITE(2,100)
71                WRITE(2,250)
72        . 250 FORMAT(1H+,44X,7HPOISSON)
73                WRITE(2,260)
74          260 FORMAT(11HOMEAN = 2.0)
75                FOR J=1,4
76                  WRITE(2,103)
77                  FOR K=1,5
78                    FOR L=1,5
79                      V(L)=POISSON(STREAM,2.0)
80                       WRITE(6)V(L)
81                       IV(L)=V(L)
82                      WRITE(2,220)(IV(I),I=1,5)
83                   DUMMY
84                DUMMY
85     F        REWIND 6
86       F        CALL SDEV(2.0,100,A005,A006)
87                WRITE(2,300)CMEAN,SD
88                EXIT
89                END
90                ENDSUBFILE
91                LIST(LP)
92                PROGRAM(SUBC)
93                COMPRESS INTEGER AND LOGICAL
94                INPUT 1=CRO
95                OUTPUT (MONITOR),2=LPO
96                CREATE 6=MTO/UNFORMATTED(NUMBERS)
97                TRACE
98                END
```

```
 99          READ FROM(MT,SUBC.EH)
100          SUBROUTINE SDEV(AMEAN,NO,SD,CMEAN)
101          SUMX=0
102          SUMXM=0
103          SUMXMSQ=0
104          DO 10 I=1,NO
105          READ(6)X
106          SUMX=SUMX + X
107          XM=X - AMEAN
108          SUMXM=SUMXM + XM
109    10    SUMXMSQ=SUMXMSQ + XM * XM
110          ANO=NO
111          SD=SQRT(SUMXMSQ/ANO - (SUMXM/ANO)**2)
112          CMEAN=SUMX/ANO
113          RETURN
114          END
115          LIBRARY
116          READ FROM (MT,-.SRC2)
117          FINISH
```

100 GENERATED RANDOM VALUES FROM SUBROUTINE UNIFORM (RANDOM)

RANGE = 1 TO 4

3.00	1.00	1.00	3.00	3.00
2.00	2.00	2.00	4.00	4.00
4.00	4.00	4.00	4.00	1.00
2.00	1.00	1.00	2.00	3.00
4.00	3.00	3.00	1.00	2.00

1.00	2.00	2.00	3.00	3.00
2.00	2.00	2.00	3.00	1.00
2.00	4.00	3.00	3.00	3.00
1.00	3.00	3.00	2.00	2.00
3.00	3.00	4.00	2.00	4.00

3.00	4.00	4.00	4.00	2.00
1.00	4.00	1.00	2.00	2.00
1.00	4.00	1.00	2.00	3.00
3.00	4.00	2.00	3.00	3.00
4.00	2.00	1.00	2.00	1.00

1.00	4.00	1.00	3.00	1.00
1.00	1.00	2.00	3.00	2.00
4.00	4.00	3.00	2.00	2.00
4.00	3.00	1.00	3.00	2.00
1.00	2.00	2.00	3.00	3.00

SIMULATED : MEAN = 2.48   STANDARD DEVIATION = 1.05

100 GENERATED RANDOM VALUES FROM SUBROUTINE NORMAL (DEVIATE)

MEAN = 10.0   DEVIATION = 2.0

15.27	13.31	10.36	10.77	8.55
9.36	9.02	10.96	8.56	10.98
11.50	11.63	9.75	10.22	11.21
12.94	11.65	8.97	6.67	8.43
9.65	9.23	10.72	5.63	10.29

8.42	7.20	10.27	11.54	8.36
8.20	13.32	9.18	9.23	9.06
10.74	12.19	13.18	9.43	11.81
7.86	7.30	10.17	11.84	8.80
10.05	9.38	6.85	10.44	6.79

9.15	9.57	10.32	12.05	10.38
5.49	12.91	10.73	13.61	10.34
11.00	7.19	11.47	10.12	12.18
12.80	7.79	8.22	5.92	6.44
10.82	8.63	10.55	10.09	12.76

6.95	11.13	8.31	12.97	7.37
10.18	11.68	11.26	10.01	10.53
10.71	8.50	6.66	11.21	12.44
11.18	9.93	12.08	8.58	8.13
10.94	9.16	9.69	9.78	8.75

SIMULATED : MEAN = 9.96   STANDARD DEVIATION = 1.94

100 GENERATED RANDOM VALUES FROM SUBROUTINE NEGATIVE EXPONENTIAL (NEGEXP)

MEAN = 50

59.00	17.00	92.00	18.00	121.00
22.00	3.00	115.00	39.00	37.00
10.00	35.00	54.00	12.00	14.00
12.00	175.00	75.00	46.00	32.00
55.00	90.00	76.00	30.00	22.00

58.00	25.00	25.00	116.00	54.00
0.00	3.00	15.00	36.00	257.00
3.00	29.00	74.00	28.00	10.00
18.00	7.00	158.00	102.00	35.00
101.00	55.00	36.00	17.00	4.00

177.00	107.00	28.00	15.00	31.00
28.00	5.00	34.00	92.00	71.00
59.00	130.00	61.00	122.00	74.00
6.00	35.00	80.00	105.00	26.00
23.00	40.00	30.00	20.00	1.00

124.00	59.00	135.00	45.00	45.00
27.00	9.00	42.00	52.00	213.00
18.00	47.00	107.00	4.00	14.00
31.00	9.00	62.00	198.00	80.00
118.00	179.00	96.00	7.00	16.00

SIMULATED : MEAN = 56.64   STANDARD DEVIATION = 52.19

100 GENERATED RANDOM VALUES FROM SUBROUTINE POISSON

MEAN = 2.0

```
0    2    1    2    3
2    2    2    3    2
3    3    8    4    2
5    2    4    1    2
1    0    3    1    3


0    3    4    2    0
1    1    0    2    6
2    2    5    1    2
5    1    4    1    4
4    3    4    3    6


4    1    1    3    2
4    1    2    2    2
2    3    4    1    2
1    3    2    2    0
6    2    0    3    1


2    2    1    1    0
0    2    0    0    4
2    2    3    2    2
1    3    1    2    1
1    0    6    5    0
```

SIMULATED : MEAN = 2.24   STANDARD DEVIATION = 1.62
NORMAL EXIT

A Dispatch Problem: Table of Lorry Loading

First day

Arrival time	Load (tons)	Loading started	Loading finished
7.05	2	7.05	7.15
7.15	3	7.15	7.20
7.40	3	7.40	8.05
7.45	5	7.45	7.55
7.45	5	7.55	8.40
8.00	2	8.05	8.20
8.15	3	8.20	8.40
8.30	4	8.40	9.15
8.40	1	8.40	8.50
8.50	6	8.50	9.25
9.05	2	9.15	9.40
9.45	5	9.45	10.45
10.00	2	10.00	10.30
10.25	5	10.30	11.20
10.40	3	10.45	11.20
11.10	1	11.20	11.50
11.30	1	11.30	11.50
12.00	2	12.00	12.20
13.15	3	13.15	13.45
14.00	6	14.00	15.45
14.00	2	14.00	14.35
14.15	1	14.35	15.05
14.25	3	15.05	15.20
15.15	2	15.20	15.35
15.30	4	15.35	16.15

Second day

Arrival time	Load (tons)	Loading started	Loading finished
7.00	1	7.00	7.30
7.05	2	7.05	7.35
7.10	3	7.30	7.55
7.30	2	7.35	9.35
8.00	4	8.00	8.20
8.00	3	8.20	9.00
8.15	1	9.00	9.05
8.25	5	9.05	9.45
8.30	2	9.35	9.50
8.35	3	9.45	10.05
8.50	6	9.50	10.40
9.05	1	10.05	10.25
10.00	6	10.25	11.20
11.05	3	11.05	11.45
12.00	3	12.00	12.10
12.15	4	12.15	12.35
13.10	2	13.10	13.30
14.00	5	14.00	14.55
14.00	2	14.00	14.45
14.00	5	14.45	15.35
14.10	6	15.05	16.15
15.05	3	15.35	15.55
15.15	5	15.55	16.30
15.20	2	16.15	16.40

Third day

Arrival time	Load (tons)	Loading started	Loading finished
7.05	5	7.05	7.25
7.30	2	7.30	7.50
8.00	3	8.00	8.50
8.00	5	8.00	8.55
8.15	6	8.50	10.00
8.30	2	8.55	9.20
8.40	4	9.20	9.30
9.05	3	9.30	10.10
10.10	4	10.10	10.50
10.10	5	10.10	10.55
10.20	2	10.50	11.20
10.35	1	10.55	11.25
11.00	2	11.20	12.05

Third day—*continued*

Arrival time	Load (tons)	Loading started	Loading finished
12.15	1	12.15	12.35
12.50	4	12.50	13.20
13.05	3	13.05	13.25
13.30	5	13.30	14.35
14.00	2	14.00	15.00
14.30	1	14.35	15.10
14.40	3	15.00	15.35
14.50	2	15.10	15.55
15.00	6	15.35	16.30
15.00	3	15.55	16.25
15.15	1	16.25	16.50
15.25	3	16.30	16.50

Fourth day

Arrival time	Load (tons)	Loading started	Loading finished
7.00	2	7.00	7.25
7.05	4	7.05	7.10
7.20	3	7.20	8.00
7.30	5	7.30	7.55
7.45	2	7.55	8.25
7.50	4	8.00	8.40
8.10	5	8.25	9.35
8.30	3	8.40	8.50
8.40	6	8.50	10.05
9.05	1	9.35	9.50
10.00	3	10.00	10.20
10.15	6	10.15	10.55
11.10	2	11.10	11.25
11.30	2	11.30	12.05
12.15	3	12.15	12.40
12.35	1	12.35	12.55
13.00	5	13.00	13.50
13.25	2	13.25	13.45
14.05	5	14.05	14.50
14.10	1	14.10	14.40
14.30	3	14.40	15.30
14.30	2	14.50	15.05
14.50	1	15.05	15.30
15.15	5	15.30	16.10
15.45	3	15.45	16.40

Fifth day

Arrival time	Load (tons)	Loading started	Loading finished
7.15	1	7.15	7.30
7.50	2	7.50	8.30
8.00	2	8.00	8.20
8.15	3	8.20	8.35
8.25	6	8.30	9.10
8.30	5	8.35	10.50
8.35	1	9.10	9.40
8.50	4	9.40	10.25
9.00	3	10.25	10.50
9.25	3	10.50	11.10
10.05	2	10.50	11.20
10.15	1	11.10	11.30
11.00	2	11.20	11.35
12.10	3	12.10	12.40
13.00	5	13.00	13.35
13.05	2	13.05	13.30
14.05	3	14.05	14.45
14.15	5	14.15	15.05
14.25	1	14.45	15.00
14.30	5	15.00	15.40
15.15	3	15.15	16.00
15.35	2	15.40	16.00
15.50	4	16.00	16.30

Appendix 16

Random Number Tables

```
97 58 55 23 12   87 39 84 32 23   26 91 01 11 26   01 24 06 58 20   33 46 38 86 23
84 95 87 34 95   31 23 12 64 75   89 28 38 15 91   81 89 08 86 08   88 20 02 11 67
11 52 38 09 94   32 47 35 42 67   39 33 89 97 16   28 94 86 93 86   96 13 43 85 99
38 69 94 97 10   44 42 85 46 88   56 56 63 58 22   89 19 26 82 25   94 15 54 65 62
23 99 36 33 41   99 76 22 29 19   92 53 92 15 71   47 57 74 69 03   65 57 90 53 17

09 15 95 74 87   09 63 82 63 29   84 57 45 80 07   13 57 40 58 34   21 93 90 39 21
55 75 91 36 57   38 30 89 64 42   01 84 83 12 79   32 09 56 03 81   90 88 00 71 02
84 62 29 92 42   03 92 37 46 19   90 75 68 84 49   53 80 62 19 20   31 14 42 11 17
79 25 70 07 80   85 32 53 87 11   33 79 14 20 04   12 40 31 74 39   80 21 37 65 20
40 10 91 52 27   21 18 64 61 04   85 55 16 90 71   31 95 15 86 74   87 80 75 71 27

93 18 86 63 72   22 12 44 23 89   38 06 46 04 79   67 77 33 21 75   40 51 74 60 53
63 71 69 30 23   53 85 90 05 07   67 33 56 52 60   21 50 72 26 28   48 67 31 87 61
05 29 95 78 06   10 41 62 18 37   42 91 98 43 33   20 58 62 80 65   19 90 07 84 49
30 04 29 90 89   64 25 66 36 41   99 59 15 43 86   34 10 05 99 83   08 02 18 01 22
75 50 83 42 46   80 76 77 34 16   04 05 06 28 86   60 70 04 13 28   98 76 78 43 69

68 82 44 11 33   11 20 42 00 22   40 03 06 12 45   06 32 34 44 18   01 26 36 78 42
51 38 78 69 65   25 98 73 40 31   12 04 99 51 09   49 04 32 68 68   54 64 15 25 68
98 41 81 63 70   58 43 39 93 18   54 46 98 33 01   47 85 39 81 11   48 84 07 64 76
08 44 37 01 53   59 67 11 11 53   16 98 16 52 52   39 32 22 18 22   04 03 06 77 17
17 30 92 82 09   42 37 88 43 35   11 54 89 05 61   10 46 27 43 33   88 92 72 62 01

74 87 89 10 02   19 45 29 65 70   77 81 98 78 67   05 62 57 08 79   30 32 62 91 87
61 81 52 99 80   11 55 21 98 02   08 26 01 20 16   07 42 88 56 51   31 96 14 85 49
55 08 43 08 22   50 28 03 18 00   80 79 60 18 33   92 36 13 50 41   43 59 82 16 65
44 38 47 15 16   96 03 51 42 15   35 96 40 87 91   56 91 13 58 85   40 06 36 04 30
12 45 97 68 57   62 36 61 03 29   46 60 79 85 99   91 13 99 95 58   75 14 74 88 12

19 95 23 05 45   01 87 81 18 92   36 94 07 14 08   90 32 51 29 61   50 60 34 92 25
71 55 86 72 94   77 08 55 65 50   33 53 94 81 52   36 31 53 12 74   88 59 99 35 95
07 32 94 03 20   66 29 98 75 65   70 30 56 59 08   24 51 75 48 73   11 29 77 08 36
10 35 58 59 25   89 62 60 77 71   24 13 38 20 83   02 48 11 67 95   38 97 15 58 18
62 99 34 08 06   81 46 09 16 82   95 17 13 46 36   51 36 87 56 10   80 79 40 48 82
```

Source: From Table F, appendix II of Croft: *Applied Statistics for Management Studies,* published by Macdonald and Evans, London. Reproduced by permission of the author and publishers.

Appendix 17

Chi-Square Tables

The quantity tabulated is the value of χ^2 which must be exceeded for significance at the level given

d.f.	P = 0.05	0.01
1	3.84	6.63
2	5.99	9.21
3	7.81	11.3
4	9.49	13.3
5	11.1	15.1
6	12.6	16.8
7	14.1	18.5
8	15.5	20.1
9	16.9	21.7
10	18.3	23.2
11	19.7	24.7
12	21.0	26.2
13	22.4	27.7
14	23.7	29.1
15	25.0	30.6
16	26.3	32.0
17	27.6	33.4
18	28.9	34.8
19	30.1	36.2
20	31.4	37.6
22	33.9	40.3
24	36.4	43.0
26	38.9	45.6
28	41.3	48.3
30	43.8	50.9

For degrees of freedom greater than 30 $\sqrt{2\chi^2}$ is distributed as normal with mean $= \sqrt{20 \times 1}$ and variance $= 1$

Source: From Table C, appendix II of Croft: *Applied Statistics for Management Studies,* published by Macdonald and Evans, London. Reproduced by permission of the author and publishers.

Normal Tables

The quantity given is the probability that Z would be exceeded for a measurement drawn from a standardised normal distribution

second decimal place of Z

Z	0	1	2	3	4	5	6	7	8	9
0.0	0.5000	0.4960	0.4920	0.4880	0.4840	0.4801	0.4761	0.4721	0.4681	0.4641
0.1	0.4602	0.4562	0.4522	0.4483	0.4443	0.4404	0.4364	0.4325	0.4286	0.4247
0.2	0.4207	0.4168	0.4129	0.4090	0.4052	0.4013	0.3974	0.3936	0.3897	0.3859
0.3	0.3821	0.3783	0.3745	0.3707	0.3669	0.3632	0.3594	0.3557	0.3520	0.3483
0.4	0.3446	0.3409	0.3372	0.3336	0.3300	0.3264	0.3228	0.3192	0.3156	0.3121
0.5	0.3085	0.3050	0.3015	0.2981	0.2946	0.2912	0.2877	0.2843	0.2810	0.2776
0.6	0.2743	0.2709	0.2676	0.2643	0.2611	0.2578	0.2546	0.2514	0.2483	0.2451
0.7	0.2420	0.2389	0.2358	0.2327	0.2297	0.2266	0.2236	0.2206	0.2177	0.2148
0.8	0.2119	0.2090	0.2061	0.2033	0.2005	0.1977	0.1949	0.1922	0.1894	0.1867
0.9	0.1841	0.1814	0.1788	0.1762	0.1736	0.1711	0.1685	0.1660	0.1635	0.1611
1.0	0.1587	0.1562	0.1539	0.1515	0.1492	0.1469	0.1446	0.1423	0.1401	0.1379
1.1	0.1357	0.1335	0.1314	0.1292	0.1271	0.1251	0.1230	0.1210	0.1190	0.1170
1.2	0.1151	0.1131	0.1112	0.1093	0.1075	0.1056	0.1038	0.1020	0.1003	0.0985
1.3	0.0968	0.0951	0.0934	0.0918	0.0901	0.0885	0.0869	0.0853	0.0838	0.0823
1.4	0.0809	0.0793	0.0778	0.0764	0.0749	0.0735	0.0722	0.0708	0.0694	0.0681
1.5	0.0668	0.0655	0.0643	0.0630	0.0618	0.0606	0.0594	0.0582	0.0571	0.0559
1.6	0.0548	0.0537	0.0526	0.0516	0.0505	0.0495	0.0485	0.0475	0.0465	0.0455
1.7	0.0446	0.0436	0.0427	0.0418	0.0409	0.0401	0.0392	0.0384	0.0375	0.0367
1.8	0.0359	0.0352	0.0344	0.0336	0.0329	0.0322	0.0314	0.0307	0.0301	0.0294
1.9	0.0287	0.0281	0.0274	0.0268	0.0262	0.0256	0.0250	0.0244	0.0238	0.0233
2.0	0.0227	0.0222	0.0217	0.0212	0.0207	0.0202	0.0197	0.0192	0.0188	0.0183
2.1	0.0179	0.0174	0.0170	0.0166	0.0162	0.0158	0.0154	0.0150	0.0146	0.0143
2.2	0.0139	0.0136	0.0132	0.0129	0.0126	0.0122	0.0119	0.0116	0.0113	0.0110
2.3	0.0107	0.0104	0.0102	0.00990	0.00964	0.00939	0.00914	0.00889	0.00866	0.00842
2.4	0.00820	0.00798	0.00776	0.00755	0.00734	0.00714	0.00695	0.00676	0.00657	0.00639
2.5	0.00621	0.00604	0.00587	0.00570	0.00554	0.00539	0.00523	0.00508	0.00494	0.00480
2.6	0.00466	0.00453	0.00440	0.00427	0.00415	0.00403	0.00391	0.00379	0.00368	0.00357
2.7	0.00347	0.00336	0.00326	0.00317	0.00307	0.00298	0.00289	0.00280	0.00272	0.00264
2.8	0.00256	0.00248	0.00240	0.00233	0.00226	0.00219	0.00212	0.00205	0.00199	0.00193
2.9	0.00187	0.00181	0.00175	0.00169	0.00164	0.00159	0.00154	0.00149	0.00144	0.00140
3.0	0.00135	0.00131	0.00126	0.00122	0.00118	0.00114	0.00111	0.00107	0.00104	0.00100
3.1	0.00097	0.00094	0.00090	0.00087	0.00084	0.00082	0.00079	0.00076	0.00074	0.00071
3.2	0.00069	0.00066	0.00064	0.00062	0.00060	0.00058	0.00056	0.00054	0.00052	0.00050
3.3	0.00048	0.00047	0.00045	0.00043	0.00042	0.00040	0.00039	0.00038	0.00036	0.00035
3.4	0.00034	0.00032	0.00031	0.00030	0.00029	0.00028	0.00027	0.00026	0.00025	0.00024
3.5	0.00023	0.00022	0.00022	0.00021	0.00020	0.00019	0.00019	0.00018	0.00017	0.00017

Source: From Table A, appendix II of Croft: *Applied Statistics for Management Studies,* published by Macdonald and Evans, London. Reproduced by permission of the author and publishers.

Poisson Tables

See following facing pages.

The quantity tabulated is the probability that r occurrences will be observed in a Poisson distribution mean = m

m \ r =	0	1	2	3	4	5	6	7	8	9	10	11	12	13	14	15
0.02	0.9802	0.0192	0.0002													
0.04	0.9608	0.0384	0.0008													
0.06	0.9418	0.0565	0.0017													
0.08	0.9231	0.0738	0.0030	0.0001												
0.1	0.9048	0.0905	0.0045	0.0002												
0.2	0.8187	0.1637	0.0164	0.0011	0.0001											
0.3	0.7408	0.2222	0.0333	0.0033	0.0002											
0.4	0.6703	0.2681	0.0536	0.0072	0.0007	0.0001										
0.5	0.6065	0.3033	0.0758	0.0126	0.0016	0.0002										
0.6	0.5488	0.3293	0.0988	0.0198	0.0030	0.0004										
0.7	0.4966	0.3476	0.1217	0.0284	0.0050	0.0007	0.0001									
0.8	0.4493	0.3595	0.1438	0.0383	0.0077	0.0012	0.0002									
0.9	0.4066	0.3659	0.1647	0.0494	0.0111	0.0020	0.0003									
1.0	0.3679	0.3679	0.1839	0.0613	0.0153	0.0031	0.0005	0.0001								
1.1	0.3329	0.3662	0.2014	0.0738	0.0203	0.0045	0.0008	0.0001								
1.2	0.3012	0.3614	0.2169	0.0867	0.0260	0.0062	0.0012	0.0002								
1.3	0.2725	0.3543	0.2303	0.0998	0.0324	0.0084	0.0018	0.0003	0.0001							
1.4	0.2466	0.3452	0.2417	0.1128	0.0395	0.0111	0.0026	0.0005	0.0001							
1.5	0.2231	0.3347	0.2510	0.1255	0.0471	0.0141	0.0035	0.0008	0.0001							
1.6	0.2019	0.3230	0.2584	0.1378	0.0551	0.0176	0.0047	0.0011	0.0002							
1.7	0.1827	0.3106	0.2640	0.1496	0.0636	0.0216	0.0061	0.0015	0.0003	0.0001						
1.8	0.1653	0.2975	0.2678	0.1607	0.0723	0.0260	0.0078	0.0020	0.0005	0.0001						
1.9	0.1496	0.2842	0.2700	0.1710	0.0812	0.0309	0.0098	0.0027	0.0006	0.0001						
2.0	0.1353	0.2707	0.2707	0.1804	0.0902	0.0361	0.0120	0.0034	0.0009	0.0002	0.0001					
2.1	0.1225	0.2572	0.2700	0.1890	0.0992	0.0417	0.0146	0.0044	0.0011	0.0003	0.0001					
2.2	0.1108	0.2438	0.2681	0.1966	0.1082	0.0476	0.0174	0.0055	0.0015	0.0004						

2.3	0.1003	0.2306	0.2652	0.2033	0.1169	0.0538	0.0206	0.0068	0.0019	0.0005	0.0001					
2.4	0.0907	0.2177	0.2613	0.2090	0.1254	0.0602	0.0241	0.0083	0.0025	0.0007	0.0002					
2.5	0.0821	0.2052	0.2565	0.2138	0.1336	0.0668	0.0278	0.0099	0.0031	0.0009	0.0002					
2.6	0.0743	0.1931	0.2510	0.2176	0.1414	0.0735	0.0319	0.0118	0.0038	0.0011	0.0003	0.0001				
2.7	0.0672	0.1815	0.2450	0.2205	0.1488	0.0804	0.0362	0.0139	0.0047	0.0014	0.0004	0.0001				
2.8	0.0608	0.1703	0.2384	0.2225	0.1557	0.0872	0.0407	0.0163	0.0057	0.0018	0.0005	0.0001				
2.9	0.0550	0.1596	0.2314	0.2237	0.1622	0.0940	0.0455	0.0188	0.0068	0.0022	0.0006	0.0002				
3.0	0.0498	0.1494	0.2240	0.2240	0.1680	0.1008	0.0504	0.0216	0.0081	0.0027	0.0008	0.0002	0.0001			
3.1	0.0450	0.1397	0.2165	0.2237	0.1734	0.1075	0.0555	0.0246	0.0095	0.0033	0.0010	0.0003	0.0001			
3.2	0.0408	0.1304	0.2087	0.2226	0.1781	0.1140	0.0608	0.0278	0.0111	0.0040	0.0013	0.0004	0.0001			
3.3	0.0369	0.1217	0.2008	0.2209	0.1823	0.1203	0.0662	0.0312	0.0129	0.0047	0.0016	0.0005	0.0001			
3.4	0.0334	0.1135	0.1929	0.2186	0.1858	0.1264	0.0716	0.0348	0.0148	0.0056	0.0019	0.0006	0.0002			
3.5	0.0302	0.1057	0.1850	0.2158	0.1888	0.1322	0.0771	0.0385	0.0169	0.0066	0.0023	0.0007	0.0002	0.0001		
3.6	0.0273	0.0984	0.1771	0.2125	0.1912	0.1377	0.0826	0.0425	0.0191	0.0076	0.0028	0.0009	0.0003	0.0001		
3.7	0.0247	0.0915	0.1692	0.2087	0.1931	0.1429	0.0881	0.0466	0.0215	0.0089	0.0033	0.0011	0.0003	0.0001		
3.8	0.0224	0.0850	0.1615	0.2046	0.1944	0.1477	0.0936	0.0508	0.0241	0.0102	0.0039	0.0013	0.0004	0.0001		
3.9	0.0202	0.0789	0.1539	0.2001	0.1951	0.1522	0.0989	0.0551	0.0269	0.0116	0.0045	0.0016	0.0005	0.0002		
4.0	0.0183	0.0733	0.1465	0.1954	0.1954	0.1563	0.1042	0.0595	0.0298	0.0132	0.0053	0.0019	0.0006	0.0002	0.0001	
4.1	0.0166	0.0679	0.1393	0.1904	0.1951	0.1600	0.1093	0.0640	0.0328	0.0150	0.0061	0.0023	0.0008	0.0002	0.0001	
4.2	0.0150	0.0630	0.1323	0.1852	0.1944	0.1633	0.1143	0.0686	0.0360	0.0168	0.0071	0.0027	0.0009	0.0003	0.0001	
4.3	0.0136	0.0583	0.1254	0.1798	0.1933	0.1662	0.1191	0.0732	0.0393	0.0188	0.0081	0.0032	0.0011	0.0004	0.0001	
4.4	0.0123	0.0540	0.1188	0.1743	0.1917	0.1687	0.1237	0.0778	0.0428	0.0209	0.0092	0.0037	0.0014	0.0005	0.0001	
4.5	0.0111	0.0500	0.1125	0.1687	0.1898	0.1708	0.1281	0.0824	0.0463	0.0232	0.0104	0.0043	0.0016	0.0006	0.0002	0.0001
4.6	0.0101	0.0462	0.1063	0.1631	0.1875	0.1725	0.1323	0.0869	0.0500	0.0255	0.0118	0.0049	0.0019	0.0007	0.0002	0.0001
4.7	0.0091	0.0427	0.1005	0.1574	0.1849	0.1738	0.1362	0.0914	0.0537	0.0280	0.0132	0.0056	0.0022	0.0008	0.0003	0.0001
4.8	0.0082	0.0395	0.0948	0.1517	0.1820	0.1747	0.1398	0.0959	0.0575	0.0307	0.0147	0.0064	0.0026	0.0009	0.0003	0.0001
4.9	0.0074	0.0365	0.0894	0.1460	0.1789	0.1753	0.1432	0.1002	0.0614	0.0334	0.0164	0.0073	0.0030	0.0011	0.0004	0.0001
5.0	0.0067	0.0337	0.0842	0.1404	0.1755	0.1755	0.1462	0.1044	0.0653	0.0363	0.0181	0.0082	0.0034	0.0013	0.0005	0.0002

Source: From Table E, Appendix II of Croft: *Applied Statistics for Management Studies*, published by Macdonald and Evans, London. Reproduced by permission of the author and publishers.

Appendix 20

Formulae for a 'Simple' Queue

Formulae

(1) Poisson input, unlimited queue length, single service channel with exponential service time distribution. Average rate of input λ and average rate of service μ; $\lambda < \mu$.

Traffic intensity	$\rho = \lambda/\mu$
P of n units in the system	$p(n) = \rho^n(1 - \rho)$
P of more than n units in the system	$p(>n) = \rho^{n+1}$
Average number of units in the system	$N = \rho/(1 - \rho)$
P of n units in the queue	$q(n) = \rho^{n+1}(1 - \rho)$ (for $n > 0$)
	$q(0) = 1 - \rho^2$
P of more than n units in the queue	$q(>n) = \rho^{n+2}$
Average number of units in the queue	$Q = \rho^2/(1 - \rho)$
P of no waiting (up to start of service)	$w(0) = 1 - \rho$
P of waiting from t to $t + dt$	$w(t)\,dt = \rho(\mu - \lambda)\,e^{-t(\mu - \lambda)}\,dt$
P of waiting longer than t	$w(>t) = \rho e^{-t(\mu-\lambda)}$
Average waiting time	$W = \rho/(\mu - \lambda)$
P of time from t to $t + dt$ spent in the system	$s(t)\,dt = (\mu - \lambda)\,e^{-t(\mu - \lambda)}\,dt$
P of more than time t spent in the system	$s(>t) = e^{-t(\mu-\lambda)}$
Average time spent in the system	$S = 1/(\mu - \lambda)$
P that a queue exists	$p(>1) = \rho^2$
P that a unit needs to wait for service	$p(>0) = \rho$
Utilisation of the service channel	$u = \rho$

The formulae for $q(n)$, $q(> n)$ and Q if divided by ρ^2 apply to the time during which a queue exists; those for $w(t)$, $w(> t)$ and W if divided by ρ refer to the units which need to wait.

Source: From page 108 of Houlden: *Some Techniques of Operational Research,* published by E.U.P., London. Reproduced by permission of the author and publishers. This work gives the appropriate formulae for eleven types of queueing situation.

Appendix 21

Runs Test Tables

n_1	n_2	Number of runs		n_1	n_2	Number of runs	
2	2–11	–	–	10	16–18	8	19
2	12–20	2	–	10	19	8	20
3	3–5	–	–	10	20	9	20
3	6–14	2	–	11	11	7	17
3	15–20	3	–	11	12	7	18
4	4	–	–	11	13	7	19
4	5–6	2	9	11	14–15	8	19
4	7	2	–	11	16	8	20
4	8–15	3	–	11	17–18	9	20
4	16–20	4	–	11	19–20	9	21
5	5	2	10	12	12	7	19
5	6	3	10	12	13	8	19
5	7–8	3	11	12	14–15	8	20
5	9–10	3	–	12	16–18	9	21
5	11–17	4	–	12	19–20	10	22
5	18–20	5	–	13	13	8	20
6	6	3	11	13	14	9	20
6	7–8	3	12	13	15–16	9	21
6	9–12	4	13	13	17–18	10	22
6	13–18	5	–	13	19–20	10	23
6	19–20	6	–	14	14	9	21
7	7	3	13	14	15	9	22
7	8	4	13	14	16	10	22
7	9	4	14	14	17–18	10	23
7	10–12	5	14	14	19	11	23
7	13–14	5	15	14	20	11	24
7	15	6	15	15	15	10	22
7	16–20	6	–	15	16	10	23
8	8	4	14	15	17	11	23
8	9	5	14	15	18–19	11	24
8	10–11	5	15	15	20	12	25
8	12–15	6	16	16	16	11	23
8	16	6	17	16	17	11	24
8	17–20	7	17	16	18	11	25
9	9	5	15	16	19–20	12	25
9	10	5	16	17	17	11	25
9	11–12	6	16	17	18	12	25
9	13	6	17	17	19	12	26
9	14	7	17	17	20	13	26
9	15–17	7	18	18	18	12	26
9	18–20	8	18	18	19	13	26
10	10	6	16	18	20	13	27
10	11	6	17	19	19–20	13	27
10	12	7	17	20	20	14	28
10	13–15	7	18				

Note: Table shows 5 per cent levels for runs test.

Source: From page 325 of Langley: *Practical Statistics,* published by PAN, London. Reproduced by permission of the author and PAN Books Limited.

Appendix 22

r Tables

If the calculated value of *r* exceeds the table value of r_α, a significant correlation has been established at the α significance level.

d.f.	$r_{.1}$	$r_{.05}$	$r_{.02}$	$r_{.01}$	$r_{.001}$
1	0.98769	0.99692	0.999507	0.999877	0.9999988
2	0.90000	0.95000	0.98000	0.990000	0.99900
3	0.8054	0.8783	0.93433	0.95873	0.99116
4	0.7293	0.8114	0.8822	0.91720	0.97406
5	0.6694	0.7545	0.8329	0.8745	0.95074
6	0.6215	0.7067	0.7887	0.8343	0.92493
7	0.5822	0.6664	0.7498	0.7977	0.8982
8	0.5494	0.6319	0.7155	0.7646	0.8721
9	0.5214	0.6021	0.6851	0.7348	0.8471
10	0.4973	0.5760	0.6581	0.7079	0.8233
11	0.4762	0.5529	0.6339	0.6835	0.8010
12	0.4575	0.5324	0.6120	0.6614	0.7800
13	0.4409	0.5139	0.5923	0.6411	0.7603
14	0.4259	0.4973	0.5742	0.6226	0.7420
15	0.4124	0.4821	0.5577	0.6055	0.7246
16	0.4000	0.4683	0.5425	0.5897	0.7084
17	0.3887	0.4555	0.5285	0.5751	0.6932
18	0.3783	0.4438	0.5155	0.5614	0.6787
19	0.3687	0.4329	0.5034	0.5487	0.6652
20	0.3598	0.4227	0.4921	0.5368	0.6524
25	0.3233	0.3809	0.4451	0.4869	0.5974
30	0.2960	0.3494	0.4093	0.4487	0.5541
35	0.2746	0.3246	0.3810	0.4182	0.5189
40	0.2573	0.3044	0.3578	0.3932	0.4896
45	0.2428	0.2875	0.3384	0.3721	0.4648
50	0.2306	0.2732	0.3218	0.3541	0.4433
60	0.2108	0.2500	0.2948	0.3248	0.4078
70	0.1954	0.2319	0.2737	0.3017	0.3799
80	0.1829	0.2172	0.2565	0.2830	0.3568
90	0.1726	0.2050	0.2422	0.2673	0.3375
100	0.1638	0.1946	0.2301	0.2540	0.3211

Source: From Table VII of Fisher and Yates: *Statistical Tables for Biological, Agricultural and Medical Research,* published by Oliver & Boyd, Edinburgh. Reproduced by permission of the authors and publishers.

Index

Activities in CSL 101
Arithmetic tests in CSL 117
Arrays
  ARRAY statements in CSL 112
  DIMENSION statements in FORTRAN 86
  subscripted variables in CSL 112
  subscripted variables in FORTRAN 86
Arrival patterns analysis 45, 137, 141
Attributes in CSL 112

BASIC 105
  examples see PRAC and PRAS
BOWS
  data 119, 153
  description of problem 153
  output 153
  program explanation 125
  statement illustrations 110, 111, 112

CAPF
  data 205
  general description 205
  interpretation of results 209
  output 206, 209
  statement illustrations 81, 82, 84, 85, 86
  use of UNIFM and NORM 101
  variable incrementing 208
Classes in CSL 110, 112
Combined units
  allocation of random numbers 16
  FORTRAN program 19
  histogram of failure patterns 15

manual simulation 14
worksheet 17
see also COMF
COMF statement illustrations 89
Correlation 169
  coefficient of 169
  correlogram 170
  serial 170
CSL
  compilation and execution 124
  FORTRAN statements and segments in 123
  general description 110
  history 109
  structural words 112, 135
Critical path analysis 31
Cumulative average use of 18, 151

Data
  accuracy of 32, 60
  operations in CSL 114
  operations in FORTRAN 81
  simplification example of 146
  structure in CSL 112
  structure in FORTRAN 80
  variability considerations of 144
Decision trees 54
Dispatch problem 140
DO statements in FORTRAN 88, 101

Econometric models 172
ELEM
  general description 194
  interpretation of results 196
  outline of program 90
  output 196
  statement illustrations 84, 86, 88

Index

Entities in CSL 110, 112
Errors
　detection and correction in
　　FORTRAN 97
　logical example of 69
Exercises suggested 220
Exponential smoothing 173
　smoothing constant 174
　trend allowing for 173, 175
　Trigg's tracking 178
　see also FORE

FIND statements in CSL 118
FOR statements in CSL 115
FORE
　general description 179
　interpretation of output 181
　output 180
Forecasting 165, 178
　adaptive 166, 173
　econometric model 172
　leading indicators 167
　moving averages 173
　routines see FORE
　size of error 165, 177
　statistical methods 171
　techniques 29
　time series analysis 171
　see also Correlation
　see also Exponential smoothing
FORTRAN
　basic 76
　compiler 76
　ICL 1900 implementation 103
　library subroutines 104
　MASTER segment 104
　program description segment 103
　rules for expressions 81
　use of magnetic tape 102
Frequency distributions
　as FORTRAN input 86
　binomial 38
　exponential 44
　FORTRAN programs 101
　in CSL 119
　inter-relationships 45, 137
　negative exponential 44, 137
　normal 42
　Poisson 40, 137

see also Histograms

Graphs
　arithmetic probability 207
　cumulative use of 143, 152
　semi-log 48

Histograms
　example production scheduling
　　204
　example profitability analysis 217
　in BASIC example of output 214,
　　216
　in CSL 111, 122
　in CSL example of output 154,
　　156, 157, 162
　parameters selection of 213
HOCUS 62

Industrial dynamics 65
Inventory control 28, 181
　alternative systems 183
　basic principles 182
　formulae 185, 186
　lead time variation 189
　main variables 183
　reorder level 189
　safety stock 184, 188
　stock-out risk 187, 190
　validation of program 69
　see also STAN

Leading indicators 167
Linear programming 28
LOAD
　description of program 202
　'diagnostic' output 203
　discussion of results 204
　general description 199
　histogram of excess hours 204
　input and output 200
　interpretation of results 204
　Poisson distribution for daily in-
　　take 199

MAD see Mean absolute deviation
Maintenance problems see COMF
　ELEM SOMB
Management approaches to 20

Manual simulation examples of 14, 140
Mathematical models
example of 23
measure of effectiveness 24
use of in business 25
see also Simulation models
Mean absolute deviation 166, 172
Mobile patrols, see PSIM
Models see Mathematical models

NORM
Normal distribution 101
machine-hour example 206
use in inventory control 188

Operational research
applications of 26
basic concepts 22
development of 21
mathematical model example of 23
relationship to statistics 27
relationship to work study 27
techniques, resume of 27

Pareto law 205
Plant capacity problem see CAPF
Poisson distribution
applied to work load 199
see also Frequency distributions
PRAC
discussion of results 215
general description 215
histogram of profitability 217
output 216
PRAS
general description 213
histogram selection of parameters 213
input phase 106
interpretation of results 215
output 214
Probability
examples of cumulative output 214, 216
see also Statistics
Production control 198
analytical approach 198
load and capacity 199

Pareto law 205
throughput times 199
see also CAPF and LOAD
Production scheduling problem see LOAD
Profitability problems 211
discussion of comparative methods 211, 217
see also PRAC and PRAS
Program development 100
PSIM
data 155
description of problem 155
description of program 158
output 155
statement illustrations 110, 112, 118

Queueing systems see BOWS PSIM SIMQ and SOMB
Queueing theory 29
examples of 22, 137, 138
factors 137, 155
formulae 138
general description 136

Random numbers
allocation of 14, 143
tables 14
use in simulation 14
use of in CSL 111
RECYCLE, in CSL 134
Refuelling aircraft see BOWS
Repair and re-issue problem see SOMB
Replacement theory 30
Results
interpretation of
see also BOWS CAPF ELEM FORE LOAD PRAC PRAS PSIM SIMQ SOMB STAN
Routing techniques 31

Sets in CSL 110, 112
Significance testing 49
SIMQ
description of program 150
nature of input 149
output 149, 151
statement illustration 83

Index

Simulation
    accuracy of 32, 60
    diagnostics 97
    languages 109
    length of 18, 155
    manual example 14
    meaning of 13
    programming check list 74
    usefulness of 13
    use of computers 76
    use of cumulative average 18
    use of decision trees 54
Simulation models
    construction of inter-relationships
      62
    development of 219
    for inventory control 28
    for queueing problems 29
    for replacement problems 30
    for routing problems 31
    HOCUS 62
    identifying relevant factors 54
    industrial dynamics 65
    interpretation of results 220
    statistical aspects 58
    summary of considerations 219
    terms of reference 52
    use in forecasting 29
    use of significance tests 50
    validation 69, 219
    with critical path analysis 31
    with linear programming 28
    see also BOWS CAPF ELEM FORE
      LOAD PRAC PRAS PSIM SIMQ
      SOMB STAN
SOMB
    description of problem 160
    description of program 162
    interpretation of output 161
    output 161
STAN
    general description 190
    interpretation of output 191
Statement numbers

in CSL 114
in FORTRAN 78
Statistics
    calculation of expectation 36
    concept of probability 33
    relationship to operational research
      27
    significance testing 49
    see also Frequency distributions
Stock control see **Inventory control**
Stock control analysis problem see
    STAN
Students 't' test 169
SUBC statement illustrations 116,
    123
SUBF statement illustrations 101,
    102
Subroutines
    CSL library 125
    FORTRAN 90, 101, 104, 123
    FORTRAN library 104
    frequency distributions 100

Terminals
    'conversational' output 106
    on-line use of 105
Time advance in CSL 110
Time cells in CSL 110
Transfer statements
    in CSL 115, 117
    in FORTRAN 85, 88, 101

Validation of model 69, 219
    monitoring progress 151
    use of 'diagnostic' output 97, 203
Variable incrementing, example
    of 208

Worksheet
    for combined units example 17
    for dispatch problem 148
Work study relationship to operational
    research 27